AMERICAN PHILOSOPHIES
OF RELIGION

AMERICAN PHILOSOPHIES OF RELIGION

BY

HENRY NELSON WIEMAN

Professor of Philosophy of Religion
The University of Chicago

BERNARD EUGENE MELAND

Professor of Religion and Philosophy
Central College, Fayette, Missouri

WILLETT, CLARK & COMPANY

CHICAGO   NEW YORK

1936

Our knowledge is a torch of smoky pine
That lights the pathway but one step ahead
Across a void of mystery and dread.
Bid, then, the tender light of faith to shine
By which alone the mortal heart is led
Unto the thinking of the thought divine.

— GEORGE SANTAYANA

PREFACE

THIS book arose out of the effort to interpret the religious thought of today to college and university audiences. It is therefore, in part, simply a survey of contemporary types of thought in American philosophy of religion. Yet it aims beyond the mere photographic reflection of present trends. It seeks to clarify the current confusion in modern thought by providing a perspective with which to view the present scene. To accomplish this we have sought to single out the distinctive strands of thinking and to bring together those that issue from a common source and which bear similarities arising from a basic kinship. We have thus tried to achieve an orderly arrangement of current views that is organic rather than arbitrary or mechanical.

The full force of our efforts will be lost unless this perspective is acquired at the outset. In Chapters I and III we set forth the point of view at length, but there may be value in calling attention to its broad outlines here. In attempting to give systematic presentation to the various philosophies of religion now current in this country, we found ourselves grouping certain men and books together as proponents of essentially the same view. Their similarities pointed to common backgrounds, and in the persistent effort to delineate these commonalities underlying their thought, we were led to recognize four major traditions or channels of thought which seemed to have been the controlling magnets shaping the religious thought of the Western world, and, more particularly, that of our American commonwealth. We saw, for example, the persistent influence of super-naturalism in present-day religion. We noted, second, the dominance of idealism among certain types of religious thinkers. We became aware, further, of a distinctive emphasis among certain American liberals that seemed to lead back directly to the spirit and method of romanticism. And we discovered, finally, that a growing group of thinkers held to the procedure known as the scientific method and chose to keep within the bounds of the naturalistic order. The philosophies of each of these special groupings, upon analysis, seemed to become more comprehensible when interpreted against these respective backgrounds. Consequently, we became increasingly certain that in order to understand contemporary philosophies of religion and to evaluate their relevance to the present religious situation, careful inquiry should be directed to the sources upon which they feed and full cognizance given to the historical banners they unfurl. Naturally no present-day representative is consistent with the tradition which he continues. And the significance of each cannot be determined arbitrarily by the prestige or lack of status which the respective traditions have acquired through the years. But the temper of thought is made manifest in each case. And the degree of relevance to current ends is, in some measure, made clearer. It is therefore both as an aid to acquiring fuller insight into present-day philosophies of religion and as a guide to interpreting and evaluating their contributions to the current quest that we invite our readers to approach these modern philosophers through the historical hallways which we have designated, and to employ, although with scientific tentativeness, the classificatory labels which we have seen fit to apply, thus dividing the contemporary company of religious thinkers into supernaturalists, idealists, romanticists and naturalists.

Our purpose has been to do more, however, than simply systematize present-day philosophy of religion. We have tried to interpret the various philosophies of religion in relation to the present cultural situation with a view, not only to understanding them, but to estimating their importance as efforts to formulate a faith for our day. Accordingly, we address our remarks to everyone who would soberly ponder this urgent problem — to preachers as well as teachers of religion; to youth, baffled by the contradictory counsel of religious leaders, as well as adults, troubled by the turmoil of cultural change and shifting winds of doctrine. We have not tried to give a final word, but to call attention to directive insights in the various contemporary philosophies of religion which may be clarifying and stimulating. In certain matters of belief we have stated our own preferences freely. Nevertheless, we have tried to keep clear of dogmatizing. How far the personal biases have marred the presentation of other views, the reader himself must judge. No doubt we have been guilty of some misrepresentation and unfair judgment; for no interpreter escapes the limitations of the personal equation. But deliberate effort has been made to present fairly and adequately each of the important formulations of present-day religious thought.

Contributors to the symposium which ends this volume all had the manuscript before them as they wrote. They have been most gracious in their co-operation. Their criticisms of the manuscript, as well as their own contributions, are invaluable.

This volume is a collaboration, rather than the combined results of two writers. It was wrought out by two minds working with remarkable accord. Each has amplified and corrected the insight of the other. The book as a whole, therefore, represents the co-operative deliberations and labors of the authors, and certain sections have been written jointly. These chapters are: I, IX and XII. The independent writing has been divided as follows: Chapters II, IV, V, VI, VIII and XIII have been written by H. N. Wieman. The remaining chapters — III, VII, X, XI, XIV and XV — have been written by B. E. Meland. However, in these independent chapters, each has greatly aided the other.

THE AUTHORS

CONTENTS

A SYMPOSIUM

THE PRESENT OUTLOOK IN PHILOSOPHY OF RELIGION

PART ONE

ORIENTATION

CHAPTER I

BY WAY OF PERSPECTIVE

)MS of a searching mood are everywhere apparent
religious thinkers today. Not since the days of the
and the Reformation have the turns of thought
ıdamental in implication. This temper of inquiry
revalent in both Catholic and Protestant circles. In
m it has been manifest for some time in such popular
tendencies as the Catholic Youth Movement in Aus-
tria, the *Volksbildung Verein* in southern Germany, and in the
evangelical and liturgical movements within the Benedictine
Orders throughout Europe, especially in France and Germany.
In the field of Catholic theology and philosophy one finds a
similar searching spirit. Contemporary writers, apparently
finding present-day formulations inadequate, are eagerly at
work reinterpreting tradition and current culture in the hope
that a more satisfying synthesis of thought may emerge. The
new theology of certain German Catholic theologians, the neo-
Augustinian emphasis found in both France and Germany, and
the more widespread neo-Thomist movement are telling symptoms of a renascent spirit in Catholic thought.

Within Protestantism, the resurgent currents of new thought
are even more pronounced. Europe, having felt the impact of
recent world disturbances more keenly than America, has been
shaken more vigorously by reactionary developments issuing

from its crises. No sufficient study of recent tendencie
thought in relation to the wider cultural changes has b
made as yet to warrant confident generalizations on this n
ter, but there can be little doubt that the temper of thought n
manifest is in some measure the expression of deeper cultu
currents. Some of the more influential of these Protesta
tendencies are the Barthian movement and its correlative
actions, the high-church movements as well as the modifi
liturgical reforms, the Buchman movement, the neo-Francisc
revival, and the revival of mysticism, not to mention the ma
creative developments in European theology and philosopl
seeking a new orientation of thought, expressive of modern ii
sights.[1]

In America the search for a center has been equally wid
spread, although less articulate. Yet the present mood amon
us seems ripe for just such resurgent movements as have bee
occurring across the sea. The restlessness among our younge
American clergy and theologians with regard to the socia
philosophy of Christianity and their persistent preoccupation
with Marxian ideals, the solicitous urging of penitent liberal
churchmen to heed the call of *the New Protestantism,* and
the frequent gathering of selected groups to consider a religious rationalization of the social revolution that seems imminent are some of the obvious signs of a rising reactive
spirit.

More fundamental than any of these reactionary symptoms,
however, is the search for reality among theologians and philosophers of religion. Within the decade that has passed, more
attention has been given to the philosophical study of religion
than at any comparable time previous to this period. Literature
in the field of philosophy of religion has been appearing with
increasing regularity in America. And the present indications
are that more and more thinkers in the philosophical field will
be turning to ponder the fundamental matters of religious
thought. With this situation developing, there is reason to re-

view the course which this rising tide of reflection has been taking as well as to hazard some predictions as to the possible turns ahead.

PURPOSE AND METHOD

As one views the contemporary scene in the field of religious thought, one cannot fail to be impressed by the great variety in points of view. And listening to current discussions of religious problems here and there, one may be inclined to regard them all as a huge babel of confused and contradictory voices. But there is more order and consistency in this apparent jumble of proud phrases than the ordinary listener is apt to discern. For these many voices in religion are not just the soundings of individual cranks or sages; they are the current renderings of thought-traditions which have been developing through the centuries. Each discourse that one hears today is an earnest exposition, more or less accurate and worthy, of a great basic theme which has dominated groups of thinkers from age to age. And in most cases these basic themes are the affirmations growing out of a fundamental *slant* on the world and its life. Any man is easy, William James used to say, when you get hold of his center. The course of contemporary philosophies of religion will be more readily discerned and appreciated to the degree that one undertakes to identify these many voices with the thought-traditions out of which they speak.

The present volume is intended to bring these many diverse efforts to establish a philosophy of religion for today into clearer perspective, to make more articulate the significant tendencies and turnings in modern thought, and to provide, as it were, a bird's-eye view of the whole field of American philosophy of religion and its literature. Were it not that the undertaking is so imperative, one might well judge this effort presumptuous. For no two interpreters can hope to arrange the thoughts of their contemporaries in systematic form so as to satisfy all concerned. Yet, if it be remembered that this classified interpretation of present-day views has been attempted, not simply for the purpose of tabulating thinkers, but with a view to clarifying the cross-currents of thought that might otherwise confuse and confound, the effort may appear more justified, and the results more illuminating.

The theologies and philosophies of religion now taking form reflect the influences of four great traditions which have dominated the religious and philosophical thought of the Western world. One stream takes its rise out of the tradition of supernaturalism; another out of the tradition of idealism; a third out of the movement of thought known as romanticism; and a fourth out of the tradition of naturalism. These traditions will be discussed later, but their distinctive traits should be noted now so as to visualize the broad outlines of the field at the outset. We shall consider each briefly with regard to method and metaphysics.

1. The contemporary philosophies of religion that draw upon the tradition of supernaturalism are distinctive in method in that they hold to an authoritarian source outside of the rational processes of man as a conditioning, if not the controlling, factor in religious faith and knowledge. Revelation in some form is therefore essential to their philosophies of religion. This method arises, doubtless, out of their metaphysics, which is a thoroughgoing dualism. The realm of the divine and the natural order are in sharp antithesis to each other. The creature world being impotent to remedy the situation, the only hope of bridging the chasm lies in the divine order taking the initiative to communicate with mankind. This is felt to be possible because God is conceived of as a *personal Being* who is both aware of and interested in his creatures.

2. The idealists are pre-eminently rationalists in method. They hold that truth may be attained only through rigorous application of speculative logic. The exception to this in our classification is the modern mystic, who holds to a special theory of knowledge peculiar to the tradition of mysticism,

approaching that of supernaturalism. Metaphysically the idealists are not all alike. The absolutists and the modern mystics
embrace a monism, while the personalists revert to a modified
dualism. But they agree in designating Cosmic Mind (in some
sense) as the ultimate form of reality.

As we shall point out later, idealism has carried over also
into forms of philosophy of religion that are rooted in other traditions. For example, the ethical intuitionists under romanticism and the evolutionary theists under naturalism will be found
holding to Cosmic Mind as the metaphysical ultimate. To this
extent they must be considered idealists, but only in that respect.

3. The romanticists have this in common, that they find it
"wisdom to believe the heart," and thus make the appeal to religious experience basic in their method of attaining religious
insight. Romanticism produced two distinct emphases in religious thought: one leading to an ethical emphasis, the other
to an aesthetic interpretation of religion. Hence the romanticists are considered here under two heads: ethical intuitionists and aesthetic naturalists. The former incline toward
idealism and supernaturalism in world-view; the latter toward
naturalism.

4. The current philosophies of religion rising out of the tradition of naturalism come together on common ground in their
effort to rear a religious faith on facts made available by the
sciences. Their method, therefore, is primarily the scientific
method, but the philosophers within this group employ it with
varying degrees of consistency. They agree also in holding to
a naturalistic metaphysics. They know but one reality — that
which may be explored by scientific observation and reason.
The chief differences among them center about their interpretations of the natural order — some holding to a radical empiricism, yielding a humanistic philosophy of religion; others
pressing on to establish a new metaphysics, interpreting God in
terms of cosmic process.

OTHER BASES OF CLASSIFICATION

There are other points of view from which contemporary philosophies of religion in America might be surveyed. They might be distinguished by the metaphysics they set forth. But if that were done the question would still remain: Why did each philosopher develop his own peculiar kind of metaphysics? The only way to answer that question would be to bring to light the tradition of thought and feeling which dominated the thinker and gave him his problem, his approach and his point of view.

Again, one might try to differentiate the philosophies of religion in the United States by the respective methods of religious inquiry which they uphold. But here again the deeper problem would have to be solved: Why one method rather than another? And here likewise the answer would have to be sought in the traditions of thought which shaped the mind and provided the materials of the philosopher in question. The most potent influence in shaping any philosophy is the tradition of thought which provides the method, the materials, the objective, and the problem for the system that is constructed by the individual.

A third way of classifying philosophies of religion would be according to the major problems with which they deal. But here again the answer would be found, if found at all, in the social heritage which nourished each thinker and most potently influenced him.

Thus all classifications, when followed through to the end, lead back to the dominating traditions of thought which guide, inspire and challenge the minds of the thinkers under examination. Therefore, in studying the philosophies of religion in America, we have adopted the method of examining them in the light of the traditions of thought which seem most influential in shaping their work. These traditions are, as we have said, supernaturalism, idealism, romanticism and natural-

ism. Every modern thinker in this field has been influenced
in some measure by all of these traditions. But in each case,
some one of these streams has been more potent than others in
shaping the mind of the individual.

While our method has been that of studying present-day
thinkers in the light of these four great traditions, it may be
clarifying to note the grouping that would result if they were
studied from the point of view of their metaphysics and then
from that of their methods of inquiry. The validity of our approach by way of the traditions appears to be substantiated again
when we discover that these other standpoints, with few exceptions, bring forth the same alignment that the traditions
reveal.

Suppose one take metaphysics as the basis of study. In prevalent philosophies of religion we find three outstanding types
of metaphysics. First is the metaphysics which holds to a
dualism between God and the world, corresponding to the tradition of supernaturalism. Second is the metaphysics of Cosmic Mind, corresponding to the tradition of idealism. Third
is the metaphysics which finds ultimate reality in some process
of nature. This corresponds to naturalism.

Thus we find that the metaphysical classification corresponds
strikingly to the classification according to the dominating traditions, excepting the romantic tradition. But examination reveals that the romanticists all claim the ground and goal of the
universe to be Cosmic Mind (when they undertake to define
their metaphysics). Hence they show in their metaphysics the
dominating influence of the tradition of idealism, as we have
said. They are not idealists, however. They repudiate idealism
on several points. They doubtless get their predilection for
thinking of God as mind from traditional supernaturalism.
But idealism is the philosophic reformulation of this tradition,
adapting it to modern thought. The romantic intuitionists
take this philosophic formulation of divine mind, rather than
the unmodified traditional form found in supernaturalism.

This is true also of the evolutionary theists. Hence the tradition of idealism shows its influence in this kind of metaphysics also.

One might also distinguish the various philosophies of religion metaphysically on the basis of the conception of God that is developed. Again four types stand out: God as Being, in supernaturalism; God as Mind, in idealism and romanticism; God as Process, in naturalistic theism; and God as Symbol, in humanistic theism and aesthetic naturalism.

One of the most enlightening ways of studying our many philosophies of religion is to elucidate their several methods of religious inquiry. Here again we find our approach by way of the great traditions confirmed. Under the tradition of supernaturalism we find the authoritarian method. In the keeping of idealism is the method of rational speculation. The romanticists use a method which we shall call pragmatic, although it should not be confused with the pragmatism of John Dewey. Perhaps a more applicable term to denote their method would be "emotive," implying the appeal to practical experience. The tradition of naturalism adheres to the scientific method.

These four methods which distinguish the philosophies of religion in America today — the authoritarian, the speculative, the emotive and the scientific — are discussed and clarified much more fully in the first part of Chapter XII.

There has been a strong tendency among some students of philosophy of religion to classify these philosophies according to the same divisions as are commonly used in distinguishing the several schools of general philosophy. These are Idealism, Realism and Pragmatism. But we believe this is a mistake and only results in confusion. The main problem of general philosophy since Descartes has been that of epistemology. Hence these divisions are almost exclusively concerned with this problem. But in philosophy of religion the problem of knowledge has not been the central issue on which the different philosophies have divided. Hence to try to classify them on that issue is to throw the whole picture out of perspective.

There is another objection, even more important, for not forcing philosophies of religion into the same schema as general
philosophy. It is quite possible for two or more philosophers to
hold the same epistemology and yet be worlds apart in their
philosophy of religion. For example, E. B. Pratt, Roy W. Sellars and George Santayana all belong to that division of general
philosophy called critical realism. But one could scarcely get
three philosophies of religion more different from one another
than are those represented by these three men. Therefore in
our treatment of philosophies of religion in America we make
no attempt to correlate them with the three major divisions of
general philosophy which go by the names of Idealism, Realism
and Pragmatism.

Finally it should be noted that this old classification is getting
out of date even in general philosophy. Once it served very
well to distinguish the different philosophers, but now it is often
more a source of confusion than enlightenment. Many a so-
called idealist is indistinguishable from a realist, and vice versa.
Also there is developing a new kind of epistemology, sometimes called objective relativism, most fully developed by C. I.
Lewis, which cuts across the old divisions. Therefore it is re-
grettable when a student of philosophies of religion tries to ape
general philosophy by adopting its classification when it, itself,
is casting off that classification as being outworn and inadequate.

IMPORTANCE OF HISTORICAL BACKGROUND

Most philosophies of religion are too organic in content and
flexible in method to yield to rigid classification. No matter
how carefully the schema may be devised, it will seem inadequate as an index to the currents of thought; for thought, being
organic and mobile, overruns mechanical categories. Nevertheless, thought tends to follow a consistent curvature, owing
to the fact that it proceeds from certain presuppositions, is
dominated by certain biases and predilections, and yields at

basic points to the appeal of an accepted method. The classification of views, then, when it is done with an eye to basic traits, is simply the bringing together of formulated theories which reflect common presuppositions, biases and methods. Or we may say it is the relating of contrasting views in an orderly arrangement that reveals the degrees of their divergences.

To discover these determining or shaping elements in a philosophy, one needs to do more than consult the contemporary statement of the position; one must view the current expression in relation to the historic streams of thought that have fed into it, for it is in the broader perspective that the motivating factors come to light. Method, to be sure, is detectable within the short range of thought revealed by the contemporary view; but to sense the more subtle, motivating influences that determine the *slant of vision*, and which give rise to the inhibitory as well as the outreaching impulses, one must see the reactive tendencies that lay back of that way of thinking. The tension between supernaturalism and naturalism, for example, is something more than a logical matter. It is an historical one. It reflects, on the one hand, the rise of other-worldliness in traditional thought as a reaction against current worldly conditions; and, on the other hand, the rise of this-worldliness in much of modern thought as a subsequent reaction against supernaturalism in medieval thought. Two historical situations are involved in this tension. Neither supernatural philosophies nor naturalistic philosophies, therefore, can be considered as purely logical constructions of ideas, for the emotive elements have affected the turn of logic too materially. Similarly the wall of indifference that seems to rise at times between idealistic forms of religious philosophy and the naturalistic systems that draw heavily from the sciences reflects more than a contemporary mood. It marks an historical cleavage that goes back to the rise of modern philosophy and recalls the reactionary current that set in early in the seventeenth century against the effort to subject philosophy to the domination of the sciences. Likewise in the case of the tension between ethical intuitionism and supernaturalism on the one hand, and ethical intuitionism and naturalism on the other. In the former we have a contemporary expression of the seventeenth century conflict between the " religion of authority " in traditional theology and the " religion of the spirit " implicit in the rising liberal theology. In the latter we see the present extension of the *romantic protest against reason* as the sole arbiter in matters of religious thought.

These historical conflicts in the growth of thought have been too fundamental in basis and implication to be outgrown completely. Even after the years have softened the differences and eased the tensions, the temperamental biases persist and become active agents of thought whenever the views, dominated by one or the other tradition, come into conflict or enter upon friendly combat.

Why do these biases persist? Because the historical episodes of reaction in the history of thought are the expressions of a more deeply persistent phenomenon: namely, the temperamental differences in human nature, arising out of socio-physical conditions affecting the thinking organism. Much as we may seek to make thinking objective and purely logical, we never succeed fully in escaping the human equation. For thinking involves responding to stimuli. And responding to stimuli demands sensitivity to stimuli. It is here that the human equation asserts itself. The variation in men's sensitivity on the one hand, and the diversity of stimuli to which they become sensitive on the other, are the root conditions that determine both the line of their reasoning and the degree to which this or that idea may take hold of them, or may appeal to their reason as acceptable. Consequently a survey of contemporary systems of thought, like the history of philosophical or religious thought, is as much a disclosure of human blindness and impulse as it is an exposition of luminous insight and reason.

All this argues for great care in associating contemporary views with one another. Mere mechanical similarities and differences must not determine the classification. Neither should concern for categorical distinctions, to aid and simplify the selection of a tenable position from the variety of views, influence the procedure too strongly. There must be concern for the total nature of its thought: its spirit as well as its literal characteristics; its negations as well as its affirmations; its historical emergence as well as its current form. In working out our classification in this study, we have tried to be sensitive to all of these aspects.

Before proceeding with our analysis of contemporary thought, we turn to consider the present state of culture and human life, revealing the imperative need for the work of philosophers of religion today.

[1] The following publications contain helpful surveys of contemporary European thought: *Present Theological Tendencies:* Aubrey, Harper, 1936; *Im Ringen um die Kirche:* Heiler, Ernst Reinhardt, 1931; *Modern Man's Worship:* Meland, (Part I) Harper, 1934; *La Philosophie religieuse en Grande-Bretagne de 1850 à nos jours:* Librairie Blond Gay, 1934; *Philosophy Today:* Schaub (editor), Open Court Publishing Co., 1928; *The Religious Situation:* Tillich, Holt, 1932; *Religious Thought in England Since 1850:* Webb, Oxford University Press, 1935; *Contemporary Thought of Great Britain:* Widgery, Knopf, 1927; *Le Culte,* Vol. I: Will, Librairie Istra, 1925. A volume surveying the religious thought of Europe and America during the past half century is in preparation, under the editorship of the writer, Meland, in which scholars like C. C. J. Webb, Canon Mozley, F. Menegoz, Victor Monod and Paul Tillich are collaborating. Important surveys are to be found also in the *Journal of Philosophical Studies, The New Scholasticism, The Philosophical Review,* and *The Journal of Religion.*

CHAPTER II

THE PRESENT NEED FOR PHILOSOPHY OF RELIGION

IN AN age when the traditional religion is fairly satisfactory and needs only to be clarified and systematized, the intellectual work in religion is properly called "theology." It is very important and very useful. It gives power and depth and scope to religion. It greatly increases its effectiveness as a vital function.

But in an age when the traditional form of religion is not satisfactory, when its basic structure must be re-examined and the abstract essentials distinguished from the passing forms of concrete life, philosophy of religion comes to the front. In such a time the theologians are likely to say that there is no real difference between theology and philosophy of religion. What they mean is that in such a time the work they have to do is really that of philosophy of religion. In this they are right, although there is a difference between theology and philosophy of religion.

The theologian endeavors to present the object of religious devotion in a form that is intellectually acceptable to the people of his time and group. That means he must organize beliefs about the supremely worthful in such a way that they do not contradict one another and are not contradicted by other propositions held to be true. Thus theology gives intellectual expression to religious devotion.

But philosophy criticizes the assumptions of that devotion. It seeks to lay bare the essential characteristics which make this reality worthy of such devotion, if it has such characteristics. Philosophy of religion wants to know if the essentials are there; theology wants to make sure that the form of presentation is acceptable to the mental needs of the people of that time and place.

This distinction between theology and philosophy of religion may be made clearer if we compare religion to eating. If religion is like eating, then the reality which interests the religious person is analogous to food. In that case the theologian is the one who puts this food into such form that it is palatable and can be most readily eaten. The theologian is a good cook. But the philosopher is a dietitian. He does not prepare the food for eating. He does not present God in a form that is digestible to the ordinary religious person. That is not his business. He does not talk about jelly and fried chicken and cake. He talks about vitamins and proteins. Now, no one ever hungered for vitamins and proteins. Of course, what he really needed were these, but he could not take them in the abstract form of vitamins and proteins, although these were truly the essentials. He had to have them in the form of jelly and fried chicken and the like. The theologian talks about beefsteak and lettuce. The philosopher talks about starches and calories. Consequently, simple souls are likely to think that the philosopher is discussing something that has no connection with their yearnings. In this they are mistaken, but their mistake is very understandable.

We have come to a time in the history of the world when the religious diet must be changed. This diet has always been changing throughout history, not in respect to the essentials, not in respect to vitamins and proteins, not in respect to the reality of God, but in respect to the concrete form in which these essentials are taken. At one time they may have been taken in the form of roots and berries and slugs and insects, later in the form of raw fish or bear and deer. So also, in religion, you can trace the many forms in which men have sought and found the reality of God. That does not mean that everything that men have ever worshiped was truly God any more than everything people have ever eaten truly had in it the essentials of nutrition. There has been a great deal of religious malnutrition as well as physiological.

It is a dangerous thing to change the diet without the services of a dietitian, especially if the new food is of a sort that was never before eaten by man. Does it have the essential elements of nutrition? It must be palatable, but that is not enough. We must have the services of the dietitian as well as the cook. We must operate with those concepts which enable us to detect the essential reality in the new foods, whether that essential reality be proteins or deity.

Is the religious anemia of the modern man due to the fact that he has not been able to find in the new " isms " and religions of our time the ancient nourishment which gives to life its vitality and power? Is the ancient deity found in these new religions?

Also, there is another peculiar problem. How to keep the zest of life through a keen sense of the supremely worthful for all human living and at the same time be keenly self-conscious and critical, that is the problem. It can be solved only by a religion which has attained some sense of the supremely worthful for all human living by way of the critical understanding. But that also requires the services of philosophy.

A swift survey of the outstanding characteristics of our time will help to reveal the peculiar need for philosophy of religion in such an age as this. These outstanding characteristics come under the heads of social change, sophistication, and cultural problems.

SOCIAL CHANGE

Social change is always going on, but it has rarely been so swift and radical as it is today. In recent times the intellectual and institutional structure of life has not been able to keep up with the rapid transformation of the actual processes of living.

The process has run away from the forms, standards, ideals, affections, loyalties, objectives. Undoubtedly this maladjustment between the process and the ideology of life has occurred in the past, but perhaps never in the same degree and not in the same way.

Swift and radical change in the past has generally been due to one or more of three causes — conquest, internal disintegration, and natural catastrophe. In case of conquest, two cultures were brought together so that either they merged or one dominated the other, or both. But in such case the problem was not to rear a new moral and religious structure. It was to merge or otherwise adjust two structures already in existence. Such a task might well call for the services of philosophy, but it plainly did not so urgently demand a clarification of the basic principles on which any culture must be reared as does the present state of affairs, where the problem is not so much to merge two old cultures as to rear a new one to fit the requirements of a new way of living.

When extreme social change was due to internal disintegration or natural catastrophe, the need of philosophy was even less imperative. Such a change meant a lapse to some more simple, more primitive, way of living. In the purlieus of society can always be found some forms that can be used and developed to meet the needs of life when it thus declines.

But the cause of social change in our day is none of these we have mentioned. It is science and machinery. It is a change that has made life not more simple, but more complex. It has not diminished our powers of achievement but has increased them. It has not reduced our economic wealth but has vastly increased it. It has not made us less dependent on one another, but more so. It has not decreased the materials and opportunities for enjoyment but has brought them to a bewildering confusion. We do not mean that this change brought about by science and machinery has thus far made life necessarily more joyous or satisfying or meaningful, but only that it has increased the complexity, the power to do things, the interdependence, and the materials. Hence the social change we have undergone in the recent past is not only different from other historic changes in being more swift and deep, but is also different in kind.

The sovereign loyalties which dominated the life of the past cannot dominate ours. The affections which mellowed and sweetened past lives cannot be ours in just the same form. The objectives which lured them on cannot command our powers. The appreciations which warmed their hearts must reach us in different forms. All this means that we must give religion a new form fitted to the new way of living.

But there has been too much unintelligent tampering with religion. There has been too much changing of the form of religion without regard to the basic reality which any form must hold if it is to meet the requirements of living. There are too many new forms of religion being foisted upon an unsuspecting world. It is not enough to change the form of religion. We must first clarify those principles which essentially underlie any noble religion, and with these to guide us, and only with these, can we undertake the reformulation of religion. We must be sure the vitamins and proteins are in the new forms. This is the reason that modern social change requires philosophy of religion.

Another characteristic of change today points to the same conclusion. The difference between successive generations has become so great that the transmission of affections, loyalties and appreciations from one to the other has become exceedingly difficult. We have long passed the time when this transmission could occur automatically and unconsciously. It has become a highly technical and self-conscious process called "education." But we are rapidly coming to the place where it is impossible, or at any rate unprofitable, to do it even by professional education.

Experts in the field of education are coming to see that what we must do is no longer to attempt to transmit our loyalties, affections and appreciations, but rather give to the rising generation those methods and principles by which they may be able to develop their own objectives and ruling interests. But educators have not come to see so clearly, as yet, that this is possible only if we have brought to light the underlying principles by which any noble way of living can be shaped. It is not merely a matter of skills and techniques. It is quite as truly, and even more imperatively, a matter of having those abstract, guiding principles which must determine good life, whatever form it may assume. Until we have grasped these with a fair degree of clarity and have learned how to hand them on from generation to generation, we cannot bridge the widening chasm that separates the mature from the immature. But this chasm must be bridged, else culture will decline toward barbarism.

Still another feature of our social change should be noted. It has become so great that the individual is clearly conscious of a shift in the major objectives of life as he passes from the cradle to the grave. Thus, if he develops a satisfactory way of living in his young manhood, and clings to it, he is likely to find himself in an alien world when he becomes old, like Sir Bedivere when King Arthur's court was dissolved in ruin. Sir Bedivere, however, could lapse into a simpler way of living in a simpler world. But the man of today cannot. Rather, he must live in a more complex world. What is a man to do when the morality and religion of his youth is unworkable in his later years? Three things he might do. He might hold fast to the ways that were worthy in his youth and endure the maladjustment which such ways involve in the new and different world. Or he might cast off the old ways and shop around in the various new religions and moralities that are on display, finding nothing satisfying in any of them. Or, in the third place, if he has the basic guiding principles which an adequate philosophy of religion can provide, he can progressively modify and develop his religion and morality along with the changing world. Some few have been able to do this. They alone can live wisely.

SOPHISTICATION

There has been sophistication in every age of high civilization, but it is probable that sophistication today has gone more widely and sunk more deeply than in other times. At any rate, there is a great deal of it, chiefly because of our present means of communication and transportation.

By "sophistication" we mean that state of mind in which it is impossible for a person to accept uncritically any way of life. A sophisticated person can accept a way of life after having critically examined it. He might even adopt some very ancient system of religion and morality. Some sophisticated people have done just that. But a sophisticated person cannot do what most men through human history have done. He cannot grow up into a system of values with its loyalties, affections, standards, never asking whether it is good or bad, but simply living it as *the* way of life for any human. If he accepts any way of life, he must do it self-consciously and critically. That is what we mean by sophistication.

There are a number of causes for this widespread sophistication. In examining them, we shall be thinking especially of sophistication in religion. We have mentioned modern communication and transportation, but these are not real causes. They are only the means by which the real causes are rendered pervasive and potent.

One of the causes of sophistication is modern psychology. People have become very sensitive about "compensatory illusions," " escape mechanisms " and " wishful thinking." They have been taught that much of morality and religion is a disguised form of these, and so they are on their guard. They examine critically any way of life that may be presented to see if it be not an example of one of these. They have become skeptical, skittish, uncertain, lest they be caught in wishful thinking.

Another cause of sophistication is the obvious maladjustment of traditional religion to the modern world. This maladjustment makes traditional religion unrealistic. In its time this body of tradition may very well have been the way in which men came to grips with reality. In a very different cultural context these old words and forms had a very different meaning from what they now have. But today they often generate illusions rather than adjust to reality. Realization of this makes people critical and sophisticated toward all religion.

Again, the scientific spirit has developed in men a demand for intellectual integrity. This does not mean that people in any appreciable numbers understand science or are scientific. It only means that they have heard and felt enough about science to be more critical, more cautious, more insistent on evidence, less ready to accept a belief merely because it is handed down, or because it makes one happy, or because it is upheld by a revered person or institution, or because it is respectable so to believe, or because it gives one the zeal to do right or to resist temptation or for any other personal or social advantage, or to satisfy a subjective need. Not to be bribed into holding a belief by personal or social advantage or by subjective need, is what is meant by "intellectual integrity." While there is precious little of it in the world now as always, there is probably more of it than in most times. It is a virtue but it also makes for critical-mindedness and sophistication. It takes away the naïveté of life.

Knowledge of other religions besides one's own, with consequent comparison and criticism leading to discernment of faults in all, and possibly to dreaming of a religion better than any, is a further cause of sophistication. It also makes impossible the naïve acceptance of any religion. It is likely to make one feel that no religion is satisfactory and so cause one to stand aloof from all.

Finally, the widespread discussion of religion is both cause and effect of religious sophistication. The religious discussion so rife today is not like that of other times, which was the discussion of the objects of religious interest. A healthy religion, like a healthy hungry man, is not interested in its own digestive processes. It is interested in the objective reality. In case of religion this is God or salvation or sin. Only the sick or the sophisticated talk about religion rather than the objects of religious interest, and the digestive process rather than the food which satisfies hunger. The discussion of religion today is of this sophisticated sort, and it greatly magnifies the sophistication.

The sophisticated person can be genuinely religious in only one way, and that is to search out and test, and so be intellectually satisfied that he has to do with the reality that is supremely worthful for all human living. Only so can he give that wholehearted devotion which is religion. But to do this requires the implements of philosophy. If he is not equipped to use these implements, he may hold on halfheartedly or desperately to some form of religion which he only half believes, or he may nominally cast off all religion, the while he practices unconsciously some crude uncriticized form of religion, or he may restlessly try one kind of " ism " after another without finding anything that satisfies. Only with the tools of philosophy can he achieve a vital, personal religion which can make life noble, zestful and intelligent. By the " tools of philosophy " we mean the tools of criticism.

OUR CULTURAL PROBLEMS

Our age has certain cultural problems that are peculiar to it and which distinguish it from other ages. An analysis of these problems will further reveal our need of philosophy of religion.

The *first* of these peculiar problems is a great increase in economic goods, but produced under the control of social customs which make it impossible for the great majority of people to have abundant access to them. Our storehouses are bursting with actual and potential wealth. By potential wealth we mean that even when the actual goods are not there, we have the power to produce them in great quantities. But while these economic goods are accumulating and wasting unused, millions of people who have helped to produce them are in dire need. While we suffer bitter want, the goods, actual and potential, pile ever higher; but we block one another when we try to get at them. We reach out after them while they rot and rust and waste away, but we live under such a code that each gets in the other man's way whenever he tries to get access to these rich supplies.

This is one of the most bizarre, one of the most unbelievable situations that has ever arisen in human history. It is so anomalous and so foolish that it cannot last long. Either we shall cease to produce in such quantity and lose the power to produce, or else we shall find some way of getting at these great stores of economic wealth and using them for the common good.

What prevents us from enjoying this great wealth we are able to produce is the system of loyalties and ideals under which we live. These might be briefly described as free competition, individualism, and domination of life by the profit motive. But any ruling system of loyalties and ideals constitutes a morality and a religion. Thus the cause of our economic depression, poverty and misery is not economic scarcity or inability to produce, or lack of mechanisms for distributing these great quantities of goods we can produce, but it is the intellectual and institutional structure of our dominant loyalties. These must be reconstructed before we can hope to gain access to the economic abundance that is rightfully ours. The mastering loyalties which make us act the way we do, stupidly frustrating one another when we try to get at the goods we have produced or can produce, must be changed.

Some may ridicule the thought that philosophy can reshape our loyalties in such a way that our powers can be released to distribute and enjoy the wealth that is ours. It is true that philosophy could not do this by itself alone. But mighty pent forces are storming and pressing to break through this tangle of frustrating ideals and habits. Hence philosophy does not have to do the work alone. It only needs to show how this tangle may be straightened out in certain respects and then the great urges of life will break through to develop a new way. It can set forth certain basic guiding principles which help to release us from the tangle of outgrown habits and ideals and give some sense of an outline of the new way of life that must be developed by the processes of actual living.

The *second* great cultural problem which distinguishes our time might be stated thus: Great increase in power of achievement but no cause sufficiently dominant to draw all this power into its service. When we speak of today's marvelous increase in human power, we think first of the machines that have been invented and are now being perfected. They are a large part of it, but not all. We also have the techniques of social control, the social mechanisms, the fact-finding devices, propaganda, methods of organizing individuals into corporate bodies, executive and administrative agencies, and so forth. We can mobilize vast masses of men, not only in war but also in other enterprises, and not only their bodies but also their minds, their inventiveness, and other resources of personality.

All this power we have, actual or potential, but we do not know what to do with it. So we waste our time and energy in a dizzy whirl of trivial matters. Or we throw ourselves into dissipation to escape the ennui, or we exploit and destroy and yearn for great destructive conflicts like war in order to give us a chance to use our powers.

Here, again, the cause of the difficulty is that we have outgrown our old loyalties. The great causes of life as they are handed down to us from the past are not formulated in such a way as to absorb our energies and awaken our supreme devotion. Our machines, our social devices of achievement, our methods of procedure, our mechanisms of power, simply cannot gear into these causes because of the form in which they come to us. These forms were suited to activities of another age, not to ours.

We need to formulate the supreme objectives of life in a new way, in a way suited to make use of our present powers of achievement and our uttermost loyalties. It is not so much that we need new objectives in any ultimate sense, but we need to see these supreme objectives in new perspectives and with wider horizons and in relation to other activities. We need to get at those underlying principles which reveal the scope and diversity of these supreme causes.

The *third* peculiar cultural problem of our time is an increase in the materials and opportunities for happiness without standards adequate to guide us in our choices and appreciations. The humblest today has access to the cultural achievements of the greatest. Shakespeare, Dante, Homer, and innumerable lesser works can be gotten in paper-bound books for ten cents. The greatest singers, speakers and thinkers can be heard over the radio in the humblest home. Science and its inventions are being put into popular journals so that the high school boy can read and understand. Even history of philosophy is being written in such a way that the common man can get some sense of what it is all about.

Some may say that this popularization of truth, beauty and goodness degrades them and leaves only the sham forms of them, not the reality. The reply is that if anyone thinks he has the insight and acumen and taste to appreciate the highest and best, he can today, as never before, gain access to the original works of the greatest in history and find them more readily than ever.

However, it is true that all this abundance of culture seems to be a hodgepodge heaped up round about us but which no one is able to enjoy.   And the cause would seem to be rather obvious.   One must have standards by which one is reared from infancy in order to appreciate the cultural riches of life.   Furthermore, great achievements of truth, beauty and goodness can be fully such only in the context of some great body of culture to which they are native.   A heterogeneous assemblage of such works cannot give abundant richness to life.   They cannot be appreciatively assimilated in that way.

Nevertheless, the fact still stands that we have the materials and the opportunities, the leisure and the means, for developing a richness of life such as was never before possible.   What we lack, what modern civilization lacks, is a set of standards fitted to its genius, by which to develop capacity for appreciation, and ability to participate in the creation of an organic unity of culture wherein each work and act would help to illuminate and enhance the value of all others.   Such standards again call for that grasp of fundamental principles which it is the work of philosophy to uncover.

Such work of philosophy is not so much needed in an age in which a ripe tradition has gradually arisen which guides the individual in his development from infancy so that the interactions of society enlarge his capacity for appreciation and his powers of creative participation to the utmost of his ability. But our age has all the powers, materials, opportunities and means for the flowering of a magnificent culture, lacking only the standards.   When tradition does not supply these, philosophy must serve as a midwife to help bring them to birth. Philosophy cannot create them, but it can help to bring them to consciousness.

A *fourth* distinctive cultural problem of our time is a great increase of interdependence but without integrating loyalties, habits and sentiments which would enable us to live together co-operatively and in creative community.

Our interdependence is obvious. No longer does a man go to the well in his back yard to get a drink. He gets it out of a faucet, which means that in drinking he is caught in bonds of interdependence with a vast network of finance, industrial workers, experts, machines. When he goes to town, he no longer hitches the horse to the buggy and drives, but he gets on a streetcar; and again he is enmeshed in bonds of interdependence. He gets his ideas from a newspaper which covers the planet with a network of news-gathering and idea-formulating activities. His fears, hopes, likes and dislikes are likewise shaped by doings and sayings of others spread far and wide. When the man in Corning, Kansas, sells his goods or services, the price is ruinously lowered or lucratively increased by what is happening in Russia, China, Japan and France.

But the ideals and habits which shape our conduct and our feelings are not fitted to such a close network of interdependence. They are fitted to a much more loosely integrated system of living. For example, the traditional ideal of national sovereignty was fitted to a time when the nations were relatively independent. But they are no longer independent. Hence the way of living which is shaped by this ideal causes hideous disasters in our modern world. Or, again, the ideal of laissez faire, free competition and private initiative in making the most money you can for yourself, was an ideal which was fairly well fitted for pioneer conditions in which each man was loosely bound to the activities of others. But in our modern world, with its compact and intricate connection of each with all, such an ideal and such living spread havoc.

We need to develop loyalties, sentiments, ideals, which will enable us to reap the rare and precious values which can come out of these close bonds of interdependence if we use them to unite our forces in co-operation and creative interaction.

A *fifth* problem of our time is the drift toward collectivism with the danger of diminishing seriously our personal freedom. Collectivism is inevitable in our modern world and is all to the good, providing it does not destroy personal freedom. By "personal freedom" we here mean the stimulus and the opportunity to exercise individual initiative, to think for one's self, to experiment, criticize, invent, not necessarily machines but ways and devices for living. There can be no high culture without such freedom. There can be no richness of life unless each can develop his own unique individuality, think the thoughts, make the criticisms, and perform the acts that no one else but he could bring forth. But such freedom and uniqueness of individuality will destroy culture, especially in our modern world, with its delicate and intricate interdependence, unless each individual so functions as to stimulate the individuality of others and contribute the expression of his own individuality to the enrichment of the life of all. The life of all can be variegated and full only when it is constantly enriched by contributions of highly developed and unique individualities.

The danger is not in collectivism understood in the sense just described, but it is in that kind of collectivism which imposes uniformity, which regiments and suppresses freedom and uniqueness of thinking, acting and appreciating.

Since the end of the Middle Ages there has been a struggle, and a winning struggle, to achieve personal freedom and development of the individuality of persons and groups. But in recent years there has been a turning back toward the establishment of control, order, system, regimentation. We see it in Russia, in Germany, in Italy, in the United States, even in England and France, as well as in other countries. We see it not only in business and industry and politics. In art, also, there is a turn toward classicism and systematizing. We have the drama of O'Neill and the novels of Romain Rolland setting forth philosophies of life. In science there is a turning away from the theory and practice that science consisted chiefly in the use of specialized techniques and the accumulation of facts, toward the opposite view and practice that science strives to discover or achieve a rational order in the universe. Philosophy also is returning to rearing of cosmologies and world-enfolding systems.

This turn of history is inevitable. It is forced upon us. Civilization, with its delicate balance and finespun interdependence, could not survive if the old individualism were allowed to run rampant. Therefore it is being suppressed and will be more and more, ruthlessly if need be, in order that our whole civilization may not perish. But must we suffer also the decline of liberalism? Must we suffer the loss of that freedom to think, to criticize, to experiment, which is essential to every vital culture? Yes, we must, unless one great need is supplied.

When interdependence increases more rapidly than the cohesive tissue of society, conflict, destruction and collapse are inevitable unless coercive control and regimentation are supplied sufficiently to make up for the lack of cohesive tissue. By cohesive tissue we mean those integrating loyalties, affections, sentiments and habits which keep people working in harmony and creative community. There can be spontaneity, originality, freedom and liberalism in a closely woven system of interdependence only if this cohesive tissue has been developed sufficiently to keep the creative activities harmonious and co-operative. If not, then regimentation must be imposed.

Perhaps this is the most serious problem we face at this turning-point in history when the old individualism is being driven out by necessity. Can a new individualism be developed, an individualism in which the needed harmony and community is sustained by integrating loyalties and sentiments so that there need be no permanent suppression of individuality by regimentation?

At present we do not have this cohesive tissue. Therefore regimentation is necessary. But need it be permanent? May we not develop cohesive tissue, integrating loyalties, and unifying sentiments, sufficient to hold us into a co-operative and mutually sustaining community without the need of regimentation with its suppression of individual criticism and creativity? Certainly philosophy cannot do it. Nothing can do it except a great religion adequate to our time. Philosophy is a necessary guide and help in the growth of such a religion.

When we speak of the need of philosophy of religion, we do not mean the work of professionals who make philosophy of religion their chief business. We need such men, of course — more of them than ever before. But that is not the primary need. The primary need is for a widespread interest among great numbers of people in this problem of finding what is essential and fundamental in the passing forms of religion and holding fast to that when new forms are developing. Great numbers of people must become inquirers in religion and not merely passive believers.

In this sense philosophy of religion must become a great co-operative enterprise engaging the thought of thousands of people who make no pretense at being professional philosophers. If philosophy is to assist in the development of the religion we sorely need, a great many people must take some creative part in this endeavor to grasp the basic reality which must be found anew in the development of any great religion. We believe such widespread interest and endeavor is occurring today.

Whatever one may think of the ideas of C. G. Jung — and certainly many of them are seriously questionable — his vocation and contacts put him in a strategic position for discerning the modern temper and religious needs of the modern man. We quote him:

During the past thirty years, people from all the civilized countries of the earth have consulted me. I have treated many hundreds of patients, the larger number being Protestants, a smaller number Jews, and not more than five or six believing Catholics. Among all my patients in the second half of life — that is to say, over thirty-five — there has not been one whose problem in the last resort was not that of finding a religious outlook on life. It is safe to say that every one of them fell ill because he had lost that which the living religions of every age have given to their followers, and none of them has been really healed who did not regain his religious outlook. . . . It seems that side by side with the decline of religious life, the neuroses grow noticeably more frequent . . . everywhere the mental state of European man shows an alarming lack of balance. We are living undeniably in a period of the greatest restlessness, nervous tension, confusion and disorientation of outlook. . . . Every one of them has the feeling that our religious truths have somehow or other grown empty.[1]

These facts would seem to make plain that we must have a religion adequate to our time, else we cannot go on. No philosophy can be a substitute for such a religion. Neither can philosophy construct such a religion. But philosophy of religion is an indispensable aid in bringing such a religion to birth and to maturity.

The task that this situation imposes, however, is a sobering one in the light of the diversity of views and interests in the field of philosophy of religion today. For when differences become too marked and fundamental, concerted effort in dealing with this constructive problem is measurably frustrated, if not precluded. And the difficulty becomes accentuated when those holding varying views turn a deaf ear to one another's reasoning, or stiffen at the approach of one another's thoughts. The recognition that all are laboring toward the common end of intelligibly discerning the meaning and significance of truths that shape human life, should help to correlate our striving, even though we may project our different ends in interpreting the route toward that goal. If the present work can contribute toward a fuller understanding of the contemporary quests for truth, and increase the degree of mutual appreciation among their proponents, it will at least be a step toward achieving the larger, constructive task that confronts religious thinkers today.

[1] *Modern Man in Search of a Soul:* C. G. Jung. Pp. 264, 266, 268.

CHAPTER III

TRADITIONS SHAPING AMERICAN RELIGIOUS THOUGHT

THE religious thought of the Western world has been dominated by four great persisting influences. In the order of
their emergence within Christian thought, they may be cited
as *the tradition of supernaturalism, the tradition of idealism,
the tradition of romanticism,* and *the tradition of naturalism.*

The tradition of supernaturalism represents that magnificent
world-view that evolved in the minds of the ancient church
fathers, which found literary expression in the writings of
Dante and Milton, aesthetic rendering in the art of the medieval
Symbolists, of Giotto and Fra Angelico, and in the religious
art of Rubens, Raphael and Michelangelo, as well as in the
Romanesque and Gothic architecture, and which has become
permanently embodied, intellectually and emotionally, in the
Roman Catholic church. Not all who hold to the tradition of
supernaturalism are to be found in the Catholic church; but
all who do hold to it share with Catholicism in temper of intellect and emotional response. Protestantism, in its orthodox
form, was a break from an institution, based upon an attitude;
not a withdrawal from a world-view. Thus traditional Protestants stand within the thought bounds of their Catholic for-
bears, and share more in common than they recognize with
their Catholic contemporaries.

What are some of the distinctive traits of the supernatural tradition? It is important to note that its world-view is a syncretism of Jewish, Greek and Roman thought and culture, with stray influences from the Oriental mind. Jewish influences came in by way of the biblical background and even more directly through the intimate connections between early Christianity and Judaism. Eastern winds of doctrine were everywhere scattering the seeds of Oriental mysteries and philosophies in the soil of early Christianity. Gnosticism was the most potent of these influences. In fact, when the history of doctrine is frankly viewed, it becomes apparent that Christian thought, in its early stages, took form under the pressure of conflict with the Gnostic movement. And in this conflict, as in many another historic interaction, the conqueror emerged *conquered* by the very influences it sought to resist. If Christianity did not take directly from the Gnostics' speculations, it formulated doctrines at points of tension which had been precipitated by Gnostic aggression. And thus the Christian creeds became sorts of orthodox confessions on points raised by the speculative inquiry of this Oriental syncretism. Greek influences came about in many ways. The spread of Christianity into the Greek world occasioned a gradual orientation, on the part of Christian thinkers, in the thought-world of the Greeks and an assimilation of its ideology. Paul's efforts to adjust to the Greek mentality of his Gentile audiences are typical of this trend. The translation of Christian concepts into the thought-forms of the Greeks, as in the Gospel of John, suggests another. When early Christian theology began to be formulated, it could not escape the influence of Greek philosophy. Origen's eclectic use of Platonism in setting forth the basic truths of the church is clearly an example. Again, through Augustine, Neo-Platonism impressed itself upon the thought of the church. And in the sixteenth century, when St. Thomas Aquinas reconstructed and systematized Catholic theology, the concepts of Aristotle, filled, to be sure, with a Romanized content, infiltrated the language of western theology. The dominance of the Roman mind in the western world of affairs made inevitable the Romanizing of this syncretistic theology, once Christianity adorned its priests with the symbols of imperial recognition. The Roman mind was not creative, but organizational and practical. It brought muscle and motive power into the thought-life of Christianity by turning theological councils into a Curia, and doctrines into dogmas. Rome added to the Hebraic ideal of moral rectitude and to the Hellenistic appeal for logical order, the stern and simple philosophy of political conformity. Thus Christianity became a world-view, syncretizing three cultural ideals. The character of this tradition of supernaturalism, although composite, is well integrated. Its many aspects blend into one unified, ecclesiastically-controlled culture, a masterful achievement that must be assigned almost wholly to the medieval schoolmen of the Roman Catholic church.

This tradition should be viewed from another angle. Consider its epistemological characteristics. The temper of thought in supernaturalism is authoritarian. That is to say, belief ultimately rests upon the force of organized authority and precedent, rather than upon the appeal of logical reason. Back of every creed or dogma stands the imposing witness of the apostolic succession. Reverence for its tradition, or the compelling influence of organized forces that *do* revere it, constitutes the ground of appeal. But there is a logic to this authoritarianism after all. For back of the apostolic succession is the historic revelation that is thought to have first communicated the faith to the saints. Truth thus *once and for all time delivered,* is not *attained;* it is only *retained.* It is not *discovered;* but *recovered* and communicated. Always it is an absolute, a priori body of knowledge, independent of human frailty and beyond human comprehension. The attitude toward the free use of reason or the uncontrolled expression of individual experience in supernaturalism should therefore not be difficult to understand.

Reason is looked upon as a worthy aid to faith, provided it *deduces* facts from a proper major premise. It becomes a pathway to error, however, when it undertakes to *induce* new premises from humanly observed or derived facts. No other position is possible from the authoritarian point of view. For facts or premises apart from the historically given norm cease to be either knowledge or truth. The theory of revelation closes the circuit of religious thinking, and thus returns reasoning to the major premises established a priori through precedent and authority.

But the theory of revelation rests upon religious as well as rational ground. Revealed truth is not simply informing; it is transforming, or saving. It provides the medium of grace whereby man passes from the state of mortality to that of immortality. Dogma, in other words, is simply the officially accepted intellectual formula or framework that holds man in right relations with supernatural agencies that save him from an otherwise incurable state. Truth is illumination that relates man helpfully and effectively to the supernatural world, the source of grace; not a philosophy that explains. Consequently it becomes imperative, on the one hand, to guard this sacred wisdom lest it become obscured through human distortion, and, on the other hand, to control and guide men's mental venturing lest they lose their way and miss this illumination that leads to salvation. Both concerns lead to authoritarianism and decry the free use of reason.

For much the same reason, mysticism, or the free practice of individual experience, must be discouraged when it goes beyond the bounds of established or legitimate feeling. For just as reason may detour men's thoughts from the divine illumination, so emotions, when freed from the restraint of authority, may change the course of the "soul" and impel men toward "unholy" desires.

The tradition of supernaturalism may best be envisaged if, in addition to considering its ideas, we contemplate the men who created these ideas and sentiments. Among the early Christian thinkers should be mentioned the Apostle Paul, as well as the earlier apostles; the Apologists, and the Ante-Nicene Fathers, particularly Irenaeus, Tertullian, Clement and Origen; the Nicene Fathers, such as Athanasius, Eusebius Caesarea, Basil, Gregory of Nyssa and John Chrysostom; and the Post-Nicene Fathers, Augustine, Jerome, Ambrose, and Hilary of Poitiers. Of the medieval schoolmen, John Scotus, Anselm, Abelard and Thomas Aquinas are outstanding. On the Protestant side, the names of Martin Luther, John Calvin, Ulrich Zwingli, John Wesley and Jonathan Edwards are important.

Of all the traditions, this one perhaps is the most ambiguous and the most difficult to focus. We have chosen to interpret its contemporary manifestation solely in terms of Protestant philosophy of religion. It is represented in two groups of American thinkers: (1) the traditional supernaturalists: Machen, Mullin and Patton; and (2) the neo-supernaturalists: Tillich, Pauck, Richards, Niebuhr brothers, Lewis and Cell.

THE TRADITION OF IDEALISM

Modern philosophy arose simultaneously with the advance of the scientific movement, and was to some extent shaped under its stimulus. But there developed a division in the ranks of philosophers: some turning back devotedly to the master minds of the classical period; others persistently pursuing the alluring implications of Bacon's magic phrase, " Knowledge is Power." Out of the one philosophical temper have come the idealistic types of philosophies, concerned, it would seem, with reconstructing a world-view that would retain the emotional climate of the ancient religious world, without sacrificing the integrity of intellect, possessed with modern knowledge. Out of the other have come the realistic types, and more particularly, the empirical sort. However concerned they may have been to retain the emotional warmth of earlier outlooks, the rigorous demands of the mind have always triumphed over the sentiments of the heart in these philosophies. The one might be described as a mind lured by a warm heart; the other a heart dominated by an invincible mind. The one has sought to save the world for ideal values; the other has undertaken to bring the world to a courageous reckoning with real existence. The former has worked to keep the fire of hope alive in man's breast; the latter has encouraged men to discipline their hopes in the conviction that hope was possible only when reality, rather than illusion, ruled their lives.

These distinctions go back to a prior divergence in temperament. The outlook of the former accords with the world-view of the classical philosophical outlook, sometimes referred to as " the great tradition." The outlook of the latter is more akin to the world-view of modern science. Thus, while modern philosophy embraces both of these temperaments, we may speak of the tradition of idealism as a distinct influence, perpetuating the *ideal* emphasis of the classical school, and at the same time bridging the world-view of supernaturalism with that of the natural sciences. And we may speak of the tradition of naturalism as a thoroughgoing naturalizing influence upon modern thought, concerned to bring to light what in nature may rightfully command supreme devotion of human living through a philosophical understanding of the implications of the scientific method.

We turn now to a more definitive consideration of the tradition of idealism. Between the supernatural world-view of the Middle Ages and the world-view of the modern period, to which both idealism and naturalism belong, stands the age of the Renaissance. " That period of the intellectual life of Europe which is known as the age of the Renaissance," writes Höffding in his *History of Modern Philosophy,* " is characterized, on the one hand, by the breach with the shackled, disconnected and limited conception of life of the Middle Ages, and on the other, by the extension of view to new spheres and the unfolding of new powers." The Catholic church had given to the Middle

Ages a Latinized version of Greek thought and culture. The Renaissance broke through the Latin wall, and recovered Greek thought and ideals in their native form. In doing so, it opened two dykes in the ancient dam, one releasing a stream from Plato's thought, which later became the fountain source of philosophical idealism; another releasing a stream of Aristotle — not Aristotle the philosopher, but Aristotle the scientist. Out of it came the stimulus which eventuated in the scientific movement.

It would not be correct however to say that the tradition of idealism issued directly from Platonic philosophy. For this tradition emerged more as a reaction against the scientific emphasis in philosophy than as a gradual outgrowth of classical philosophy. To quote Höffding again:

The three great systems developed by Descartes, Hobbes and Spinoza all established a strictly mechanical interconnection of Nature with regard to the material side of existence. In these systems were deduced the logical consequences of principles, the establishment of which had been made possible by the birth of the exact sciences. To many men of the old school these new principles and systems appeared the essence of arbitrariness and godlessness. A reaction may be traced under different forms toward the end of the seventeenth century. While retaining genuinely scientific acquisitions, they sought to find a way which would lead out beyond this view, and to reconcile it with the ancient and medieval conception from which men had so emphatically turned away.[1]

The tradition of idealism, then, may be regarded as a turning back upon the scientific movement to recover values that had been lost to the age as a result of the scientific reaction against medievalism. This I think is significant. The shadow of the supernatural never quite vanishes from the philosophical systems that have developed under the influence of idealism.

The philosophers whose writings, considered as a consistent stream of thought, constitute the tradition of idealism, are Leibniz, Shaftesbury, Berkeley, Kant, and the German Romanticists, Fichte, Schelling, Hegel and Lotze. What are the traits in these philosophers that bring them all under the common denominator, idealists? One distinctive trait is their refusal to be content with building a philosophical picture of the world purely on the basis of the sciences. They accepted the Copernican point of view. They were open to the insights of the sciences. Yet, being sensitive to the limitations of the scientific procedure, they refused to give unqualified loyalty to its demands. They had more confidence in speculative reasoning than in scientific reasoning based upon observation. The reason for their wariness in regard to the scientific method lay in their philosophic " hunch " that there existed something beyond what we can see and describe. Thus they came back to a REALM, with capital letters, disturbingly similar to the *other-world* of supernaturalism. Plato's eternal essences, Leibniz' doctrine of monads and substance, Kant's *thing-in-itself,* and the *realm of the absolute* in Absolute Idealism are suggestive of this tendency. This awareness of an over-realm impelled them toward a *faith-attitude,* qualitatively akin to the mental response of the supernaturalists. In all this they differed from the philosophers, dominated by the tradition of naturalism.

How do they differ from those who adhere to supernaturalism? To be sure, the idealists at the outset made terms with the Copernican system. Their distinctive difference from the supernaturalists, however, appears in their epistemology — their theory of knowledge. The supernaturalists' otherworld is removed from man's world by a veil which man, himself, is helpless to penetrate or draw apart. *Revelation,* the process whereby God invades man's presence and illumines his mind and heart, is the only means by which man may communicate with that other world. The philosopher dominated by the tradition of idealism has bridged this chasm with the ladder of reason. In idealism, *Mind* is the unique emissary from the transcendent realm which enables man to have visions and thoughts of God. What truth is known, or is to be known, has been, or is to be, found by way of logical processes of thought. Accordingly, from this point of view, the logical consistency of a proposition is the criterion of validity. No other authority need be invoked.

It should be noted, of course, that recent forms of idealism have taken over the monistic conception of the world. This has had the effect of further accentuating the mystical tendency that was always latent there.

The tradition of idealism has become diversified and eclectic today. Its impetus has burst like a skyrocket and its spray of sparks has become absorbed in a variety of thought-streams. The purest embodiment of its influence is to be found in the philosophies of religion of absolute idealists, of which Josiah Royce and William Ernest Hocking are the chief contemporary representatives in America. Also, in modern mystics like Rufus Jones and Charles A. Bennett, its influence is marked. To a less degree, but with obvious affinities, the philosophy of the personalists of the Bowne tradition is also indebted. These are the three major movements in contemporary thought that seem to have been dominated by the idealistic tradition. But there are evidences of its pervasive influence in many forms of contemporary thought that make no claim to its inheritance, as in the pragmatic philosophies, the intuitionists and certain of the naturalistic forms of theism.

THE TRADITION OF ROMANTICISM

The Romantic Tradition in western religious thought arose with the period contemporary with Schleiermacher. Its underlying motive has been the freeing of thought from dogmatic, rational restraint to the end of bringing religious reflection nearer to the report of *experience*. Historically it may be regarded as the theological expression of the Romantic Movement. Schleiermacher and Coleridge, who may be considered the pioneer religious romanticists in their respective countries, were also active participants in the wider literary circles of romanticism.[2] The same reaction against rationalism that impelled the literary romanticists to insist upon the validity of emotions and the appreciative response, also led theologians like Schleiermacher and philosophers like Coleridge to extend the appeal to religious experience.[3] Schleiermacher did so by a direct emphasis upon the primal place of *feeling* in religion. Coleridge undertook to accomplish this end by exposing the limitations of language, as in his *Aids to Reflection*. It is commonly recognized that the writings of Coleridge provided the medium through which the German Romanticists filtered into the thought-world of the English-speaking countries. While this is true enough, the direct influence of Coleridge's own reflections is not to be minimized. Out of these two significant sources emerged two lines of theological thinking that were destined to merge in the Christocentric movement of the nineteenth century in America, continuing later in the liberal theology of the present century.[4] The first line of theological thought took its rise in the writings of the eminent German theologian, Albrecht Ritschl, who was directly influenced by Schleiermacher, and spread beyond Germany into England and America. The second line developed from the mind of the great American theologian, Horace Bushnell, who in turn had steeped his thoughts in Coleridge's *Aids to Reflection*. The influence of Bushnell was confined to this country, largely to New England; yet the depth of his insight and the reach of his mind exceeded that of the more widely read German theologian, Ritschl.

Ritschlian theology, while it continued the emphasis upon feeling and experience which had characterized the thought of Schleiermacher, narrowed the appeal to experience to a specific object within the Christian tradition. That object was the *person* of the historic Jesus. Accordingly the appeal to Christ, or more particularly, the appeal to the immediate experience of the person of Christ, replaced the appeal to experience, based upon the " sense of dependence."[5] Partly in the effort to assure the full force of the ethical imperative, which the Ritschlians felt issued from the experience of Christ, the leader of the movement, Ritschl, developed strong antipathies toward metaphysical speculation and mysticism.   In this he doubtless was carrying over a line of emphasis that had been justified by the " Critiques " of Kant.   Not all of the followers of Ritschl however concurred in his reaction against philosophy and mysticism.   None of the American Ritschlians took over this phase of his thought.   A. C. McGiffert and G. W. Knox were more inclined than other Americans to adhere to the ethical theism of Ritschl, Harnack and Herrmann, but that was due more to the field of their theological interests than to any pronounced intellectual bias.   But William Adams Brown, Henry Churchill King and G. B. Foster all reveal marked eclectic tendencies. And the theology and philosophy of religion that has been developing among more recent religious liberals has become increasingly eclectic; so much so, in fact, that the Christocentric emphasis, once basic in liberal theology, has become overladen with a mixture of modern influences drawn from philosophy, mysticism, science and social ethics.

Bushnell's penetrating mind and poetic spirit has had less attention in the way of a following in this country than his genius deserves; yet no religious thinker of the modern period within the romantic tradition has escaped his influence.   Beyond adding to the religious insight of his day, Bushnell gave force to the intuitive approach to religious truths.   He was essentially a preacher, and therefore inclined toward the practical and mediating role.   Yet his outreach was so profound that his mind became searching and venturesome.   But here the influence of the Romantic reaction, mediated through Coleridge, was clearly marked.   Like Coleridge, he felt that words were too limited as vehicles of divine truth to yield adequate insight; [6] consequently he urged humility and tolerance of thought where " high truths " were concerned, and at the same time warned against too great confidence in reason as a means to truth.   This sensitive nature in Bushnell made him at once humble, yet daring; tolerant, yet confident of his own intuitive grasp. He remained open to the appeal of insight, however or wherever it might come; yet he undertook to deal with it selectively on the basis of reasonable judgment and practical experience.

Thus the liberalizing temperament was here clearly in evidence, and it has been a cogent influence in shaping American religious thought.

This same temper of mind is reflected in the writings of another New England theologian, William Newton Clarke, who in some respects has had wider influence upon the religious thought of America. Clarke's mind, while not so far-ranging as Bushnell's, was more systematic. Through his *Outlines of Theology* and subsequent publications,[7] he infused into theological thinking a pervasive spirit of reasonableness; not alone the reasonableness of rational justification, but the reasonableness of sympathetic understanding issuing from an inclusive spirit. This trait has become a marked characteristic of recent religious liberalism.

How widely this tradition of romanticism has influenced and shaped American religious thought, no observer can hope to discover. But that it has permeated the minds of certain Christian theologians and philosophers in America, the writings of present-day religious eclectic-liberals clearly reveals.

Romantic Liberalism was many-sided. Its reaction against the rationalism of the period was motivated, not only by a concern to get beyond the sovereignty of mind to the appeal to experience, but also by a desire to leap beyond the strictures of literal truth to the fuller vision of imaginative insight. Schleiermacher's thought lent itself to both of these objectives. Thus, in addition to the trend that led, through Ritschl, to ethical theism and the liberal theology of the practical eclectics, there issued also the emphasis upon the appreciative approach to religious reality that has come to be called aesthetic naturalism.

The term aesthetic naturalism is not altogether clear in its historical meaning. It has generally been applied to that type of thought which interprets religion in terms of appreciative symbols, and which tends therefore toward an emphasis upon ritual and its accompanying arts, rather than toward moral or ethical interests. Randall, for example, in his *Making of the Modern Mind,* says that

> The one tendency speaking of aesthetic naturalism is exemplified by men who find the religious experience and the religious feelings primarily a matter of appreciation of and communion with the great religious leaders and systems of the past; they see in religion the highest of the arts, the noblest imaginative embodiment of human ideals, and seek in the great religious traditions, in their rich fruitage in storied cathedral and ancient ritual and poetic doctrine, the satisfaction of their natural yearning for beauty and piety and aesthetic adjustment to human life.[8]

Accordingly, Randall finds aesthetic naturalism leading naturally to an esoteric Catholicism and High Church Anglicanism. But in aesthetic naturalism of this type, the only naturalistic trait that can be pointed to is its abandonment of a literal belief in the historic dogmas and the emphasis upon sensuous appreciation in religion.

Whether or not this tendency toward formalism and retrospection is inevitable in aesthetic naturalism is open to question. The aesthete does, to be sure, turn more agreeably to that which has become stable and static, for judgment of value is then more dependable; hence the aesthetic interest in the things of antiquity. The same motive that impels appreciation of antiques leads to the kind of reverence for ritual and religious symbols that is found in high-churchism. Other factors enter in here to be sure, but the principle of appraisal is the same. History bears out, of course, that churches and religious temples with their fondness for form and ornamentation have kept company with art and the artist. Yet here the affinity, particularly on the part of the artist, is largely a vocational relationship. The fact that is overlooked in the insistence that the aesthetic attitude in religion leads to an emphasis upon established form and historic values is that the aesthetic response is not necessarily passive. It may be creative. It *is* creative in individuals like the artist, the poet, and the mystic. At least in some of them. If it led to the worship of the Catholic church in John Newman, it led to the free, open, mystic communion of Romantic Liberalism in Schleiermacher. If it turns T. S. Eliot and George Santayana to a renewed emphasis upon the significance of tradition, it impels Oppenheim and Brownell to find the full meaning of existence in the " integrative moment of living."

It is important to recognize, therefore, that the aesthetic attitude in religion may take the form of an expansive outreach toward the yet unattained. It may thrust one with heroic abandonment toward the *perilous open* to attain new possibilities of experienceable value. Where sense of wonder and open awareness enter into the aesthetic response, the course of aesthetic naturalism turns forward, not backward.

Perhaps we are dealing here with two fundamentally different forms of aesthetic response. Then again it may be simply the difference between aesthetic appreciation that has become fixed upon a single ideal of cultural value, and the aesthetic response that continues to reach out eagerly toward the new frontiers of experience. There is a traditional temper in aesthetic naturalism, and there is also a creative mood. The aesthetic naturalism that goes beyond tradition has generally taken the form of nature mysticism. This is the obvious course; for the appreciative response, whatever the world-view, is directed toward that which communicates reality. Where conceptions of reality have become fixed, obviously the symbols and patterns for communicating reality also become fixed. This leads to the aesthetic emphasis upon tradition and its accompanying ritual, a tendency we have already noted. Where conceptions of reality are in flux, however, the appreciative response becomes a philosophical attitude, directed toward cosmic sources or the world of nature. This more open form of aesthetic naturalism or nature mysticism was clearly in evidence throughout the Romantic period. The nature-centered philosophy of Rousseau inspired it to an exaggerated degree. Poets of the period like Goethe, Wordsworth and Coleridge gave it lyric expression.[9] And its mystical note has been continued in American nature mystics like Whitman, Emerson, Thoreau and Burroughs.

This aesthetic phase of the romantic tradition has had influence in two directions among contemporary writers. On the one hand, it has given impetus to the Anglo-Catholic developments and on the other hand, has kept alive the appeal of nature mysticism, which, in its contemporary form, tends to become more realistic in both a philosophical and psychological sense.

THE TRADITION OF NATURALISM

Naturalism is an ancient tradition. Were we to consider it in its naïve expressions, we should have to deal with it first. For the history of religions makes plain that early man's religious response arose out of an awareness of impressive happenings within his natural environment and that, so far as we are able to tell, his explanations of his experiences involved no bifurcation of nature. That dualistic conception, positing the world of the supernatural beyond the natural, was a mental achievement of high order, and came only after men's reflective abilities had been developed to where imaginative hypotheses were possible.[10] Supernaturalism, then, overlies the naturalistic layer of thought in the archaeological story of the growth of mind.

But the naturalistic tendency continued to filter through even after supernatural theories came to dominate the world-view of men. Among the Greeks, in fact, it took precedence over supernaturalism. Strange as it may seem, the Greeks never took the view of an overarching supernal realm with the degree of seriousness that characterized their Mediterranean neighbors. And the priestly form of religion that normally accompanies such a world-view never took root in Greece.[11]

The philosophic expression of this naturalistic tendency first appears in the writings of the Ionian nature-philosophers. Its theological implications begin to take form in the tenth chapter of Plato's *Laws* and in *Timaeus,* in Aristotle's *Metaphysics* and in the sober views of the Stoics. This natural theology was carried forward into Christian thought by the Medieval Schoolmen, Anselm, Abelard, Thomas Aquinas, Raymond of Sebonde, and by the Renaissance theologian, Pomponazzi. Thomas Aquinas, more than any other theologian of this period, furthered the teleological arguments for the existence of God. It is instructive, therefore, to note with what inevitableness the Neo-Thomist movement among Catholics of our day seems to be tending toward a position of natural theology strikingly similar to that of the theistic evolutionists in Protestant theology.

Natural theology, as it is commonly conceived among Protestant thinkers, began to take form among the Deists of the seventeenth century, when reason was in conflict with revelation. They undertook to resolve this conflict by showing how reason and revelation had been but two means of making known the *one* God to man. Chief among these naturalistic apologists was Lord Herbert of Cherbury, whose book *De Veritate* appeared in 1624. Other eminent expositions of this view were *The Reasonableness of Christianity* by John Locke (1696), *Christianity as Old as Creation* by Tindal (1730), Butler's *Analogy* (1736), Paley's *Evidences* (1794) and *Natural Theology* (1799) and writings by Tillotson, Blount, Wollaston, Clarke and Reimarus.

The next important wave of natural theology followed the publication of Darwin's *Origin of Species* (1859). Having passed through a period of intense conflict with the evolutionary scientists of the 'sixties, and the agnostic philosophers of the 'seventies, Christian theologians in the 'eighties undertook to come to terms with the theory of evolution and to turn it to the service of theology in interpreting the operations of God in the natural world. Scientists like Le Conte and Agassiz contributed immeasurably to this impetus. But the constructive achievements were formulated largely through philosophers like John Fiske, who defined evolution as " God's way of doing things." Simultaneous with the efforts of these American evolutionists, was felt also the influence of Henry Drummond, the English philosopher-scientist, through his memorable volumes, *Natural Law in the Spiritual World* (1883) and *The Ascent of Man* (1894). This point of view came to be known as *theistic evolution*. Its most systematic formulation is to be found in *The Theology of an Evolutionist* by Lyman Abbott. Other influential expressions of it are the books, *Through Science to Faith* (1904) and *Constructive Natural Theology* (1913), *Christian Faith in an Age of Science* (1903) by W. N. Rice; *Christian Faith and Evolution* by E. E. Lane; *To Christ Through Evolution* by L. M. Sweet, as well as many other books on theology in which the gap between the Christian and the scientific world-views is bridged through harmonization.

The contemporary successors to these theistic evolutionists are the evolutionary theists, who undertake to give a religious formulation of the insights of the new physics, modern astronomy and the new biology.

It is important to observe that this tradition of natural theology has come into prominence following the revolutionary impact of some branch of physical science, precipitating a crisis in theological thought. Aquinas gave stability and systematic formulation to Christian thought following the Copernican revolution. The Deists countered the rationalistic attacks upon religious faith, growing out of the scientific movement during the seventeenth and eighteenth centuries. The theistic evolutionists, as we have seen, met the incursions of the biological sciences into religious thought toward the end of the nineteenth century. Almost before theology could muster its resources of thought to cope with the devastating implications of behavioristic psychology, psychologists themselves provided an alternative theory of psychology, more agreeable to the insights of religion, in the Gestalt school.[12] While this view continues to speak in terms of a *behavioristic* standpoint, its emphasis upon the *pattern* renders its thought more inclusive of relations considered important to religious interpreters, than the descriptive behaviorism of the Watsonian school. Gerald Birney Smith once remarked that the only branch of physical science that had not precipitated tension and conflict in religious thought was the field of physics. And he explained this fact by saying that this science was comfortably removed from that area of reflection that considered man in his relation to reality. But Dr. Smith lived to see the growing implications of the revolution in physics. Today we are confronted with changes in the mental outlook, more fundamental perhaps than those incurred by the Copernican revolution of the sixteenth century. That religious thought is being affected by this condition, no observing thinker will deny. But the unexpected has happened. Instead of precipitating a conflict between science and theology, modern physicists are placing philosophy on the defensive but in the opposite role. For the new physicists are the idealists, and the critical skeptics are the philosophers. Meanwhile certain modern philosophers with spirited concern for the religious implications of their philosophizing, are undertaking to give logical formulation to the idealism which the physicists preach. Almost coincidentally with the development of operational concepts in modern physics, and the emphasis upon *pattern* in Gestalt psychology, modern biology has been formulating a new conception of environment, representing man and life, not *in* environment, but *as* environment. Out of this convergence of organismic thinking has developed a concept that has become the key-word of the new idealism, *emergence.*[13] In this concept, contemporary philosophers of religion who continue the tradition of natural theology have a suggestive insight that may forever break the spell of the mechanistic outlook. But there is danger as well as promise in the horizon because of this concept. Some interpreters are already pointing out the legitimacy of a new vogue of mysticism in the light of Heisenberg's principle of unpredictability.[14] Over-eager apologists for religion will be only too ready to seize upon this discovery and make the most of it, resulting in the familiar kind of obscuranticism that finds its justification chiefly in what we do not know. But the concept of emergence is an important insight, and it is destined to have an influence upon modern thought, comparable to the influence that the concept of *orderliness* and natural law had upon the thinking of the period when the scientific movement first made itself felt, and that the concept of evolution had upon the thought of the late nineteenth century. Modern philosophy has already appropriated its insight with impressive vigor.[15]

THE NATURALISM OF THE SCIENTIFIC MOVEMENT

Naturalism, as it is generally regarded today, is rather an extension of the influence of the scientific movement in philosophy than a continuing phase of natural theology. This expression of the tradition of naturalism is motivated by a radically different interest than that which issued in natural theology and theistic evolution. The latter, as we have seen, was impelled largely by a concern to save religion from the onslaught of science. The former was influenced by the intellectual impulse to bring religion to its *proper* dimensions in the light of scientific knowledge. Accordingly, the one has sought to moderate scientific findings to harmonize them with the essential affirmations of religion; the other has proceeded to trim religion down to the pattern of the scientific outlook. Both motives have influenced some modern thinkers, but the two groups divide where one or the other motive becomes dominant. This in fact is what differentiates the evolutionary theists from the rest of the naturalistic thinkers in our classification.

The tradition of naturalism in its scientific expression in

western philosophy is generally said to date from Francis Bacon's *Novum Organum,* in which he develops the inductive method and applies it to the interest of philosophy as well as to theology and ethics. As a matter of fact, however, the scientific method had been used and demonstrated by Leonardo da Vinci, Kepler and Galileo. "Thoughts which are generally ascribed to Galileo or to Bacon," writes Höffding, "had already found utterance in Leonardo, but they lay buried in his manuscripts, which have only been studied quite recently." If we were to characterize this tradition in terms of world-view, we would have to go back to Copernicus, whose work marks the emergence of the scientific view of the world of nature, or even to the Humanists of the Renaissance, who turned the tide of thinking toward natural man. In any case, we may say that the tradition of naturalism took its rise during that strenuous and tumultuous period of the early sixteenth, if not in the fifteenth, century.

We do well to note at the outset that the thinkers who launched the tradition of naturalism definitely abandoned the traditional cosmology, based upon Ptolemaic astronomy, which had been assumed by the Catholic church. I mention this because it denotes something of the temperament of the thinkers involved. Intellectually they worked outside of the church tradition. They apparently had no genuine sentiment for this tradition. This indifference to church tradition has been a persistent trait throughout the succession of philosophers who have been dominated by naturalism. They have shown no concern to reconcile truth, scientifically attained, with dogma or faith. A comparison with the philosophers within the idealistic tradition is instructive at this point. They differed from the naturalists in this respect. In fact the idealists have been the great reconcilers through the centuries. They left the traditional world-view reluctantly, and struggled with their metaphysics until they recovered at least the semblance of the older outlook. One should not make too much of this comparison, for exceptions can be cited, to be sure. But on the whole, there is something " tough-minded " to use James's language, about these philosophers who could construct mechanical worlds, write books like *The Leviathan,* fashion philosophies on the basis of the survival of the fittest, and establish God as a brutal fact, as real as a toothache.

The world-view espoused by these naturalists, then, was from the start Copernican. It was *sun-centered,* and the attitudes regarding man, his status, and his place in the scheme of things developed accordingly. There never has been the strong anthropocentric bias in this type of thinking that is found in the traditional theologies and in the idealistic philosophies. Furthermore, the systems of thought dominated by this tradition have gone hand in hand with the developing sciences. Consequently, there has been a direct feeding from the findings of such sciences as geology, archaeology, biology, sociology, psychology and physics into this tradition. Naturalism, in other words, has *taken its science straight.* Here again we see a contrast between this tradition and traditional forms of philosophy, which have insisted upon running scientific conclusions through the sieve of apologetics; and idealistic forms of philosophy, which have at least felt the need of tempering these scientific conclusions with a value-guaranteeing interpretation. The idealistic adaptation of the theory of evolution, giving rise in theology to the doctrine of *theistic evolution,* is a striking example of this tendency.

A final fact to observe in connection with the world-view of naturalism is that within this tradition, reality has always been identified wholly with the world of experience. Rarely does one find philosophers of this tradition bringing in irrational overtones approximating supernaturalism. They have stepped out of that world-view once and for all. I do not mean to say that they have no overtones or mystical dimensions; but always they are overtones that yield to exploration. The philosopher may not have the instruments or method sufficiently perfected to carry on his observations and experiments in that area, but the realm is within bounds of approach. He might enter that promised land some day.

In keeping with this point of view, the naturalist has always regarded man forthrightly as a creature of earth, not a pilgrim here, heaven bound; not even as foreordained " philosophic dust," destined to return to the feast of the wise. Man is of this world, earth-born and earth-sustained. Yet the naturalist finds a great deal of significance in that relationship. It does not detract in the least from the quality of his philosophizing.

The tradition of naturalism is distinguished from the other traditions most readily by its theory of knowledge. Obviously it abandons revelation and all approaches to truth consonant with it. It goes along with the tradition of idealism in adopting reason, but goes beyond it in adding observation and experiment. And its peculiarity is that it places emphasis upon the latter. To the naturalist, observation is the aggressive quester for fact; reason is the refiner and the order-giving instrument that builds facts into more comprehensive insights and truths. Thus the philosopher, dominated by the tradition of naturalism, adheres rigidly to the demands of the scientific method, combining reason and observation.

In this discussion of the tradition of naturalism, I have aimed to touch upon characteristics and tendencies which bring out its distinctive traits. Perhaps the best way to get at its primary bent is to consider its motivation. Naturalism has been esssentially practical in motive. It has retained the spirit and objective of science, aiming to understand the forces of nature with a view to controlling them in the cause of mankind. It is instructive to recall Höffding's comments concerning the rise of this tradition in this connection:

Humanism (that is the humanism of the Renaissance) developed out of the political and social relations of the Italian states, and out of Humanism, as a tendency making itself felt in practical life, there grew in turn a new doctrine of Man. Similarly, the mechanical science of

Nature developed out of the prosperous industry of the Italian towns. In order to procure the means for power and magnificence, the rulers had to support trade and hand-industries, and the personal force and self-assertion of the burgesses of the towns found vent in a wise and zealous activity within the sphere of manufactures and industrial invention. With regard to these a rivalry sprang up between the towns. Each sought to surpass the other in technical skill and jealously guarded new inventions and machines. This practical turning to account of the forces of Nature increased the knowledge of their mode of working and could not fail to arouse interest in the discovery of their laws. The appearance of a Leonardo or a Galileo is only comprehensible in connection with the Italian industry.

The naturalistic philosophies which have built upon this tradition have retained this practical temper. They have kept fairly close to the human scene. Seldom have they lost themselves in the intricacies of metaphysics. And in some cases they have been known to set the metaphysical problem aside altogether, lest they lose their grounding in *experienced* reality.[16]

As a closing comment, we might note that the tradition of naturalism is essentially a western tradition. It has no important antecedents, reaching back into the Oriental or Mediterranean cultures of antiquity, unless we should consider the limited experimentation of Aristotle a source. In its method and emphasis, it is a product of western Europe, and the course of its influence has continued westward through succeeding centuries. It is significant to note that the two great philosophies of recent time which have been considered native to American soil were born and reared within this tradition. To-day America may be said to be the homeland of naturalism.

The men who contributed to the tradition of naturalism are: Copernicus, Bruno, Kepler, Galileo, Francis Bacon, Descartes, Hobbes, Spinoza, John Locke, Newton, Hume, Comte, John Stuart Mill, Charles Darwin and Herbert Spencer. Many others belong in this list; but these are the significant names.

The American philosophies of religion which feed upon this tradition include the cosmic theists like Whitehead, Noble,

Conger, Overstreet and Northrop; the Religious Humanists and the Empirical Theists, Ames and Dewey, Mathews and Wieman.

These, then, are the philosophical traditions that have shaped western religious thought and which continue to dominate the religious reflections of our own day. To be sure, present-day philosophies of religion are in no way to be considered identical with systems of philosophy that have gone by the names of these traditions. No philosophy is a pure embodiment of the currents that have influenced it. But each tends to take up into its perspective, its emphasis, and its formulations, traits that are peculiar to the dominant temper or mood of thought that has environed it, or, in basic ways, motivated it. In many cases the characteristics of more than one tradition have entered into a single philosophy of religion. For example, modern mysticism is a synthesis of the elements of supernaturalism and idealism. Again, certain philosophies of religion designated as idealistic in emphasis, have absorbed elements from evolutionary naturalism. And theistic views regarded as expressions of the naturalistic tradition have strong symptoms of an idealistic bent. But in every case there is manifest a decisive preference for one or the other temper of thought. To discover these basic leanings in the philosophies of religion of today contributes measurably to the clarity of perspective, not only because of what is revealed as background, but for what is disclosed regarding the motivation of thought and the *pitch* of perspective.

---

¹ *History of Modern Philosophy,* Vol. I, p. 332.

² This statement must be qualified in regard to Coleridge. For while the seeds of romanticism were in his seminal mind, and were later to develop into a liberalizing movement, Coleridge himself leaned toward tradition and the revival of the Anglican church. Consequently his influence tended toward high church interests and doubtless was a factor in the rise of the Oxford Movement.

³ The word experience, as used by the romanticists, did not connote empirical and experimental implications, as in the naturalistic philosophies; it implied more the persuasive impact of emotional feeling.

⁴ The influence of Coleridge was more diversified, to be sure. Through James Marsh it permeated and shaped the thought of Transcendentalism, and through John McVickar gave impetus to new developments among the American Anglicans.

We are considering here, however, the more singular influence which he had through Bushnell. This developed more directly as a forerunner of liberal theology.

[5] This emphasis upon the historic Jesus, as the object of Christian experience which yielded the sense of dependence, was incipient, however, in Schleiermacher.

[6] See his essay on language in *God in Christ.*

[7] *Use of Scriptures in Theology; the Doctrine of God.*

[8] *Making of the Modern Mind,* p. 545.

[9] Coleridge did not identify himself with this extreme expression of nature mysticism, although his view lent itself to such interpretation. In so far as he contributed to the aesthetic tradition, his influence moved toward high-churchism, and actually paved the way for the Oxford Movement.

[10] See *Birth and Growth of Religion:* G. F. Moore, Part I, for a discussion of this point.

[11] The mystery religions that provide an exception here, popular as they were, were alien to the essential spirit of Greek religion. They represent the invasion of the oriental mood among the Greeks.

[12] An excellent comparison of the metaphysical implications of the behavioristic and organismic views is given in *The Psychological Review,* July 1935, by Raymond H. Wheeler, a proponent of Gestalt psychology in an article on "Organismic vs. Mechanistic Logic."

[13] The significance of this development in modern thought is ably discussed by J. E. Boodin in his recent book, *Three Interpretations of the Universe,* Chapters I–III. Macmillan, 1935.

[14] See "The New Vision of Science" by P. W. Bridgman, *Harpers,* March 1929, and "This Mysterious Universe," J. W. N. Sullivan, *Atlantic Monthly,* Jan. 1935.

[15] The most representative successors of the naturalistic tradition as natural theology in modern thought are the organismic philosophies of religions which emphasize teleology, *e.g.* the works of Boodin, W. P. Montague, W. K. Wright, H. W. Wright and R. L. Calhoun.

[16] This characterization would not apply to the cosmic theists.

PART TWO

ROOTED IN TRADITION
OF SUPERNATURALISM

CHAPTER IV

TRADITIONAL SUPERNATURALISTS

MORE than any other of the prevalent philosophies of religion, traditional supernaturalism is a system of thought by which an established way of living is justified and guided. In times of social stability this is always the chief function of any philosophy of religion. Also this is pre-eminently the function of a theology. Hence in such times philosophy of religion tends to become theological.

But in times when great cultural transition seems to demand extensive changes in the established way of religious living, philosophies of religion take on two further functions which are more distinctively philosophical as over against the theological. The first of these further functions is to theorize in an exploratory and experimental manner in the endeavor to bring to light the outlines of that new and different way of religious living which may meet the requirements of this cultural transformation which is going on. The second of these two further functions is to criticize the old way and point out what seems to be better. Thus, philosophy of religion has three functions in respect to the actual conduct of religious living: to sustain, to explore and to transform.

Of these three functions, traditional supernaturalism is chiefly devoted to the first. Other contemporary philosophies of religion in varying degrees are concerned with the second and third. The reason for this is quite apparent. Traditional supernaturalism is precisely that way of life and system of thought which resist change in response to cultural transformations that may be going on round about it. Of course nothing can keep from changing in some degree. But traditional supernaturalism resists change more than any form of Christianity in the United States.

Nevertheless traditional supernaturalism is forced, by need of protecting itself from the undermining and frontal impact of modern life, to construct its foundations anew and build up bulwarks of defense. This calls for something more than theology. Theology is the articulate and systematic formulation of religious beliefs and of the theory that underlies religious practice. Philosophy of religion goes beyond this by examining the underlying presuppositions of this whole system of thought and way of life. It does this by seeking to ascertain if these presuppositions are consistent with whatever theory may seem to underlie all the rest of life. All the rest of life means the total cultural organization of life which happens to prevail at that time. Traditional supernaturalism has been forced in self-defense to examine its own presuppositions in this way. Hence it has a contemporary philosophy of religion. Its outstanding representative in American Protestantism is J. Gresham Machen. The book in which Machen formulates this philosophy is *Christianity and Liberalism.*

ITS POWER AND PREVALENCE

The majority of religious people in the United States still follow the way of traditional supernaturalism. For many this is what religion means and the modernized forms of religion seem to them to be not only alien to Christianity but outside the pale of all religion. For them it is not so much a matter of beliefs, it is not the system of thought, it is not the moral principles; it is the feeling. Traditional supernaturalism as a way of life gives them a certain feeling. What gives them this feeling is the true religion. What does not is false religion, not real religion at all. This feeling is the feeling of security, the feeling of peace and rest and refreshment. It is the feeling of being removed from the cares and perplexities and dangers of ordinary life; the feeling of being at the portals of another world where all is so much better than the dull routine or the alarming changes or the gnawing pain of this world.

We have said that for the masses traditional supernaturalism is a feeling more than it is a set of beliefs, a system of thought or principles of conduct. But whence comes this feeling if not from beliefs and conduct? It comes from an ancient tradition. There is no other tradition in modern life having any distinctness of outline which is more ancient than this. It is transmitted to individuals by symbols that generate the characteristic feeling it carries. Any group which has the feeling transmits it to one individual member by music, by intonations of the voice, subtle movements of body through rhythms and liturgies.

In sum, the power and prevalence of traditional supernaturalism is due to the fact that it is the most ancient tradition preserving distinctness of outline in modern life. Doubtless there are other pervasive influences shaping our lives which are much more ancient than this, but no other influence has a distinct social organization, set of symbols, body of officials, public gatherings and system of beliefs all set up and functioning for the sole purpose of perpetuating the influence. Traditional supernaturalism has all of these.

While its power and prevalence among the masses is not due directly to its system of thought, indirectly its system is very important. This body of thought has a clarity and systematic completeness not found elsewhere. Without it, traditional supernaturalism could have no powerful and effective leadership. Without it, no thinking man could preserve his integrity in this movement, and without integrity he could have no power. Hence this body of thought is required to win and to train leaders of ability. The need of such leadership in perpetuating the tradition among the masses is obvious. Thus in this indirect way the system of thought and philosophy of traditional supernaturalism is of utmost importance, even when great numbers of its followers know very little about it and care less.

A third source of its power is the fact that it presents a realm of thought and feeling which stands in glowing contrast to the rest of life. When a religion offers one little more than a survey and perspective of the life he is living all the time anyway, it has little appeal to many a man. When it simply exhorts him to be more strenuous in the life that is too hard already, to shoulder responsibilities that he does not want to carry, to face this world in all its fullness when he wants to turn away from it, he is not likely to be very enthusiastic about it. But when it opens up to him another world, or rather another realm of experience, refreshingly different from his daily life, sometimes gloriously different, he may well turn to it with eagerness.

When we speak of this " other world or other realm of experience," we do not mean merely the belief in a life after death. This is certainly included in traditional supernaturalism, but it is a mistake to think its chief power lies in such a belief. This belief is simply a corollary and addendum to the whole order of life which it presents. Its power lies in the fact that it does present an order of life that is so different from the routine, so different from the problems, from the limited hopes and fears, from the drab and meager scope, of daily life. This other realm, or at any rate belief in it, provides the feeling, which one cannot get anywhere else, which refreshes and renews because it is so different from the feelings of the daily grind. It is the feeling of a hidden glory which the observable facts of life do not reveal.

Finally its power and prevalence is due to the undeveloped state of any alternative way of religious living. It requires generations to build up a new way of religious living, deeply imbedded in the social tradition and transmitted to each new individual and generation in the form of feelings engendered by association with people who have them and who quicken and deepen them in one another by manifold interactions. It takes generations to do this even in a stable social order where traditions can be continuously developed. It is even more difficult when the social order is highly unstable as it is today and has been increasingly so since the Middle Ages, and especially when the established order of society is disintegrating and the outlines of the new order are not yet visible. In such a time we are living. No wonder, then, that other ways of religious living different from traditional supernaturalism have not had opportunity to develop beyond the immature and impoverished state of early beginnings. Add to that the fact that no other philosophy of religion has yet been sufficiently developed which can command the respect and loyalty of the majority of thinking people. Most if not all other philosophies have been retreats from traditional supernaturalism and concessions to the basic theory of modern culture, rather than aggressive, constructive and triumphant grapplings with the problem of rearing a system of religious thought and life which will express the true genius of our culture and meet its deepest needs.

Here, then, we have the sources of power for traditional supernaturalism: (1) the ancient tradition and deep-laid sentiments, (2) the clarity and systematic completeness of its thought, (3) the contrast it offers to daily life, (4) the weakness or immaturity of all other ways of religious living that have been offered in its place. Here lies the strength of Roman Catholicism as well as the strength of all those forms of Protestantism which come under the heading of traditional supernaturalism.

It must be admitted, however, that its strength is waning. It is stronger than any of its competitors, and none of these as yet show signs of inheriting its power. But its ancient hold on western culture is markedly reduced. There is nothing to indicate that it will recover its hold, although it is being revived in some quarters. Whether it comes back will depend not on any

.renewed zeal, purity, clarity or other improvement within itself, but upon the turn of events in the transition of culture which is now occurring. If science is taken from its present high place of domination and given some lowly place of service; if human activities are subjected to coercive and authoritative control to avoid disaster, suppressing free inquiry, independent thinking and experimental living; if the difficulties of organizing human life under intelligent control become so baffling that we find it impossible and seek some other world and some other power to help us out of our difficulties; then traditional supernaturalism may come again to its high place in western culture. But even so, it will doubtless undergo considerable change.

ITS DISTINCTIVE TRAITS

Traditional supernaturalism has certain traits which set it forth in characteristic distinction from other philosophies of religion. One of these is its rigidity. Of course, it does not present an exception to the universal rule that all things in the world must change. But perhaps it has changed less through the centuries than any other formulation of life found in the modern world. At any rate the devotees of this kind of religion have tried harder to preserve their tradition unchanged and have put up more bulwarks against change, than any other group of Christian devotees in the United States. Feudalism may rise and fall, monarchy may come and go, democracy may begin and flourish, capitalism may spring from small beginnings, reach its zenith and decline, but traditional supernaturalism claims to be perennially the same and puts forth every effort to preserve itself intact.

Throughout the rest of the modern world change is said to be the most common and inevitable fact. Almost everywhere else it is welcomed as affording opportunity for improvement as well as giving hazard of loss. Even the religionist of the sort we are here considering recognizes the place of change in other areas of life. But in the field of his religious tradition he repudiates it. He not only quotes the phrase, " Christ is the same yesterday, today and forever," but seems to understand that to mean that his religious beliefs and feelings and practices must be changeless. So far as anything in this world is concerned, the chief cause he serves in his religious devotion is to preserve entire and without modification the revelation of God in Jesus Christ which he believes is embodied in this tradition. Hence all his powers are consecrated to the resistance of change in this body of thought and this form of life. This is the primary demand of his religious devotion.

The second distinctive trait of this philosophy of religion is that it seeks the most important truth about life outside the resources of insight and knowledge which prevailing culture may provide. It turns to what is called revelation. In the Bible, it claims, there is a supernatural revelation of truth which could not be known to man if it were not transmitted to him by way of this sacred book. All other resources of knowledge-getting, all other paths of penetration into the nature of reality and the meanings of life fall short. The most indispensable kind of knowledge for human living, they cannot give. In these other ways we get knowledge of nature, but not of super-nature. But knowledge of nature is as nothing compared to knowledge of the supernatural. Therefore one of the marked traits of this philosophy of religion is a turning to a source of light that lies wholly outside the resources of culture, scientific, artistic, philosophical, as well as those of common sense, of " religious experience," and anything else which contemporary life might afford.

A further trait is that it magnifies belief. This kind of belief which is held to be central is called faith. It means accepting certain doctrines as finally true, and seeking those sources of grace and salvation which these teachings declare to be necessary if man is to have access from this world of nature into the blessed realm of the supernatural.

Of course one cannot intelligently adopt any way of life without accepting the beliefs required for that way of living. In this sense every philosophy of religion, and every philosophy of every other human activity, must set forth certain beliefs as required for that kind of procedure. But the uniqueness of traditional supernaturalism is that it presents these beliefs for acceptance, not on grounds of rational or empirical evidence, but because they are revealed and because they are necessary to salvation. One cannot find God nor live for God, nor enter into the riches of life's fulfillment, without them. On these grounds they are to be accepted, and not because ordinary evidence of any kind supports them.

In this way belief takes on an importance for traditional supernaturalism that it does not have for any other form of Protestant Christian religion in our country. Within this tradition the faithful are called " believers," in contradistinction to all others.

Other-worldliness further characterizes this formulation of religion. In vulgar form the other world is identified with life after death; but, as stated before, the philosophy of this form of religion does not so limit it. Other-worldliness in its best philosophical presentation means the incomparable superiority of the supernatural as over against the natural. But we have access to the supernatural, or rather the supernatural has access to us, here and now. We cannot seek it out by our own powers. But when we meet certain conditions, one of which is to accept as true certain teachings, it seeks us out. It lays hold upon us and transforms us. It fits us for another kind of existence, gloriously different from this. If the supernatural power has claimed us for its own, we become strangers and pilgrims here. Our home is far away, upon a foreign shore. We belong to the realm of the blessed, where sorrow and sighing shall flee away. Thither the ransomed of the Lord shall return with everlasting joy upon their heads.

Along with this profound and ever newly quickened appreciation of the other world which is supernatural, goes a relative depreciation of this world which is natural. This does not mean that all supernaturalists are hypochondriacs or pessimists. How one will view this world largely depends on one's temperament, which modern science declares goes back in no small part to the functioning of the glands as well as to other physiological and psychological conditions. Supernaturalists are just as susceptible as any others to these conditions affecting their view of the goodness or evil of the world. Therefore they may view this world in as rosy a light as any other *except* by contrast to that other world. Where they differ from others is not that they necessarily think so badly of this world; but they think so highly of that other that, by contrast, their appraisal of this world seems pessimistic and generally depreciative. Also, there is the desire to turn the interests of men to that other world, and one great aid to this end is making them see that this world is very unsatisfactory.

It is only with these qualifications that we can say the traditional supernaturalist denounces this world and looks upon it with gloom. There is nothing in his religion which impels him to gloss over the evils of this world or in any way try to make things appear to be better than they are. The sentimental, hypocritical, unrealistic endeavor of many religionists to magnify the good and obscure the evil, and confuse the issues of good and bad in order to sustain their religious convictions, is wholesomely absent from the supernaturalist. He may err in the opposite direction. He may blind himself and others to the genuine and rich values of this world and to the opportunities to make it better; but at any rate he is not afraid to face all the evils that may be found here. After having faced them, he may not be as intelligent and energetic in trying to overcome them, because his interest and his hope is otherwise focused. But he does acknowledge them.

Perhaps all these traits of traditional supernaturalism which we have mentioned are derivatives of the one characteristic which we call cultural intransigence. It holds itself aloof from the culture in which it functions. Of course any worthy religion, and any idealistic striving, will be critical of much that is going on in life. That is inevitable, precisely because it strives for something better. But an idealistic striving may do this in two different ways. It may do it as an alien to the culture criticized, or it may do it as the noblest outreach after the highest fulfillment of that culture. Traditional supernaturalism does it as an alien. It claims to be the representative on earth of a way of life, of values, of a realm, call it what you will, that is essentially opposed even to the best that the prevailing culture can ideally seek. Culture belongs to nature. But this religion is the representative on earth of the supernatural. Even the highest fulfillment of the natural is evil as compared to the supernatural, unless it offers itself to be abolished and abandoned as soon as it has lifted one toward the supernatural as far as it can. The natural is good only when it delivers itself up to the supernatural and perishes in so doing.

In this way traditional supernaturalism stands in irreconcilable opposition to the prevailing culture. It considers any rapprochement as a compromise and concession to the evil of this world. It glories in what has recently been called a " tension " between the demands of highest and best cultural aspiration and the requirements of this realm that is so incomparably superior to the very highest hope and aspiration of any worldly culture.

All the traits previously mentioned follow from this and are necessary to preserve this intransigence. A tradition which thus holds itself independent of the cultural milieu as much as possible will be rigid in the presence of cultural changes. It will not look to the resources of that culture for the light and guidance of truth. Since it seeks to preserve a body of truth and cherished experiences independently of that culture, it will emphasize the importance of believing without dependence on evidence and reasoning found in that culture. Finally, the only home of the soul which can be found in this world is the culture in which one is reared. If one repudiates that, he must be an outcast forever unless he can find a home of the soul in some other world. Hence the other-worldliness of this philosophy. Thus all its characteristics may be said to issue from its cultural intransigence.

If we were not so familiar with it, we would think it amazing that any way of living could be thus maintained with such independence of its cultural milieu. It is as though a stream of water would flow down the midst of a river and not mix with the other waters. Such an astounding phenomenon cries out for an explanation. We must look into the historical background and origins of this tradition to see if we can find the cause for this trait which it so strikingly displays.

ITS HISTORICAL ORIGINS

There are three ways in which a religion may be related to its surrounding culture. First, it may be native to that culture. This is the most common and natural way for a religion to function. This is the way almost all the primitive religions developed. Such was the religion of the Greeks and the Romans and the religion of the Jews before the dispersion. When a religion that is native to its surrounding culture functions properly, it illuminates the highest possibilities of that culture and provides the most powerful inspiration to their fulfillment. It clarifies and purifies the most characteristic and noble expression of it and stimulates its highest fulfillment. Of course a native religion may become degenerate, just like any other religion. We do not mean to suggest that such a religion is better than others simply because it is native. We are simply pointing out what it can do, when it does its best.

The second way a religion may be related to the surrounding culture is to invade it from the outside, as Buddhism entered China or Islam conquered Persia in the seventh century. Then the religion may stimulate and fertilize the culture with foreign elements, if we look at the best it can do. But it will be transformative, rather than expressive. It will criticize, correct and redirect, rather than purify and promote to highest fulfillment the unique genius of that culture. Of course such a religion may be gradually assimilated to the surrounding culture, rather than criticizing and transforming it. Most likely, both processes will occur.

Thirdly, a religion may develop in the midst of a conglomeration of cultures, so that it is native to none. In this polyglot mixture it may develop to high maturity, absorbing much from many cultural sources; but not being absorbed by any. Then, if this mixture of cultures represents a sick and dying civilization, it may develop an order of life of its own, which will enable it to go on as the old culture dies and become the dominant teacher and cultural power over the new life that springs up when the old civilization perishes. This last is the peculiar historical origin of Christianity.

Christianity began as an offshoot of Judaism. But it was disclaimed by Judaism, so that it could not be a native of the life of Israel. It grew up in Hellenism, absorbing much of Greek thought and appropriating the Greek language. But the cultured Greeks regarded Christianity as an upstart and intruder. It was rejected by Greek culture. When Roman culture succeeded that of Greece, Christianity was still an outsider. It came to the Romans as an expression of the life of Greece, yet it was not truly Greek. For some time it made its home in the Roman Empire and became more and more Roman. It might in time have merged with this culture. Indeed it moved a long way in that direction, and had become the recognized religion of the Empire. But just when this merging of Christianity with the prevailing culture seemed about to be consummated, Roman life moved rapidly toward disintegration, and the face of Europe took on the cultural aspects of the barbarians of the north.

Then ensued the most decisive influence of all, giving to traditional supernaturalism the traits which it still bears. During its sojourn in the Roman Empire it had developed not only a way of life and a faith which embodied much of the culture then prevailing, but also a social order and an institutional structure. Precisely because of the declining strength of the Roman organization of life, Christianity was stimulated to develop an order of its own. It was a society, as well as a faith and a way of life. In this form it entered the Dark Ages and the Middle Ages. For a thousand years it struggled to maintain this culture, this order, this way of life and this faith in the midst of barbarism. This struggle of a thousand years gave to traditional supernaturalism the marks it now bears.

In order to preserve this order, faith, way of life and social organization inherited from the Greco-Roman culture, and carry it through the stormy barbaric conditions that then prevailed, it developed the life of the monasteries and the mighty organization whose head was the Pope at Rome. Time and again the prevailing ways of life threatened to submerge the Christian order. But again and again it was saved by the mighty efforts of St. Augustine, St. Benedict, St. Boniface, St. Bonaventura and Pope Gregory X and other heroes of the faith.

It is plain that the peculiar conditions under which Christianity originated, and the thousand years of struggle to preserve itself in the midst of a barbaric culture, would develop just the traits which we find in traditional supernaturalism. It would develop an unyielding rigidity against the influences of any surrounding culture. It would turn away from the resources for seeking and testing truth which the cultural environment might afford, and put its faith on some internal depository of truth. It would insist on believing the traditional doctrines, without regard to what was believed and taught by the people outside this tradition. Hence it would magnify belief. Above all it would turn away from the culture that prevailed round about, denouncing it as an unfit home for the human spirit, and turn to some other world. Hence it would be other-worldly.

Thus the history of Christianity enables us to understand traditional supernaturalism. It is true that the history we have been discussing is that of the Roman Catholic church, while the contemporary traditional supernaturalism we are chiefly considering is that of Protestantism. But these traits were put upon Christianity before Protestantism arose as a separate form of Christianity; and, what is more important, the reformers who originated Protestantism broke away from the Catholic church in great part precisely because at that time Christianity was again moving toward closer and closer rapprochement with the prevailing culture. Hence the movements of reform in the Catholic church, both those that issued in Protestantism and those that did not, were attempts to preserve these very traits we have been noting.

Last of all it should be said that when the medieval era was drawing to its close, Christianity began to merge with the prevailing culture and thus lifted it to its height. This occurred most notably in the twelfth to the fourteenth centuries. The great lives and works of that time show how a great religion can make a great culture and a great culture can make a great religion when the two merge. Here for the first time in its history, excepting perhaps toward the close of the Roman Empire, Christianity ceased to be an alien to the culture that prevailed and entered into communion with it. What was the result? This was the age of St. Francis, of St. Thomas, of Dante, and of St. Louis, the great Christian ruler. And the list could be lengthened. Some of the greatest lives and the greatest achievements of Europe appeared then. But the peculiar fate of Christianity still continued. Just when it began to be quite completely integral to this culture, it also, like that of the Roman Empire, began to disintegrate and give place to a totally different order of life. This disintegration of the two great cultures with which Christianity joined itself, occurring just at the moment when Christianity became naturalized to them, was due to causes wholly other than this conjunction with Christianity, of course.

St. Francis of Assisi is the best symbol and expression of this union between Christianity and western culture.

But it was in St. Francis of Assisi that this new spiritual culture bore its final and most perfect fruit. He is the embodiment in flesh and blood of the new spirit of Western Christianity. Hitherto though Christianity had been the great formative power in western culture it had been a foreign power that was still, as it were, something external to the nature of Western man, its real centers of life were in the monasteries, those camps of the disciplined *militia Dei,* which were scattered over the half pagan soil of Europe like fortresses in newly conquered territory. With St. Francis for the first time, we see Christianity breaking through the barriers of race and social tradition and achieving an organic and complete expression in Western man. There is no longer any conflict or inconsistency between religion and culture, between faith and life. The whole man is Christian, and the Christian spirit is united with the Western nature as intimately and inseparably as the union of soul and body.

Nothing could be more spontaneous, less artificial and " cultured " than the genius of St. Francis, yet he is the final fruit of a long process of spiritual cultivation. He marks the coming of age of Christian Europe and the birth of a new consciousness.[1]

It has been the peculiar fate of Christianity to be an alien to every culture with which it has been associated. All the more striking is this fate when we note that on the only two occasions when it did begin to make itself at home in the culture with which it was connected, that culture happened to be on the brink of its own decline and disappearance. But all this should help us to understand traditional supernaturalism.

ITS CONTENT AND THOUGHT

While we have not explicitly stated the content of thought found in the philosophy of this form of Christianity, much of it has become discernible from our discussion of other aspects of the problem. This content, like that of any other philosophy of religion, can be analyzed under six heads: (1) the idea of

God, (2) the theory of value, (3) the theory of knowledge, (4) the cosmic orientation of man, (5) the pattern it presents of human hopes and aspirations, and (6) the type of social enterprises to which it leads.

These can be sought out in Machen's *Christianity and Liberalism,* or any other well-rounded statement of this philosophy as found in works by E. Y. Mullins or F. L. Patton.

---

1 *Medieval Religion:* Christopher Dawson. Pp. 50–51.

CHAPTER V

NEO–SUPERNATURALISTS

THE most striking manifestation of religious thought and life in the Western world today is the appearance of two extremes. An extreme form of supernaturalism and an extreme form of naturalism stand over against each other. The one is called neo-supernaturalism and the other non-theistic religious humanism.

THE DIFFERENTIA OF NEO–SUPERNATURALISM

It is important to note wherein neo-supernaturalism differs from traditional supernaturalism. The chief point of difference is that neo-supernaturalism extricates the supernatural from all entangling alliances with this natural world. Traditional supernaturalism did not. Most of the difficulties of traditional supernaturalism have been due to these entanglements of its beliefs with beliefs about the world of nature. Let us note some of these troublesome alliances which traditional supernaturalism maintained, but which neo-supernaturalism has repudiated. This will help to set forth the distinguishing traits of neo-supernaturalism.

The first was alliance with reason. It is true that traditional supernaturalism declared that God and God's will, our future destiny and other matters of primary religious concern are revealed. They are not discovered in a saving way by the natural reason of man nor manifest in any of the processes of the natural order. So far, so good. That is supernaturalism and the new version of it holds to this declaration along with the traditional. But traditional supernaturalism did not remain on this high ground. While it said that the natural reason cannot find God and God's will in a saving way, nevertheless human reason can be harmonized with revelation. Human reason, rightly exercised, supports revelation.

This is the first entangling alliance which neo-supernaturalism has rejected. The latter teaches that we must not put our trust in reason even as an aid or a support to revelation. If we do, we are caught at once in all the uncertainties, controversies, errors of the schools of philosophy. Traditional supernaturalism has been dragged and mauled and trampled in the conflict between the warring systems of philosophy and science until its lineaments have been badly marred. Hence neo-supernaturalism cuts free from all connection with reason. Reason has its place in seeking the way of life through nature. It must show what is right and wrong in morals, how the state should be organized, what should be done with industry and the like. But when it comes to the things that are directly concerned with God we must cast off all connection with reason. God makes himself known directly to the individual and is apprehended by faith.

A second troublesome alliance which traditional supernaturalism formed with the natural world was its dependence on the authority of the church. Now the church is an historical, social institution. Of course, one can speak of the church as a supernatural entity, an invisible, spiritual community not in the process of history and society at all. But if one does that one must not confuse it or connect it with the social institution that plainly is a part of the historical and social process. The teachings and practices of this latter are the thoughts and works of men having all the fallibility and imperfection of human beings. Hence when traditional supernaturalism looked to the church for guidance and light concerning God and the ways of God, it found itself involved in the natural process with the evils and limitations of this order of being. Neo-supernaturalism denies that the church as an historical, social institution can show us God.

A third error of traditional supernaturalism, so the neosupernaturalists say, was to exalt the Bible as the only infallible rule of faith and practice. The Bible is a book which developed in history. Its many authors lived under historical and social conditions. Thus the Bible in its authorship, in its transcriptions and redactions and interpretations is mixed with the order of nature. Here again traditional supernaturalism has been put to no end of trouble by the higher critics and other investigators. So the neo-supernaturalists repudiate the Bible as an authority in the sense in which traditional supernaturalism so held it. God reveals himself through the Word and the Word may come to a man through reading the Bible.[1] But the Word of God is not the Bible as a total collection of writings. The neo-supernaturalists accept all the findings of the higher critics. One of their most prominent leaders in Europe, Bultmann, is himself a very radical higher critic, rejecting a great part of what has been held to be the teaching of Jesus by the traditional supernaturalists.

What is this Word? It is God's direct revelation of himself to the individual. It may come to one by way of preaching and the ministrations of the church, and it may come through the Bible. But it is not the church and it is not the Bible. These may have all the faults, errors and limitations which can be discovered in them as products of history and society. God, who completely transcends society and history, is not thereby in any way affected, and his revelation to the individual is not thereby impaired.

Still another weakness of traditional supernaturalism lay in its glorification of the historical Jesus. Here is another source of its many troubles. Jesus as a man who lived at a certain time and place can be studied as a product of the natural order. He has been so studied with increasing intensity; and in that blaze of light he does not look at all like the Christ of Christian faith. But this was another mistake due to an admixture of the supernatural with the natural order which neo-supernaturalism has corrected. The historical man who lived in Palestine is not important to the neo-supernaturalist except as the medium through which the transcendent God made himself known to the world. The important thing about Jesus was not his teachings, not his ideals, not even his moral character. The important thing was his obedience, his complete submission to God. For him God's sovereignty was absolute. He lived for God and for God only. It is the reality of God that thus shines through the historical figure that is important. But this reality does not shine through in the form of any concept of God nor in the form of any program for living as individuals or as a society. It shines through simply as that reality to which all human life must be subjected absolutely, unto uttermost death and destruction if necessary, as was the case with Jesus. It shines through as that reality for which and for which alone we must live.

Knowledge of God and God's will is not attained in specific form either intuitively or rationally or through the Bible. But we know the reality of God and God's demand of absolute obedience. This we know by faith, a faith which God himself puts into us. When all our living is thus dominated by the supreme will to obey God we can be disinterested in the midst of the lures and strifes and passions of life. Through this dominant obedience to God, we do not know what is right and wrong, but we are then able to use our intelligence freely and fully to discover what is right and wrong in the light of the best standards available to us. We must not assume that these standards are God-given or God's own. They are not. But through our obedience to God we have a corrective of human perversity. Absolute obedience to God who transcends completely every-

thing in this world releases human intelligence from the egocentric bias. Also it releases it from the bias that comes from
belonging to a particular class, group, nation, culture, race or
epoch. We still cannot use any other standards of judgment
save those which our class, group, and so forth provide us. We
still have no more knowledge than our culture can endow us.
But we can be objective in the use of our knowledge, our standards and all our resources. That is to say, we can be as disinterested and fair as it is possible for a man to be who has all
other limitations, but is dominated by no obsession or fear for
anything in this world by reason of a higher obedience that
rules him.

Our living for God is not measured by the rectitude or effectiveness of what we do. It is measured by the completeness of
our obedience, the absolute commitment of all our lives, to
God; and the consequent disinterestedness with which we
become able to treat all the problems of personal and social
living.

Thus far we have noted the difference between neo-supernaturalism and traditional supernaturalism. Now we must
look at its differentia as over against mysticism.

Mysticism declares that God is made known to us by way of
inner experience. Neo-supernaturalism rejects inner experience as a manifestation of God. The mystic way is rejected because it involves the natural order. All inner experience is
subject matter for the natural science of psychology. These
ecstasies, these emotions and thrills, these visions and voices, are
natural phenomena of the human mind and have their explanation according to the laws of the natural mind. For example,
the *numinous* feeling of Rudolf Otto is simply an effect of the
human psycho-physical organism, say the neo-supernaturalists.
To identify God with that is to drag God down into the natural
order and make him a rather trivial phenomenon of human
mentality. So with all the raptures and throbs and other mental states of the mystics. They have nothing particularly to do

with God, declare the neo-supernaturalists. They reveal some of the peculiarities of human nature; in some cases, perhaps, they reveal sublimities of human nature. But they do not reveal God.

The mystics say God is so intimately close to us and so pervasive in our world that the human intellect cannot grasp him in his fullness and richness. The neo-supernaturalists say God is so alien to human mentality and all our world that our reason cannot reach to him. Thus while both mystic and neo-supernaturalist reject reason as a guide to God, they do so on grounds totally different one from the other.

The mystics are filled with deep peace because of the pillowing presence of God in human living and in nature. The neo-supernaturalists are filled with tension and anxiety because God is opposed to human living and quite removed from nature. The mystics are optimists because they feel the sustaining presence of God. The neo-supernaturalists are pessimists with respect to this world and all its works because they are convinced that these all stand under the condemning judgment of God.

It would not be correct to say, however, that the neo-supernaturalists are pessimists in any ultimate sense. They trust in God absolutely and they know that God is right. They know that God is almighty and holds absolute sovereignty over this world and every happening in it. Therefore for him who has given himself in complete obedience to God all is well ultimately, however he may fare in this world. This does not mean merely that he will go to heaven. The neo-supernaturalists have very little to say about heaven. Some of them seem to indicate that they scarcely believe there is any continued existence of the individual after death. In any case, that is not the point when they say all is well. They mean, rather, that what they live for completely, that to which they give uttermost and absolute obedience, however inadequate their deeds, is sovereign and perfect, holy and triumphant. Hence, by reason of what they live for, by reason of this obedience, devotion and loyalty, their lives also are triumphant, no matter what may happen to their existing selves and this existing world.

The difference between neo-supernaturalism and idealism scarcely needs discussion after what we have said.

Romantic liberalism, which is the most popular form of religion today among the educated classes, draws more of the wrath of the neo-supernaturalists than any other form of religion. This may be due partly to the fact that most neo-supernaturalists today passed through a stage of being liberals before they came over to neo-supernaturalism. The biography of many of them would run like this. In childhood reared under the teachings of traditional supernaturalism. In youth and young manhood breaking with this tradition under the teachings of romantic liberalism. In later life returning to supernaturalism but with those improvements over traditional supernaturalism which we have indicated. Since they have had to drive romanticism out of their own lives, its deficiencies and evils are most vividly in their minds. However that may be, the romantic forms of religion are constantly denounced by them.

The romantic tradition is a mixture of all the other prevalent forms of religion which we have been describing — traditional supernaturalism, mysticism and idealism. It is generally marked with the high optimism that is common to the idealist. The presuppositions on which idealism is based make optimism most natural, and the romantic philosophy of religion has taken over some of these presuppositions. But it also makes use of what it can assimilate from mysticism and traditional supernaturalism. Because it is a mixture, and because it is more interested in the practical conduct of life than in any system of thought, and because it has no strongly developed and tenaciously held system, it is more subject to the winds of doctrine than to any other and, most important of all, it readily identifies God and God's will and the supreme goal of life with the point of view and social cause that happens to dominate at any particular time and place.

All this makes romantic liberalism in practice very this-worldly, whatever its theory may be. It always bears the marks of time and place. Therefore it is diametrically opposed to the purpose and claim of neo-supernaturalism which sets God and God's purpose high above every time and place. God is the eternal, beyond all times and places, say the supernaturalists. It is sacrilege, blasphemy, contemptible weakness and recreance to God to be forever clothing God in the garments of the day. He is transcendent and should always be held as such. Thus the neo-supernaturalists set themselves over against the liberals with more emphasis than against any others. Yet the liberals, precisely because they do take on the color of their time and place, are most likely to become neo-supernaturalists.

SOURCES OF NEO–SUPERNATURALISM

The neo-supernaturalism in the United States did not originate here, and is not nearly so widely and strongly developed as in some quarters of the world. Its chief source and home is Europe, with Karl Barth and his followers among the most conspicuous proponents of it. It is also to be found in England, not only in the Barthian form but also in native dress. John Oman has given one of the most persuasive formulations of neo-supernaturalism,[2] although his influence in the United States does not extend much beyond the circle of students who make it their business to study theology and philosophy of religion. Paul Tillich has reached the United States not only in his writings but also in person, and wields considerable influence. In the early stages of his career he belonged to the subterranean fellowship of Karl Barth but since then has developed a point of view of his own. His influence in the states is mediated chiefly through Wilhelm Pauck and the Niebuhr brothers who are very devoted followers of him. They have considerable leadership.

Neo-Thomism might be called a form of neo-supernaturalism although it has characteristics of its own which quite clearly distinguish it from any neo-supernaturalism in Protestant circles. Since we are chiefly concerned with the latter, it lies outside our province to discuss neo-Thomism except to mention it as one of the sources of the great ground swell of neo-supernaturalism which is sweeping the world and is beginning to show itself in America. Each of these sources we have mentioned will be briefly discussed because they are directly connected with neo-supernaturalism in the United States.

THE BARTHIAN INFLUENCE

Scarcely anyone in this country will call himself a Barthian, although great numbers are fascinated by the teachings of this man and his representatives. This fascination shows that the teachings of Barth strike a responsive chord. They are too alien to our ways of thinking and living to be wholly accepted. But there is a widespread discontent, scarcely conscious and articulate, with the prevalent forms of religion, and a craving for something in the way of religion that will satisfy a need which is scarcely conscious. The Barthian expression of religion does not fit the need exactly, and yet it has in it something possessing a powerful appeal.

Since neo-supernaturalism is not a native development in America and since its representatives here mostly echo the teaching of the originators, we cannot discuss the American expression of it without studying the teaching of those who are echoed. The two men whose teachings provide almost the total content for American neo-supernaturalism are Karl Barth and Paul Tillich. We must examine their thought. Barth seems to have three main doctrines: God's absolute otherness, his absolute sovereignty and the absolute crisis in human living.

God is absolutely other, meaning that there is no aspect or form of nature, no achievement of the human reason, no formulation of human ideals, hopes or values, that can be identi-

fied with God. It is the height of blasphemous idolatry to identify God with any of these. There is no form or structure of
human life, no aspiration or vision or inner experience which
can be set up as peculiarly the manifestation of God. God is
other than all these. God is a dark abyss, a mystery. Human
values have their place in our world, but they must not be connected with God. God stands over against it all as the judge and
condemner. God has his own ways and they are vastly different from ours. " God is in heaven and thou art on earth," is one
of the favorite expressions of this teaching.

God is absolutely sovereign. His power is without limit.
Everything is subject to his might. One might think there
would be difficulty in reconciling this almighty power of God
with a world so alien to God's nature. It is true that all other
prevalent forms of religion, except extreme naturalism and this
neo-supernaturalism, have such difficulty. But the latter escapes the problem on two grounds. In the first place, God is
not good in any human sense of goodness. Our standards of
right and wrong, of good and bad, all our norms of valuation,
are inapplicable to God. Hence any attempt to judge God's
goodness by human standards is out of the question. In the
second place, any attempt to give a rational account of God,
or to remove logical inconsistencies in our statements about
him, is foolish because God is super-rational. Thus God's absolute sovereignty stands unquestioned despite the vast and
manifest evils in the world.

God injects into human life an absolute crisis. In every concrete situation every individual faces the ultimate crisis of his
life. This ultimate crisis is the necessity of deciding for God
or against God. This crisis does not arise once only, but in
every case where a decision must be made. What does it mean
to decide for God? It cannot mean that one specific set of
values represents God, while other ends are against God. It
cannot mean that this procedure is God's and the others not.
It can only mean that my primary concern shall be to stand for

God. Doubtless whatever I do will be deeply infected with evil, because everything is enmeshed in the evils of this world. But I decide for God when every interest, every value, every hope and ideal and course of action is held by me subject to God's judgment and will. Thus I am released from fears, passions, envies, prejudices, obsessions and can view the situation disinterestedly. I am delivered from all these distortions of judgment because I am under the mastery of God alone. None of these can claim to be wholly God's way. I can examine all possibilities on their merits, not enslaved to the lure or the fear of any.

The most baffling aspect of this philosophy of religion is the theory of knowledge. How do we know anything about God or even know there is a God when all human powers of knowing are incapable of reaching to God? We know because God reveals himself to those whom he may choose. But how do we know what is God's revelation and what is not? God himself will cause us to know. There is nothing more to say about it. We know by faith but faith is the work of God in us. We know through the Word spoken in Christ. But the Word cannot be identified with the Bible, nor can Christ be identified with the historic Jesus. God speaks to us through these media.

Since all forms of rational discourse and inquiry are incompetent to deal with God, the neo-supernaturalists resort to myth and paradox. Anything one can say about God must be put into paradoxical form. It is true and yet it is not true. Its contradictory can also be said.

The great merit of this formulation of religion is that it opens a way to disinterestedness. Since God is over and above the world, and one's whole devotion is given to God, one can view everything in the world without passion or fear and with an objectivity which is so urgently needed in the turmoil of our present social confusion.

JOHN OMAN

Since John Oman's influence in America is so slight outside narrow academic circles we need say very little about him, despite the intrinsic worth of his philosophy.

According to Oman we become aware of God when we are sensitive to the qualitative richness of the world. This is not stating it accurately, for this qualitative richness does not really belong to the world of nature. The world of nature is just what the physical sciences say it is. It is a mechanism. It has no qualities of color, fragrance, emotion, aspiration, love, joy, tragedy and sublimity. All this qualitative abundance belongs to mind. But plainly the human mind does not originate it. It pours into our minds in rare moments when we are most sensitive and open to it. The poet, the lover, the mystic, the artist in all his many forms, have it most fully.

But this qualitative fullness cannot be reached by reason nor by the kind of observation employed in scientific method. All these procedures give us only the mechanism of the world, with perhaps a few tatters and fringes of the qualities which the inquiring intellect has not been able to strip away entirely. Thus there are two ways of knowing: the way we know the natural world, which is that of reason and scientific inquiry, and the way we know God, which is that of open awareness. The God we thus know is not in nature. He is supernature. But he uses nature as a medium through which to communicate himself.

PAUL TILLICH

Paul Tillich sometimes repudiates what he calls supernaturalism. But that is due to his use of words. By supernaturalism he means the breaking into this world of something so totally alien to all our ways of thinking and living that it could not mean anything to us at all. It would be meaningless. Hence supernaturalism is self-contradictory, and he accuses Barth of that kind of teaching.[3]

But Tillich is a neo-supernaturalist in the sense in which we are using the word. He holds that the reality of God wholly transcends this natural world of existence. God is so completely transcendent that we cannot say God exists, for existence is a category which applies only to nature. God is beyond existence, and yet he has almighty power. This total world of existence is maintained by God. It could not exist without God. It is not self-sufficient. God is the necessary ground of this existing world.

If we put the difference between Barth and Tillich in a single statement it would be this: Barth says that God condemns the natural life of man as evil; Tillich says that the natural life of man becomes evil only when it claims self-sufficiency or is conducted as though it were self-sufficient. The whole meaning and the only meaning of natural existence is found in the unconditioned reality of God. This meaning is wholly beyond our comprehension. But man lives as he should only when everything he does and thinks and feels, every successful achievement and every failure is treated not as having meaning and worth in itself but only having meaning and worth in God, the unconditioned.

A brief quotation may serve to express this idea of Tillich. He is writing about education:

Now every educational method which does not rest upon a common relationship of both teacher and taught to something ultimate, to the eternal, is inadequate. For in the sphere of the finite every goal that is set up, every method which is employed, is doubtful, limited, ultimately irresponsible. Only the Unconditioned can create unconditioned responsibility and therewith a relationship of teacher and taught which rests upon mutual responsibility and the possibility of unqualified loyalty. Given this common basis, the technique of communicating forms, which is the real problem of scientific pedagogy, becomes a question of the second order.[4]

In the quotation education merely serves to illustrate the principle. The same thing applies to everything else — industry, politics, art, sex love, friendship, eating, walking, anything. Just as soon as anything is done for its own sake, it is sin. Just as soon as anything is done for the fulfillment of all human history, it is sin; for the fulfillment of all human history is as nothing compared to the unknowable vastness and richness of the Unconditioned. Nothing in nature must be done for nature, not even for the most comprehensive totality of all nature, actual and possible. Everything must be done for its true meaning, which totally transcends nature and which is nothing else than the Unconditioned. This Unconditioned is so diverse from nature that it cannot even be described as having existence.

Nevertheless, this unconditioned reality of God is closely akin to the human spirit. It appears in us not as any specific ideal or quality of consciousness. It appears in us in the fact that we are able to regard every achievement, every fulfillment, every event, as pointing on to something infinitely vaster. It appears in our sense of anxiety or discontent with every attainment. It is this outreach toward the Unconditioned which shows our kinship with God.

The great evil of human life, which is constantly with us, is our failure to keep up this outreach, this discontent, this turning from everything in existence and turning toward the Unconditioned which is the real meaning and goal of everything in existence. This outreach, this discontent, this turning away toward the Unconditioned is always flickering and dying in us. We are always reverting to the life of " self-sufficient finitude." We are constantly settling down and making ourselves at home in this world of nature.

This evil reaches its greatest height in what Tillich calls demonic religion. Demonic religion is a religion that takes any human ideal, any cause of social reform, any utopia, any actual or possible form of existence and sets it up as the objective of religious aspiration and devotion. True religion gives devotion to the Unconditioned, which infinitely transcends any possible objective that can be specified. More than that, it infinitely transcends any actual or possible state of existence, no matter how perfect that state might be. Indeed, the more perfect any state of existence might be, even though it included the perfection of all existence, the more evil it might become by reason of taking on the form of self-sufficient finitude. Imperfection and catastrophe is far better, if that keeps us always giving our devotion to the Unconditioned, and not to any state of nature, actual or possible.

Here we see in Tillich, as we saw in Barth, the most noble and precious trait of religious living. This trait consists in what some other interpreters have called "detachment." It is the ability attained through high religion to view everything that happens and every possibility without any of those fears and passions that distort the judgment. It is poise, objectivity, disinterestedness, in dealing with every concrete situation, and with every issue no matter how fateful to human destiny, and no matter how alluring or dreadful it may be from the standpoint of everything in existence. It is the ability to treat every triumph and every failure, every rapturous joy and every misery, every fulfillment and every disaster, with glowing warmth and appreciation, and yet with all the powers of intelligence, judgment and appraisal freely active and undistorted by fascination or dread, fear or hope. When all our devotion is given to the unconditioned reality of God, we can in this way triumph over the world and every vicissitude of fortune. Any formulation of religion that fails to provide for this is weak and incompetent. It fails to set forth that one thing which is the preeminent function of religion in human life. We do not mean to say that this philosophy of religion called neo-supernaturalism is the only worthy philosophy. We believe this supreme function of religion can be safeguarded by other philosophical formulations. We only wish to point out this greatest point of excellence. High religion should always release to the utmost the free and unbiased exercise of all the powers of intelligence and evaluation in dealing with the most critical problems of personal and social living where the most powerful passions are involved.

AMERICAN REPRESENTATIVES OF NEO–SUPERNATURALISM

We have discussed at length the views of Karl Barth and Paul Tillich, rather than American exponents of neo-supernaturalism, because the Americans are so deeply indebted to the teachings of these men. G. W. Richards is an outstanding representative in this country of the Barthian school, while Wilhelm Pauck and the Niebuhr brothers uphold the teachings of Paul Tillich. A very stirring exposition of the neo-supernaturalistic gospel has been set forth by Edwin Lewis, an American Methodist, in the widely read volume, *A Christian Manifesto*. Lewis does not attempt a philosophical formulation. He gives voice to the sentiment rather than a systematic presentation. Another notable expression of this view is G. C. Cell's book, *The Rediscovery of John Wesley*. Perhaps the most systematic statement of this viewpoint among American writers is to be found in *Beyond Fundamentalism and Modernism* by George W. Richards. Richards is clearly an American Barthian.

A few quotations from his book will show the character of his thought.

Thus the act of God becomes a fact and a force in the life of man — not a palpable fact such as is found in nature or in history, that can be accounted for and explained by previous conditions and present circumstances; nor can its reality be proved by investigation of science or by process of reason. Assurance of it comes only through obedience of faith.[5]

When one asks: " But how can I believe? Whence comes faith to me? " the answer is that man cannot make himself believe any more than he can lift himself by his boot-straps. Neither the joy nor the sorrow of life begets faith in men. One is not taught it by circumstances. One does not learn to believe from one's self or from one's condition. Faith comes from God through His word and Spirit each moment, and when it comes, one can say nothing else, astonished and perplexed, but " Lord I believe, help thou my unbelief." [6]

The gospel, says Richards, is not a fund of information which God gives in a supernatural way to his people through direct communication or through the teaching of a prophet or sage. Rather it is a call to action. But in religious tradition this gospel all too frequently becomes perverted into something else.

The word of God, instead of being what it was intended to be — a call to action — is turned into an object of man's contemplation and theoretical knowledge, a *Weltanschauung* or a metaphysic.[7]

It is a serious mistake that has caused much controversy, bitterness, and injury to life and happiness, to assume that the gospel of God is to supersede, or is in conflict with, the work of the biologist, the psychologist, the social scientist, the moral reformer, humanitarian activities. These men, however, are to carry on their work in the power of the gospel. Again, it is an equally serious error, with woeful consequences, to assume that the scientist, the artist, the statesmen, the social servant, are sufficient unto themselves and have no need of the gospel. To neglect or to ignore the one or the other error is to develop a stunted manhood that is true neither to God nor to man. The gospel is not a supplement to the fund of rational or scientific knowledge. So it has been understood and treated in the theology of the Roman Catholic and of the Protestant church. The fundamental thesis upon which scholasticism rests, whether in the middle or the modern age, is that the content of faith and the content of reason are equivalent. Revelation, it is assumed, only forestalls the action of reason and furnishes faith with the truths which the intellect later appropriates. When the mind of man is sufficiently developed the passage from faith to knowledge is readily made.[8]

The view of the matter expressed in the quotation is rejected by Richards. He goes on to say what he thinks is the true nature of the gospel in respect to the powers of the human reason and scientific inquiry.

In contrast to rationalism one might term the gospel " irrational." This is true in so far as reason cannot reach beyond the limitations of man into the transcendental order. It is false, however, if the term irrational is identified with the gospel and one thinks one is speaking of God when one speaks of the irrational. The term can be applied to the gospel only to describe the mystery of man's being and of God's revelation. In this sense it is rather other than rational, not irrational, in its character and way of approach.[9]

What was glad tidings for a comparatively small people, the Jews, is still gospel for all nations. We live in a world of inexorable law, and yet we trust in providence; in a world of ruthless oppression, and yet we believe in the coming of righteousness and freedom; in a world of stern justice, and yet we find comfort in pardoning grace; in a world of sensuality and vice, and yet we will be chaste and temperate; in a world of selfishness, and yet we are rich; in a war-stricken world, and yet we have peace; in a world that is proud and haughty, and yet we find strength in meekness and humility; in a world of falsehood and ugliness, and yet we pursue truth and beauty. In a time of religious depression and moral dearth we have the rock-fast conviction that God reigns and reveals his purpose of righteousness and love in man. This deep unshakable abiding faith in the victory of God's purpose, revealed through Jesus Christ, is the fruit of the gospel of God. It is the never-failing cruse of oil that feeds the flaming torch of prophets and heroic souls in the Church of all ages, the ever-abounding hope which sustains every struggle of individuals and groups for the fulfillment of the petition, " Thy will be done, as in heaven so on earth." . . .

They are always reaching out toward the eternal purpose yet never able to grasp it. Enough that they see Jesus! We, too, like the Christians of all the centuries, though always abounding in the work of the Lord, live by faith in the promises of God; we are as watchmen on towers scanning the signs on the horizon through the surrounding gloom. We are stedfast and immovable even in the thickest darkness.[10]

Reinhold Niebuhr is interested in problems of social reconstruction rather than philosophy of religion. But in all his teachings there is not only a profound and intense religious spirit, but always the implications of an underlying philosophy of religion. He has not made this philosophy explicit and it is often difficult to get all its outlines. It is plain, however, that he reflects quite fully the thinking of Paul Tillich and represents much the same kind of neo-supernaturalism.

The underlying theme throughout all his writing and speaking is the hideous evil of demonic religion and demonic living,

meaning that evil which in the teaching of Tillich is called
" self-sufficient finitude." Niebuhr applies this specifically to
nationalism and capitalism. The way of living which these
words suggest is a life dominated by certain objectives which
do not open out into the unfathomed reality of God. They
seek specific objectives that can be compassed by the human
mind and the human powers of appreciation. This is always
evil.

But communism and most of the other revolutionary projects
for social change are guilty of the same evil. They set up some
goal and program of social action and serve it as though it were
the supreme objective of all human living. Here again appears
the same demonic trait. The goal must never be less than the
unknowable fullness of the unconditioned reality of God which
transcends all nature and all existence and all possibilities of
attainment. The highest reach of human history will be only
one expression of the unconditioned demand of God and by no
means reach the fullness of that demand. The demand of God
is unconditioned, which means it has no limits and can be compassed by no specifications, no dreams and ideals or practical
achievements.

Here again we have expressed that highest character of all
noble religion. Any philosophy of religion which is untrue to
this character is false. However, neo-supernaturalism is not
the only philosophy of religion which is competent to provide
for this high function.

---

[1] In the neo-supernaturalism of Karl Barth it would seem that the Bible is the
exclusive medium of God's revelation, but that is not true of all the neo-supernaturalists.

[2] See his book *The Natural and the Supernatural*. Macmillan, 1931.

[3] See Paul Tillich's "What is Wrong with the 'Dialectic' Theology?" *The
Journal of Religion*, Vol. XV, No. 2, April 1935.

[4] *The Religious Situation*: Paul Tillich. Holt, 1932.

[5] *Beyond Fundamentalism and Modernism*: George W. Richards. Scribner, 1934.
P. 3.   [6] *Ibid.*, p. 4.   [7] *Ibid.*, p. 6.   [8] *Ibid.*, p. 9.   [9] *Ibid.*, p. 9.
[10] *Ibid.*, pp. 324–26.

PART THREE

ROOTED IN TRADITION OF IDEALISM

CHAPTER VI

ABSOLUTISTS

IDEALISM is the most complicated and many-sided system of thought in the modern world; due to its long history, many co-creators and many diverse ideas assimilated into it. It is therefore difficult to say anything about it to which all idealists would subscribe. Nevertheless it may be said to have three basic doctrines. They are: (1) what we know most surely and directly is mind, pre-eminently our own minds; (2) if our knowledge of the external world is to be trustworthy, that world must also somehow be the manifestation of mind; (3) the good is the ultimately real while the evil is not.[1]

Of these three doctrines the first sets the pattern for the logic and theory of knowledge of idealism, the second determines its metaphysics, and the third its ethics and philosophy of religion.

Absolute idealists are distinguished from other representatives of idealism by adding to the three doctrines mentioned the further doctrine of the Absolute. This is a difficult teaching. The Absolute is absolutely all-inclusive, absolutely permanent and changeless, absolutely perfect.

The Absolute is all-inclusive. All the past, all the future, all the present, all that might have been, all that may be, are gathered up into its unity. Every unique individual mind and personality is but a fragment, a facet, a peculiar expression of the infinite fullness of the Absolute. All the multiplicities of the world, all the incompatibilities and contradictions and conflicts are somehow brought into a unity that is completely organic, so that every part is needed by every other part. The infinite wealth of diverse and unique individual entities that we find in the world, including personalities, would be meaningless were they not all needed to express the infinite fullness of the total unity of the Absolute. The total meaning of each is the totality of the Absolute. Diversity and uniqueness are precious only because they all are needed to make up this perfect unity.

The Absolute is permanent and changeless. Change is precious and meaningful only because the kaleidescopic changes of time, and every fleeting moment, have back of them the infinite, eternal and changeless Absolute. Time flies swiftly on because every second is needed to bring out some further element of eternity. Time and change are but the moving image of the Absolute. Let us use a very crude illustration. The Absolute is like a wheel. As it revolves it brings first one bit of its surface against the earth, then another. Time is the way first one bit of the Absolute is brought down to the earth, then another. But the Absolute does not change. What changes is that aspect of the Absolute which is manifest to us. Time is the successive manifestation of the diverse aspects of the one and changeless Absolute.

The Absolute is perfect in goodness. There is evil in the world. The absolutists do not deny that for a moment. They are not Christian Scientists. But evil is the way the perfect goodness of the Absolute is brought to fulfillment. Here we have, perhaps, the central problem of idealism as a philosophy of religion. How is evil the fulfillment of the perfect goodness of the Absolute?

Hegel answers that question by saying that evil is the way in which our experience grasps certain stages in the process of thesis and antithesis rising to a higher synthesis which is always

the greater good. Royce took the truth in this but found it insufficient and so added his further contribution to the solution
of the problem. According to Royce, the goodness of God
without evil would be the superficial goodness of innocence.
Only when God grapples with evil, struggles and suffers with
it, does the tragic glory of God's goodness rise to its sublime
perfection. God overcomes evil, conquers it completely, not
in time, for God is not temporal, but conquers it eternally.
We cannot say that God *will* overcome evil. Neither can we
say he *has* overcome it, or is now in process of overcoming, because all these expressions are in terms of time. God's complete overcoming is an eternal fact. But it is done at the cost
of unutterable struggle and unutterable suffering. Hence it is
a tragic overcoming and the goodness of God is a tragic goodness. But that is the only kind of goodness which can reach
the supreme heights of sublimity.

Hocking accepts the insights of Hegel and Royce but adds
something further of his own. He points out two remarkable
facts in human experience. One is that evil is the medium in
which associates can reach the deepest and sweetest community.
Blessed are they that mourn for they shall be comforted. Comfort is this deeper community found in suffering. But the
greatest sorrows and sufferings are just where human associates
fail us. The deepest anguish is precisely the failure of fellowship with the one who is dearest and closest. But here is where
divine fellowship enters. God is the "infallible associate."
This deeper community in suffering transmutes the evil into
blessedness.

The second fact noted by Hocking is that evil in another
person can be overcome not by direct attack, but by turning
from it and appealing to the best that is in him. The evil must
be faced squarely, acknowledged fully. But to overcome it one
must turn from it to the good that is in the other. Now this
applies not only to human personalities. It applies to the Absolute. The evil in the universe tends to shrivel and die when,

after facing and acknowledging it for what it is, we appeal from it to the goodness of God. This is the creative and fighting value of worship. In worship we turn completely to the goodness of God and thereby we overcome evil. But this can work only when we have fully faced the evil.

Let us summarize all this teaching about the Absolute in its threefold aspects of unity, changelessness and perfection. In the world there is multiplicity, conflict, discontinuity. But underneath all this swarming chaos of the world is the complete organic unity of the Absolute which gives meaning and value to the multiplicity since the infinite fullness of the Absolute can find expression in no other way than by just such multiplicity. In the world there is ceaseless change. But all this change only serves to give sequential expression to the all-inclusive, complete, eternal and changeless reality. In the world is evil, dire and very genuine. But evil brings to sublime fulfillment the perfect goodness of the Absolute.

The two towering figures representing idealism in the United States are Josiah Royce and William Ernest Hocking. We shall attempt to state the central thought of these men as it bears upon religion.

JOSIAH ROYCE

Perhaps we have already stated the greatest thinking Royce did on the problems of religion when we discussed the Absolute and the way evil is necessary to the tragic glory of sublime goodness. While we discussed that under the general head of American idealism, we were really following the thinking of Royce. Doubtless very few are satisfied with the conclusions reached by Royce on this matter of evil. We suspect Royce himself was satisfied least of all. But his great contribution lay not in the conclusion, but in the way he apprehended the magnitude and tragedy of evil and made others see it. Perhaps the greatest work of any religious and philosophical teacher is to make men see, not the final ends and solutions, but the nature and enormity of the problems and issues. This Royce does in his teaching about evil and the Absolute.

We are impelled to quote a passage from Thomas Mann's novel, *Joseph and his Brethren,* because it is so highly expressive of the spirit of Royce in his struggle with the problem of evil. Mann depicts Jacob grieving over the death of his wife Rachel. Royce in the wrestle of his thinking about evil is very much like Jacob. Rachel is dying in childbirth. Jacob is at her side.

Then it was that he [Jacob] directed upwards into the silvery light of those worlds above their heads, almost as a confession that he understood, his question: " Lord, what dost thou? "

To such questions there is no answer. Yet it is the glory of the human spirit that in this silence it does not depart from God, but rather learns to grasp the majesty of the ungraspable and to thrive thereon. Beside him the Chaldean women and slaves chanted their litanies and invocations, thinking to bind to human wishes the unreasoning powers. But Jacob had never yet so clearly understood as in this hour, why all that was false, and why Abram had left Ur to escape it. The vision vouchsafed him into this immensity was full of horror but also of power; his labor upon the godhead, which always betrayed itself in his careworn mien, made in this awful night a progress not unconnected with Rachel's agonies. And quite in the spirit of her love it was, that Jacob, her husband, should draw spiritual advantage from her dying.[2]

But Royce must speak for himself. Only his own words can show how, in him, a ruthless rigor of thinking was combined with a mighty and quenchless religious devotion.

You are reverent, we may say to the man who regards philosophic criticism as a dangerous trifling with stupendous truths; you are reverent, but what do you reverence? Have a care lest what you reverence shall turn out to be your own vague and confused notions, and not the real divine Truth at all. Take heed lest your object of worship be only your own little pet infinite, that is sublime to you mainly because it is yours, and that is in truth about as divine and infinite as your hate. For this is the danger that besets these vague and lofty sentiments. Unreflected upon, uncriticized, dumbly experienced, dumbly dreaded, these, your religious objects, may become mere feelings, merely visceral sensations of yours, that you have on Sunday mornings, or when you pray. Of course, if you are a worker, you may actually realize these vague ideas, in so far as they inspire you to work; if they do, they shall be judged by their fruits. Otherwise, do not trust too confidently their religious value. You, individually regarded, are but a mass of thought and feeling. What is only yours and in you, is not divine at all. Unless you lift it up into the light of thought and examine it often, how do you know into what your cherished religious ideal may not have rotted in the darkness of your emotions? Once in a while, there does come to a man some terrible revelation of himself in a great sorrow. Then in the tumult and anguish he looks for his religious faith to clothe his nakedness against the tempest; and he finds perhaps some moth-eaten old garment that profits him nothing, so that his soul miserably perished in the frost of doubt. Such a man has expected God to come to his help in every time of need; but the only god he has actually and consistently had, has been his own little contemptible private notion and dim feeling of a god, which he has never dared fairly to look at. Any respectable wooden idol would have done him better service; for then a man could know where and what his idol is. Such is only too apt to be the real state of the man who regards it as profanity to think clearly and sensibly on religious topics.

We claim, then, the right to criticize as fearlessly, as thoroughly, and as skeptically as may be, the foundations of conduct and faith. For what we criticize are, at the outset, our own notions which we want to have conform to the truth, if so be that there is any truth. As for doubt on religious questions, that is for a truth-seeker not only a privilege but a duty; and, as we shall experience all through this study, doubt has a curious and very valuable place in philosophy. Philosophic truth, as such, comes to us first under the form of doubt; and we never can be very near it in our search unless for a longer or shorter time, we have come to despair of it altogether. First, then, the despair of a thoroughgoing doubt, and then the discovery that this doubt contains in its bosom the truth that we are sworn to discover, however we can — this is the typical philosophic experience.[3]

Religious philosophy, says Royce, seeks what in all being is worthy of worship by reason of its goodness. We cannot find any such reality in the world known to the natural sciences. For one thing that world can be known only by conjecture, for mind alone can be known with assurance.

Here we have, standing forth in clear silhouette at once, the basic presupposition of idealism. All we can know, certainly and directly, is mind, because all experience is obviously mental. Hardness, softness, pressure, color, sound, fragrance, light, the perspectives of nearness, distance, direction, angle of vision — all these are mental. They have no being except in our minds or in relation to our minds. Hence all we can know experientially is mind. If we have any assured knowledge of anything beyond our own minds, it must be other mind. Only by virtue of the experience of some other mind, could all these data of sense experience, all these perspectives, all these magnitudes and directions, have any reality beyond our own experience.

In Royce's time the startling revelation made by the physical sciences that the world, as known to the most exact and thoroughly verified knowledge, has none of the qualities we seem to experience in it, had not yet been thoroughly assimilated into human thinking. Indeed it is not so even yet. Hence thinkers scarcely knew what to do with this declaration of the exact sciences except to say that it proved that there must be a cosmic mind else all knowing and all science is invalid. Since Royce's time other well-established philosophical treatments of this problem have developed, such as neo-realism, critical realism and, perhaps most important of all, objective relativism.[4] The conclusion that Cosmic Mind is necessary to validate all knowledge, seemed much more inevitable in the time Royce wrote than it does now, for much thinking on the problem has been done since then.

But there is a second reason why we cannot seek with any hope of success for a reality worthy of worship in the world made known by the natural sciences. This second reason is of greater moral and religious significance than the difficulty of achieving valid knowledge in a world which has none of the qualities and perspective of human experience. From the standpoint of pure logic and epistemology this reason looms big. But from the standpoint of morals and religious devotion the second is determinative. Also this second difficulty has received far less study and thorough treatment than the first.

The second difficulty in the way of finding God in the world as made known by the natural sciences lies in the fact that this world is made up of a plurality of forces without any unifying power to give them order and direction. Now a multiplicity of forces may bring about a great deal of good. Indeed these many unorganized tendencies may drift on in such a way as to achieve an ever increasing good for an indefinite period of time. But if they are ultimately a multiplicity, if they are not controlled by an underlying unity, all this increasing good is but an accident. It is due to some fortunate concatenation of these many forces working together. That, for example, is all that evolution can be as a phenomenon of nature. For progress to have any religious significance, it must be the symbol of eternity. Thus Royce puts behind him the world of nature known to the sciences and common sense. It has no genuine religious significance except as it leads us on to something deeper.

There is a deeper reality. We know it first of all as a postulate of faith, just as science knows by faith. The postulate of science is that universal rational order is at the heart of things. The postulate of religion is that universal goodness is at the heart of things.

But idealism goes further. Idealism undertakes to demonstrate that the whole world of nature is comprehended in the mind of an All-knower. Two gateways lead us to this knowledge. One is sense experience. We have already followed this argument. Sense experience is mental. Therefore it can give us no knowledge of an external world unless that external world is also mental. The second gate is error. We certainly have the experience of error. But error is impossible unless there be truth. But every truth that is less than absolute, universal and perfect truth is to some degree error. Therefore the reality of error demonstrates the reality of absolute, universal and perfect truth. But such truth necessarily involves an absolute, universal and perfect Mind.

The experience of evil leads on to the reality of perfect goodness, even as the experience of error leads on to the reality of the perfect truth. If I experience what is truly evil, it can be so only by virtue of the reality of something better. In like manner any better is evil in relation to something better still, until we get to the supreme perfection of Goodness. Hence we have the absolute of perfect goodness and perfect truth found through the experience of evil.

Royce's little book *Loyalty* is of perennial importance, despite the criticism and even ridicule that has been directed upon it. The greatest moral requirement of human life is to be loyal. One must be loyal first to what is nearest and dearest. But this should lead on to more inclusive objects of loyalty. Thus there will be concentric circles of loyalty leading out to the fringes of all reality. Above all one must learn to be loyal to the spirit of loyalty in other people, even when one cannot agree with them, for this is the mark of nobility in every man. Thus the supreme object of loyalty will be the spirit of loyalty. We believe the implications of this are not different from what Whitehead says religion is. Religion, says Whitehead, is world loyalty. This highest loyalty was certainly religious in its implications for Royce.

Another great religious teaching of Royce was the " Beloved Community." Where two or three are gathered together with the right attitude, there is something more present and potent than the several individuals taken by themselves. There is something that makes these individuals think and act differently and brings to them an enrichment and fulfillment far greater than would be the sum of their several isolated endeavors. M. P. Follett has carried this idea to high fulfillment and application in her *Creative Experience*. Follett does not explicitly set forth any religious significance for this fact. She contents herself with demonstrating the psychological and social facts involved. But for Royce it was a vision and insight into the present reality and potency of God. He endeavored to show how all the distinctively human activities, when rightly conducted, such as economic activity, borrowing and lending of money in banking, insurance, communication, forever work to order and multiply the interests of men in such a way that the good of each is the good of all.

We must again let Royce speak for himself to show the high religion that dominated his work. In the following he states in the form of a parable two convictions, the reality of God and the inadequacy of all his thinking about God. The roses of the child are his own teachings about God and the child's going to sleep is his own death.

And so at worst we are like a child who has come to the palace of the King on the day of his wedding, bearing roses as a gift to grace the feast. For the child, waiting innocently to see whether the King will appear and praise the welcome flowers, grows at last weary with watching all day and with listening to harsh words outside the palace gate, amid the jostling crowd. And so in the evening it falls asleep beneath the great dark walls, unseen and forgotten; and the withering roses by and by fall from its lap, and are scattered by the wind into the dusty highway, there to be trodden underfoot and destroyed. Yet all that happens only because here are infinitely fairer treasures within the palace than the ignorant child could bring. The King knows of this, yes, and of ten thousand other proffered gifts of loyal subjects. But he needs them not. Rather are all things from eternity his own.

Perhaps Royce's prophecy about himself is coming true. The forms of absolute idealism which he taught, the roses he brought to the King, are being scattered by the wind and trodden under foot. But can we ever forget the spirit of the man! Jacob worn with the struggle to know what God is, and finding something about God in the depths of sorrow and loss — that is Royce.

WILLIAM E. HOCKING

The tradition of absolute idealism, modified in the light of contemporaneous thinking, is carried on by W. E. Hocking.

He has made some statements which indicate that he does not hold to an inclusive Absolute. He has implied that the worship and devoted living of religion requires a distinctness and independence of the individual over against God, which the doctrine of the Absolute does not provide. Thus he moves in the direction of the personalists we are to discuss a little later. Nevertheless it is generally held that he supports the tradition of absolute idealism more faithfully than any other thinker of commanding importance in America. One difficulty in treating him is that he has not yet made a systematic and comprehensive statement of his philosophical position. His *Meaning of God in Human Experience* comes nearer to this than any other book by him. But this was written twenty-five years ago and it was written to deal with a special problem in religion rather than to present a rounded system of philosophy.

The special problem which Hocking treats in his *Meaning of God* is that of the relation between feeling and reason in religion. The idealists had magnified the importance of reason. Reality is Idea and we discover idea and Idea by thinking. Nevertheless it is an obvious fact that feeling plays a very large part in religion, perhaps a larger part than reason. Is this a mistake? Does it indicate the weakness and foolishness of man? Is it a distortion of what true religion ought to be? Or is the fault on the other side? Is it idealism that has been in error in holding that reality is Idea and must be found through thought and only through thought?

The answer which Hocking gives is unique. He claims that neither religion nor idealism has been at fault. The seeming contradiction is resolved when we see that feeling is always idea in process of being born. We first discern concrete reality in a vague, dim way through feeling. Meager abstract features of reality can be discerned clearly in distinct ideas. But the more individual, the more concrete, the more rich and precious the reality, the more difficult it is to grasp it in the form of a clear, rational idea. It is Idea. All reality is Idea. But our minds are small and weak; we must gradually develop clear discernment. We do this by first feeling the reality. We develop more and more comprehensive and clarified ideas of it. But always there is more to know, and this more we apprehend by way of feeling. Thus round the borders of the most clarified and comprehensive idea there is always a fringe of feeling which may be intense or mild, but is always more or less vague.

Now the most inclusive, most concrete, most worthful and rich reality is the object of religious interest. Religion is man's interest in this most worthful reality. This reality is the Absolute, in so far as Hocking is an absolute idealist, and often he speaks in this vein. At any rate this religious reality is more inclusive, rich, individual and concrete than any other reality and is named God. But such a reality is precisely the most difficult to grasp in the form of the clear and distinct ideas of reason. Yet it cannot be fully grasped in any other way. If our powers were great enough we would know God as Idea. But being what we are, we can know only abstract features of this reality in the form of clear thought. For the most part we must apprehend God by way of feeling. But it is not mere feeling. It is feeling which is the nascent form of developing idea.

There can be a kind of intellectual clarity that impoverishes our hold on this precious reality. On the other hand, there can be a kind of emotionalism which does likewise. Neither side is sufficient in itself. The use of great feeling is to keep us close to that which develops into clear idea; and the use of clear ideas is to illuminate what we experience by the feeling which fringes all our ideas and sometimes submerges them. The good of feeling in religion is to nourish thought; and the good of thought is to clarify the meaning implicit in feeling.

Thus we see where science and philosophy have their place in the service of religious devotion. Also it makes plain the equal importance of worship wherein there may be in some instances very little clear idea of any sort. Feeling, especially worshipful feeling, is the growing edge of thought; thought, especially religious thought, is the fulfillment of feeling.

However, Hocking makes very plain that all the arts and sciences, all the activities of human living, every impulse and movement, when rightly directed are concerned with the fuller experience and realization of this reality which is worshiped in religion. Thus, roughly speaking, we might say that religion is to all the arts and sciences what feeling is to thought. In religion we discern and deal with that reality which is so rich, so inclusive, so concrete and full, that only meager slices or features of it can be sufficiently clarified to come within the jurisdiction of the special arts and sciences. These latter deal with abstract features of that which, in its concrete fullness, we revere in religion.

Thus religion is man's awareness of the all-inclusive, eternal and perfect reality of the Absolute, or whatever the most inclusive reality may be. Of course men have not necessarily thought of it in any such terms. Hocking traces the antitheses through which men's idea of God has passed in the process of its development. First men think of God as personal, then as impersonal. Then they come back to the concept of personality again, and so on. First they think of God as one, then as many, then as one, then as many. First they think of him as near, then as far, through progressive alternations. First they think of him as moral, then as amoral or super-moral, then again as moral. So it is with other categories.

These antitheses are necessary because of the inadequacy of our clarified ideas which reach after this total reality which is too full of riches for us to grasp. But our idea becomes more adequate through this process of thesis and antithesis. The impersonal idea of God corrects the narrowness and limitation of the personal. The higher personal idea supplements what was left out of the concept of impersonality, and so on with all the other shuttle movements by which we attain to fuller rational apprehension of the reality of God.

But man experiences the reality of God long before he has any respectable idea of what that reality is. The history of religions makes this all too plain. His first ideas of God are exceedingly crude. But always the fuller idea is seeking emergence through the dim depths of religious feeling.

Man is not content with the world that meets his biological needs only. Why is he not content? Because he feels the stir, the intimation and the lure of this vaster, richer reality. Man is not at home in the world of nature. He is a rebel and an alien. Why? For the same reason. Man is haunted with a sense of mystery. He has the feeling of being weak, incompetent, frail. This can come only through a vague sense of a possible greater power. He feels he is ignorant, that he is evil and unholy. All these feelings indicate the same thing. They show that he is experiencing the total reality of the Absolute with its unlimited knowledge, power, holiness, complete fulfillment of all values. But in the early stages of his history man does not know whence come these feelings.

Religion is distinguished from all the arts and sciences such as industry, politics, education, fine arts, friendship, home life and all the rest. It is unique among all these because in religion we are aware of the Absolute in which is the complete fulfillment of the infinity of all values, while all these other interests of life are simply ways in which we laboriously achieve one by one the several values which go to make up the totality of the Absolute. In religion we attain all at once, in one leap, the totality of all values that ever can be achieved or ever might be, because all these are in the Absolute. But when we attain them this way we cannot discriminate them in their distinct and several qualities. We get them all merged together into one indiscriminated lump. It is the part of the arts and sciences throughout history to bring out into explicit and analyzed distinctness all the infinite riches which are merged in the total synthesis of the Absolute. The arts and sciences are the prisms which analyze the white light of the Absolute into its many colors.

According to Hocking's philosophy of religion the function of religion in human life and history is to hold fast to the Absolute so that the arts and sciences can bring forth from its infinite riches the diverse treasures which are there. To use a very crude figure, religion is the hand that holds the total apple while the arts and sciences are the teeth that nibble at it and so enable human life to assimilate its values into the practical living of every day.

Mystical experience is the moment of vivid awareness of the merged totality of value in the Absolute prior to the analytical explication of its values into their distinct qualities by the practical processes of everyday living which are called the arts and sciences of life.

Wholesome and effective living requires an alternation between these two concerns of life. On the one hand, we must worship in order to keep firm hold on the apple. On the other hand, we must engage in the practical affairs of life in order to absorb any of the apple into our living. If we do not worship we shall find ourselves in time engaged in many activities that mean nothing of importance. In other words, we shall be chewing the air or sawdust or anything else except the apple. But if we worship all the time and do not alternate between it and practical life, we shall find ourselves holding to the apple but getting no nourishment from it. Hocking sets forth clearly and cogently the evils that beset our lives when we do not at intervals renew our acquaintance with the Absolute through worship or through some other practice that will do the work of worship.

Religion is "anticipated attainment" meaning that in religion we find the merged totality of all those values which are gradually rendered explicit in the sequence of time and in daily living.

From these rich sources in Royce and Hocking there have

spread far-winding streams of religious influence throughout American life. Watts Cunningham, William Urban, J. A. Leighton, G. P. Adams, and others have made further formulations of this way of thinking.

[1] This third characterization does not apply equally to all contemporary idealists. For example, Personalists regard evil as an essential aspect of the universe. E. S. Brightman goes still further, holding evil to be "ultimately and eternally real and hence impairing the perfect reality."

[2] *Joseph and His Brethren*. Pp. 426–27.

[3] *Religious Aspects of Philosophy*: Josiah Royce. Pp. 12–14.

[4] See especially *Mind and the World Order*: C. I. Lewis. Scribner, 1929.

CHAPTER VII

MODERN MYSTICS

T HE modern mystics and the absolutists are closely akin to one another in temper and spirit. Apart from the mystic's singular emphasis upon intuition as a theory of knowledge (and even here they are not altogether at odds) the two are at one in their metaphysics: each is monistic in world view, each posits an Absolute Being, and each rests in the assurance of the ultimacy of the good. Of all the possible forms of philosophy, absolute idealism is most agreeable to the emotional pattern of mysticism. In fact, thoroughgoing absolutists like Royce and Hocking have also been mystics.

Mysticism, however, is a tradition within itself. While it has drawn from the currents of both supernaturalism and idealism at various times, its stream has been a distinctive flow through the centuries, quiet and deep. Both as a mood and as a mode of thought, the mystical strain is very old, running back to the ancient Orient, where its stream broadens into a mighty ocean. The East is the natural homeland of the mystic.

Western mysticism, while obviously dependent upon the stimulus of the East, has had a distinctive tradition of its own. The fountain source of early western mysticism was the Neo-Platonism developed by Plotinus in the third century, which was largely of a speculative character. Medieval mysticism took its rise in the saintly monk, Bernard of Clairvaux, who, in protest against the hard mind of Abelard, sought to mold Christian thought nearer to the sentiments of the heart and to the practical cultivation of the divine life. This form of mystical practice was systematically developed by Hugo of St. Victor and later became a cogent influence among pietistic groups outside of the monastery. The next great name in western mysticism is Meister Eckhart, although from the twelfth to the thirteenth century, mysticism had spread as a popular movement in reaction against ecclesiasticism and its worldliness. In this reaction, many German mystics had appeared. In Eckhart, Christian mysticism moves again toward the theoretical or speculative emphasis and tends to become independent of the church and its tradition.

The strenuous conditions of the period following Eckhart's time turned the mystical tide to more practical ends, resulting in the formation of the Society of the Friends of God, but its individualistic character inherited from Eckhart persisted. The leading mystics of this period were Henry Suso and John Tauler, both disciples of Eckhart. Contemporary with them were the eminent Netherland mystics, Ruysbroeck and Groot, founder of the Brethren of the Common Lot.

Following the Reformation, mysticism continued with marked vigor both in Catholic and Protestant circles. Within Catholicism, however, under the pressure of the counter-reformation, the speculative aspect of mysticism vanished, and thus Catholic mysticism of this period became mainly the practice of spiritual exercises. The great Catholic mystics of the counter-reformation were St. Teresa, St. John of the Cross, François de Sales and Mme Guyon. Protestantism developed a vigorous mystical strain in the Cambridge Platonists and in Boehme, Fox and Law. The former revived the mysticism of Neo-Platonism, while the latter, influenced by the current Protestant preoccupation with the New Testament, particularly the writings of the Apostles John and Paul, developed a more strictly Christian mysticism. It is out of this tradition that Quaker mysticism arose, of which Rufus Jones is the eminent American exponent.

Mysticism is an ambiguous term. Of all words in the language of religion, it is the most weighted with meaning; yet so ethereal and tenuous as to be almost meaningless. This ambiguity grows out of the paradoxical testimony of the mystic, whose experience fills him with a sense of an all-knowing, yet leaves him impotent to report his findings. The curious dilemma led the early mystics to lay claim to a special path to divine knowledge, a sort of inner sense that transcended the prosaic thought processes of the human mind and brought back to the waiting mystic, revelations so full of divine content that they overflowed the meager categories of human speech. As a theory of knowledge, this view was in thorough accord with the doctrine of revelation held by organized Christianity, except for the mystic's insistence upon the priority of individual experience. It is at this point that mystics throughout Christian history have incurred opposition at the hands of the church leaders. From Pentecost to the present, institutional leaders, intent upon unity and conformity in theological doctrine, have looked with suspicion upon mysticism. And quite naturally so, for nothing is so perilous to dogma as this subjective search for God and truth.

Were it not for the inevitable intellectual claims of the mystic, mysticism would hardly concern the philosopher of religion. For to the mystic himself, mysticism is essentially a qualitative response to life, a feeling state issuing from a great tidal wave of emotion, in which one communes deeply with the Source of Being, and from which one emerges unified and charged with new energy and incentive. But every mystic has proceeded from a world-view. The early mystics from Plotinus to Thomas à Kempis reflected the philosophy of Neo-Platonism, as did the Post-Reformation mystics of the Catholic church, St. Teresa, St. John of the Cross, and their contemporaries. Protestant mystics, such as Boehme, Fox and Law, like Protestant theologians, drew upon the philosophical insight of the Gospel of John and the theology of St. Paul; and the language of modern mystics will reveal them heavily indebted to the philosophers of their times. Mysticism thus becomes an emotionalized expression of some philosophical point of view.

Were this all, however, mysticism would not claim the attention of the philosopher of religion apart from its philosophical background. But, as Bertrand Russell has pointed out in his *Mysticism and Logic:*

> Mystical philosophy, in all ages and in all parts of the world, is characterized by certain beliefs. . . . There is, first, the belief in insight as against discursive analytic knowledge: the belief in a way of wisdom, sudden, penetrating, coercive, which is contrasted with the slow and fallible study of outward appearance by a science relying wholly upon the senses. The second characteristic of mysticism is its belief in unity, and its refusal to admit opposition or division anywhere. . . . A third mark of almost all mystical metaphysics is the denial of the reality of Time. . . . The last of the doctrines of mysticism . . . is its belief that all evil is mere appearance, an illusion produced by the divisions and oppositions of the analytic intellect. (Pp. 8–10.)

These major premises tend to establish mysticism as a distinct philosophical *slant,* and likewise determine, to some extent, the mystic's selective use of philosophies upon which to ground his mystical outlook.

The belief in insight as against analytic knowledge has perhaps characterized mysticism in the minds of people more than any other single trait. Among all the early and medieval mystics this supposition led to the insistence upon a special theory of knowledge in mysticism. The mystic, through discipline and contemplation, came to have a peculiar mystical sense or inner vision which enabled him to apprehend truths of the divine not available through any other means. Where mysticism was influenced by theology based on revelation, this inner light was considered the direct revealing of God to the soul of man. The mystic simply made his human instrument sensitive to the operations of the divine and thus received the inner revelation. Among the mystics of more recent times, whose thinking has been shaped by the thought of idealism and philosophical theism, this "inner light" has been viewed as a special functioning of the mental process in relation to Absolute Mind. Finite mind becomes open and receptive to the incursions of the Infinite and thus comes to possess the thought of the Absolute.

To the degree that the world-view of the mystic approaches the contemporary philosophical outlook — that is, the outlook shaped by modern science — this doctrine of *insight* as over against analytic knowledge takes on more acceptable meaning. The difference between the two forms of knowledge is then seen to be related to the distinction between sheer perception (immediate experience) and cognition; between unanalyzed awareness and awareness in which meaning has become clarified and sharpened.

Mysticism has had a growing influence in the Western world during recent years. Many factors have contributed to this growth, not least of which has been the expanding horizon of religion and philosophical thought, turning the western philosopher's gaze eastward to the natural home of mysticism. The eighteenth and even the nineteenth centuries were too greatly dominated by the dogmatic bias against other religious cultures to give sympathetic attention to the thought of the Orient. Schopenhauer's studies in Buddhism and Emerson's excursions into Hinduism represent rare philosophical venturing for thinkers of their times. But since the opening of our century, with the shortening of mental distance between East and West, the social and religious sciences have brought the thinkers of East and West together with unprecedented freedom and frequency. The effect has been to give prestige and vogue to the thought currents of the Orient among western thinkers. An examination of some of the recent studies in mystical thought among European and American scholars will confirm this statement.[1]

Another influence has been the change within the thought structure itself, due to the growing awareness of man as a phenomenon. Psychology began as an introspective study and thus contributed immeasurably to the interest in mysticism. The studies by William James, Starbuck, Leuba and others, to mention only American psychologists, did more, perhaps, than any other factor to popularize the mystical mood, despite the critical implications of these studies. Whether or not the mystical experience is respectable to cultivate, it is certainly a thoroughly acceptable phenomenon for scientific study.

Recent philosophical thinking received a marked mystical stimulus through the intuitional philosophy of Henri Bergson in the publication of his *Creative Evolution* in 1911. Despite the critical reactions to his theory of mind and intellect in modern philosophy, his emphasis upon the bio-mystical interpretation of life in the universe continues to be a potent influence in contemporary thought. And his recent book, *Les deux sources de la morale et de la religion* (*Two Sources of Morality and Religion*), bids fair to carry his influence further.

But mysticism in its modern forms is also the natural culmination of the subjective emphasis of the liberal theologies that have flourished since Schleiermacher. Schleiermacher grounded theology on the appeal to religious experience. Since his time, and until recent years, this method has had primary emphasis in western religious thought. In no small degree, the modern mystics of the Western world are, in one way or another, spiritually indebted to Schleiermacher and his *experience* theology.

Perhaps the greatest Christian mystics of our time are the late Friedrich von Hügel, of England; Rudolf Otto, of Germany; and our own Rufus Jones. In their company should be mentioned also Evelyn Underhill and W. R. Inge. In each of these one sees reflected a marked philosophical background. Von Hügel and Rudolf Otto are exponents of a modified form of supernaturalism, somewhat akin to the vigorous neo-supernaturalism which has been stirring European theology with new life; although in no way are they to be identified with the Barthian movement and related French tendencies.

RUFUS M. JONES

Rufus Jones may undoubtedly be considered the most eminent American mystic of recent times, if, in fact, he is not the American mystic *par excellence*. He has been in continuous association with the eminent European mystics of our day, and his publications through the years have been veritable gems of mystical insight, widely read and as widely appreciated.[2]

To try to set forth or analyze his philosophy of religion, however, seems an unrewarding task; for, like every mystic, the force of his thought is in its lyrical rather than its logical quality. This is not to deprecate in any way the soundness of his thinking, for the clarity and vigor of Jones's reasoning is what gives his writings their wide appeal. But wherever logical thought takes on elegance of expression, its strength and appeal cannot be disclosed through analysis only.

While at times his language employs the imagery of supernaturalism, Rufus Jones cannot be called a supernaturalist. His thinking is grounded in the metaphysics of Absolute Idealism, or more particularly, in the distinctively *religious philosophy* of idealism known as *spiritual monism*. This view pictures man surrounded by an environing spiritual reality, infinite in expanse. In this monism, the boundaries between the natural and the supernatural dissolve: man is one with the Infinite in kind and character. The particular is apiece with the universal. God is the all-inclusive Reality, and every particular happening finds its ultimate happening in God. In the words of George A. Gordon, "The shoreless universe surrounds man and as he advances in civilization his own humanity becomes to him of infinite concern."

In supernaturalism we have a picture of two orders of being sharply divided. Its world-view might be diagramed in this manner: The arrows represent the incursions of revelation: ab, the Bible; cd, Jesus Christ; ef, subsequent miracles. Spiritual monism has changed this picture completely. Instead it presents the view of God at the center of all life, radiating his in-

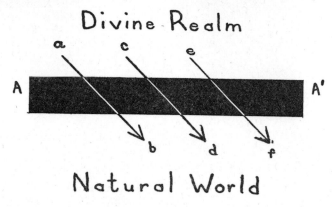

finite influence throughout the one realm of being. Its worldview might be diagramed as follows: Spiritual monism provides a dynamic conception of religion. Where supernaturalism

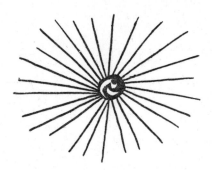

made man alien to Reality, spiritual monism represents man wholly native and within the infinite environment. Supernaturalism made clear that man needs to get acquainted with the divine through special means provided for that purpose; spiritual monism, on the other hand, implies that this reality is already so intimately a part of our being that we need only to become more fully aware of its Infinite Life coursing through our own.

> Speak to Him thou for He hears,
>   And Spirit with Spirit can meet —
> Closer is He than breathing,
>   And nearer than hands and feet.

The implications of this view are that we need simply to *live out* reality as we experience it — to *live creatively*. The key, then, to the understanding of reality is our own experience since we are part of it. If I can formulate the principles of that creative living so that it is adequately interpretative, I have at the same time formulated principles for reality as far as it goes in my own experience. To describe God, then, I describe him by an analogy with my own experience of creative living.

This point of view reaches beyond the philosophy of Rufus Jones and becomes expressive of all monistic forms of idealism which developed out of the philosophy of Fichte and other romantic idealists.[3]

Jones's thought, while grounded in spiritual monism, reflects other influences, congenial to the monistic view. Perhaps the clearest indication of a key to his philosophy of religion is found in his book, *Social Law in the Spiritual World*. Jones has drawn heavily upon the *new psychology* to illumine his conception of the " larger life " that environs it. The following passage illustrates his thought:

The iceberg with its peak of blue ice shining in the sun carries an enormously great bulk of ice submerged below the surface. Around the gulf stream of warm tropic water there is a whole ocean of cold water which has no current of its own. Beneath the lava which spouts into view through the volcano there is a molten core of earth which presses up from unexplored depths. Somewhat so the self we know is related to a larger life which belongs to it, is in some sense its own and yet lies below the margin of the primary consciousness.

Jones then undertakes to depict the facts of the inner life through a pictorial image which he constructs as follows:

In the figure (a) shows the " peak " of consciousness.   Around it (b) are the " dying peak " and the " dawning peak," i.e., the one that has just now prevailed, and the one which will succeed next.   The thought of any moment is influenced by what is just dying out and by what is

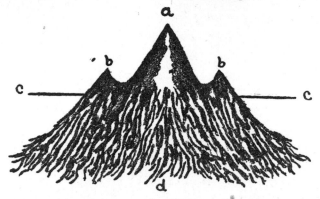

just coming in.   This makes the " fringe " around the peak.   Then (c) represents the " threshold " or horizon of consciousness.   Submerged below this line there lies (d) the vast realm of the subconscious, which, for all we know, *borders upon the infinite Life, rises out of it,* and may receive " incursions " from it.

This figure throws significant light upon the thought and language of Rufus Jones.   The closing comments of the description are particularly important: " The vast realm of the subconscious, which, for all we know, borders upon the infinite Life, rises out of it, and may receive incursions from it."   This postulate restores to Jones's metaphysics the essence of supernaturalism.   Instead of the traditional superstructure, Jones has the unfathomable ocean depths of Reality from which revelations break through into the sensory world.

A characteristic expression of Jones's philosophical method and approach in constructing the concepts of religion is given in his essay, " How Shall We Think of God? " [4]   Here his romantic idealism is apparent.

There is no future for religion, no permanence to its inspiration and lifting power, unless men and women — and the children who share their outlook and ideals — can continue genuinely and sincerely to believe in God as the ground and reality of that which is good, the spring and basis of a real moral and spiritual universe, the life and inspiration of all our aims at righteousness and truth, the Great Companion who shares with us in the travail and tragedy of the world and who is working through us to " bring things up to better."

I am convinced that the spiritual basis beneath our feet is solid. I have no fear that religion will turn out to be a slowly waning and gradually vanishing subjective dream. I am confident that *the testimony of the soul* is at least as reliable a guide to the eternal nature of things as is the witness which mathematics bears. Assertions of confidence, however, are not the same thing as facts, and optimistic statements of individual faith are not demonstrations which carry inevitable conviction to others. We must endeavor to *search out the rational foundations of our faith in God,* and we must then try to express as clearly and concretely as possible how a modern man thinks of Him. The rational foundations must of course be found revealed, if at all, in the nature of our own experience. *Reason, mind, thought, as it appears in our consciousness, is the only clue there is to that deeper fundamental Reason that holds as from one Center all the threads of reality and purpose in the mighty frame and congeries of things.* The way of approach is like that to a great mountain peak such as Mount Everest. At first there are many paths which gradually converge, and up to a certain point there are many ways of traveling, but at the very last for the final climb there is only one way up.

In the first place, knowledge of truth, truth which we discover and verify in our human experience, always presupposes something more than finite. Knowledge is something more than the formation of subjective ideas. It implies a *foundational reality* underlying and uniting the knower and objects known in a wider inclusive whole. Sense experience furnishes no adequate basis for *knowledge.* The so-called " items " presented by sense — color, sounds, tastes, odors, roughness and smoothness, weight and hardness — are no more knowledge than chaotic masses of stone, brick and lumber are a house. Knowledge involves organization, synthesis, unity, consciousness of meaning, interpretation, feeling of significance, a conviction of certainty, a sense of reality, aspects of universality and necessity. None of these features *comes in* through the senses. They belong to the nature of mind and are fundamental to mind. " To know," as a distinguished thinker of our time has said, " means more than to look out through a window at some reality of a different character." Knowledge is not something which originates within. Nor is it something received from without. It is an indivisible experience with an inner and an outer — a subjective and objective — factor, neither of which can be sundered from the other nor ever reduced to the other. Our finite minds through the process of knowledge, reveal the fact that they belong to a larger whole, a foundational reality, which underlies self and object, inner and outer, and which is the source and ground of the fundamental laws of reason through which we organize our experience, by which we get a world in common, and by which we transcend the limits of now and here, the fragmentary character of what is given to sense, and rise to something universal, necessary, and infinite in its implications, for knowledge with its element of " must be " always reveals the fact that the knower partakes in some degree of the infinite, at least he transcends the finite. We are always out beyond ourselves when we are dealing with truth.[5]

Reason, then, is one of the fundamental trails leading to awareness and certainty of God. It is the only path to that kind of experience which we call *knowledge*. But for Jones, faith in God rests upon other discoveries as well.

There is the moral experience — " The full significance of ' I ought, I must,' carries us beyond the empirical order of things and events and involves a spiritual reality of which we partake and in which we share."

Again, there is beauty — " another revelation of spiritual reality in the universe which links us up with something beyond ourselves."

The " unselfish love of friend for friend " and " loyalty to causes which concern unborn generations " are further facts of human experience revealing spiritual reality in the universe.

These, then, says Jones — beauty, truth, and goodness — are the criteria of human experience which " furnish the ground and basis of a solid rational conviction of faith in God's existence."

But these do not provide the surest ground for Jones:

The only surer ground is direct experience of God, which many persons claim to have. Arguments lead to the base of the mountain, experience alone scales it. He who has climbed the peak gets an evidence — and a thrill — of summit-vision which the dwellers in the valley-hotels can never have. My figure of the peak is not meant to refer to the solitary aspect of the man who climbs, nor to the laborious feature of the enterprise, though the experience of God is sometimes solitary and does always involve severe preparation and effort. I am only bringing out the fact that one cannot *know* the scenery and circumstances of the top unless he has been there himself. The mystic has been there, and he comes to tell us that beyond all conjectures and inferences about the reality of God is the consciousness of enjoying His presence.[6]

It becomes clear from these several quotations that we have in Rufus Jones's philosophy of religion an eclecticism that defies classification. On the basis of method, he might well have been classed with the ethical romanticists, for he reveals all of the traits of their philosophies. There is this important difference, however: he extends the meaning of the intuitive experience to a *mystical knowing*. In this respect he is even more intuitive than the intuitionists. He rests finally upon the mystical experience as the surest revealment of God. In this sense he is a genuine mystic, not simply a romanticist.

Furthermore, Jones reveals a more systematically formed metaphysical ground than is to be found among the ethical intuitionists — a metaphysics rising, as we have seen, out of the philosophy of absolute idealism. And since this rational structure is so indispensable to a complete understanding and full appreciation of his mysticism, we are impelled to place him with the idealists, despite his affinities with ethical intuitionism.

Looked at historically, it will be seen that spiritual monism was a romantic adaptation of the philosophy of absolute idealism. Its thought is rooted, therefore, in both traditions — in the soil of romanticism, but in the subsoil of idealism. Yet, considered from the standpoint of its systematic structure of thought, it is most properly designated as an expression of idealism. Perhaps *romantic absolute idealism* is its proper name.

As an expression of mysticism, Rufus Jones's thought is fundamentally in accord with Christian mysticism. But it is clearly an adaptation of Christian mysticism to the world-view of modern philosophy and psychology. What the absolutists accomplished for traditional theology, Rufus Jones accomplished for Christian mysticism. He, more than any of the modern mystics, has undertaken to bend the mystical tradition to meet the demands of modern thought.

A further distinctive characteristic of Jones's mystical philosophy is his ethical emphasis. All of the great mystics have been concerned ultimately with the ethical life.[7] But Jones has made this emphasis more explicit in his thought. This is to be explained, doubtless, by the fact that his mysticism rises out of the philosophy of spiritual monism, which, as we have seen, gives considerable attention to the relation between the human and the divine personality. Jones's ethical interest, however, is of the individualistic sort. He is concerned chiefly with man embodying in human form the full capacity of the divine life. The following quotation from one of his more recent publications, *New Studies in Mystical Religion*, is significant in this connection:

This mystical capacity in us, this capacity for another kind of world than that in space and composed of matter, *underlies,* as I have said, both our highest moral and religious attainments. . . . The moment we realize clearly that God is not in the sky, but *is Spirit,* and therefore is the Over-Spirit of our own finite spirits, all our religious problems are at once affected by the discovery. We no longer are interested in the immense structure which human thought and imagination have builded to glorify the imperial sovereign of the sky, with His court of angelic and seraphic beings and with His gorgeous pictorial heaven above the dome of the sky. Our religion ceases to be other-worldly in the ancient sense, and is primarily concerned with the opening out of our own inner selves to the divine influences of the Spirit that environs our central being. God is to be found and known, not in terms of astronomy, but rather in terms of our noblest ethical and spiritual aspirations. He is best revealed by what is best in man. In his deepest nature man is spirit, and so is in very truth made in the image of God and on the way toward Him. Finite and fragmentary we certainly are, " broken lights " of the one light, as Tennyson puts it, but in any case God and man are not sundered in the sense that mind and matter have been held to be separated by an impassable "divide." The divine and the human are not two diverse and incompatible realities, one exclusive of the other. No one can be a *person* in the full meaning of the word and not partake of God, the complete Spirit, any more than a river can be a river without partaking of the ocean, or than an atom can be an atom without partaking of electrical energy. The traits that are essential to personality are exhibited in fullness only in that complete Spirit whom we name God and who alone can say, *I am;* but even in our finite and fragmentary state we are all the time reaching beyond our own narrow limits and drawing upon the larger Spiritual Life that overspans us, as the tiny arc of a circle points to and implies the whole curve. (Pp. 195–196.)

CHARLES A. BENNETT

In the writings of the late Charles A. Bennett we have the promise of what might have been another eminent American mystic. But death cast its untimely shadow. Bennett has left two books: *A Philosophical Study of Mysticism,* and a posthumous publication, *The Dilemma of Religious Knowledge.* Neither of these reveals a fully worked out metaphysics; but his inclination toward the mystical of a supernatural sort is unmistakable.

In one of his essays in this last publication, he states his conception of religion clearly. Briefly he surveys three types of experience: Secularism, Naturalism, and Magic, in which he finds no trace of the religious element, the reason being that all three lack what he calls the sense of mystery. Where this sense appears, there religion is present. Note how he defines this sense of mystery:

> The moment religion appears upon the scene, man's universe becomes divided into two: the holy and the secular, the sacred and the profane, the visible and the invisible, that which is eternal and real over against that which is vain and transient. *The sense of mystery, in its simplest definition, is the sense of the unseen order supervening upon, shining through and transfiguring the seen.* It is this that is here proposed as the central element in religion. (P. 7.)

Bennett goes on to point out that this mystery with which religion confronts man is knowable, not in a rational sense, but in the terms of "faith." And here he reveals the characteristic temper of the mystic. Religion cannot be rationally discerned, Bennett insists, for its mystery defies understanding.

> The thing that strikes one most about the mystery of religion [he writes] is that it is foreign to the native air of our minds, that it is opaque to human intelligence. It is certainly grasped, yet it is not understood; if it reveals itself, it also conceals itself from rational comprehension. There is little or nothing that we can say about it that will withstand logical scrutiny. In spite of all the efforts of theologian and philosopher, supernature refuses to be naturalized or rationalized. It is as though in religion we came upon some surd in experience, some nonrational factor; and more and more I find myself coming to sympathize with that paradoxical assertion of the mystic that if God is to be known he must be known in " a cloud of unknowing." (P. 10.)

The mystery of religion may become known, then, only through faith. What, then, is faith? To Bennett, it is something more than an expectant venture in optimism; it is an aggressive assertion of conviction, grounded in a knowing which only religion can give. It is assurance grasped, not attained.

This is not satisfactory; not even to Bennett. But it is as far as his thinking brought him.

No cursory account of the workings of a mystical mind can be satisfactory, for its strength lies, not in the clarity of its logic, but in the suggestive insights which loom up out of the mists that gather upon the fringes of its thoughts. The mystic *feels* more strongly than he *reasons*.

There is reason to believe that Bennett's mysticism might have moved beyond his supposition of the supernatural, had he been permitted to ponder the problem further. For he had already worked out a basis for solving his dilemma of religious knowledge along more natural lines in an article on " Poetic Imagination and Philosophy " in *The Yale Review* (Vol. 20).[8] Yet, Bennett recoiled from *naturalistic* explanations, for he was by temperament a supernaturalist.

With all of his leanings toward supernaturalism, however, Bennett's view, in so far as it was constructively developed, was grounded in the metaphysics of Absolute Idealism. His writings show marked affinities with the philosophy of Hocking, and in a sense might be regarded as the mystical extension of Hocking's idealism.

Mystical thought has also had a wide rendering in more popular forms. The books by Ralph Waldo Trine,[9] Richard Jefferies,[10] Glenn Clark,[11] and Mary Austin[12] as well as the writings of Margaret Prescott Montague[13] are some of the more notable contributions.

Rufus Jones, in writing on "Mystical Life and Thought in America,"[14] rightly refers to such eminent names as Walt Whitman, Ralph Waldo Emerson, J. G. Whittier, John Burroughs, Josiah Royce and William Ernest Hocking as exponents of mystical religion. In their company might be named also the poets Walter de la Mare, Sidney Lanier, poet-philosophers such as H. Thoreau, George Santayana, William James, as well as a host of other writers possessed of a mystical temperament. For, from a certain point of view there are but two types of writers, the imaginative and the prosaic. A classification of *mystics in religion,* however, must be more definitive than such a literary distinction affords. Furthermore, in classifying modern mystics, one needs to distinguish between those who embody the mystical tradition and those who venture upon a mystical route markedly divergent from the path of the "great mystics." Rufus Jones distinguishes between "cosmic mysticism" and "Christian mysticism." Something of this contrast distinguishes mystics like von Hügel, Rudolf Otto, Rufus Jones, Evelyn Underhill and W. R. Inge from mystical writers like Whitman, Emerson, Burroughs, Thoreau and others. These latter stand outside of the great tradition of Christian mysticism. They contribute to a stream of mystical thought which was clearly nature-centered and thus may be regarded as forerunners of a mystical naturalism.

¹ See, for example, studies by Rudolf Otto, Friedrich Heiler, Baron von Hügel and W. E. Hocking.

² His better known books of a popular nature are: *The Inner Life, Spiritual Energies in Daily Life, Fundamental Ends of Life, Finding the Trail of Life, A Boy's Religion from Memory,* and *The Trail of Life in College.* Some of his more scholarly studies include: *Autobiography of George Fox, Social Law in the Spiritual World, Quakerism a Religion of Life, Studies in Mystical Religion, Some Exponents of Mystical Religion, The Life and Message of George Fox, The Faith and Practice of the Quakers, The Church's Debt to Heretics, Spiritual Reformers of the Sixteenth Century, Religious Foundations,* and *New Studies in Mystical Religion.*

³ This type of religious philosophy is implicit in all forms of absolute idealism. Among British philosophers, it is represented by J. Caird, *Introduction to Philosophy of Religion* and *Fundamental Ideas of Christianity;* A. Seth Pringle-Pattison, *The Idea of God in the Light of Recent Philosophy;* G. Galloway, *Philosophy of Religion;* C. C. J. Webb, *God and Human Personality,* and *The Personality of God.* Among American philosophers, it is expressed to a marked degree in the writings of the absolute idealists discussed in Chapter VI, as well as in the following: Samuel Harris, *God the Lord and Creator of All;* John Watson, *Philosophical Basis of Religion;* Ten Broeke, *A Constructive Basis for Theology;* G. A. Gordon, *The New Epoch for Faith;* R. J. Campbell, *The New Theology;* J. M. Snowden, *The World a Spiritual System,* and *Personality of God;* W. L. Walker, *Christian Theism and Spiritual Monism;* E. H. Reeman, *Do We Need a New Idea of God?* J. M. Shaw, *The Christian Gospel and the Fatherhood of God;* W. C. Bell, *Sharing in Creation.*

⁴ *Religious Foundations* (edited by R. M. Jones), Macmillan, 1923. Chapter I.

⁵ *Ibid.,* pp. 5–7.   ⁶ *Ibid.,* p. 10.

⁷ See *The Mystical Life:* Bastide. Scribner, 1935; and *Two Sources of Morality and Religion:* Bergson. Holt, 1935.

⁸ See the writer's *Modern Man's Worship.* Pp. 208.

⁹ *In Tune with the Infinite.* Crowell, 1897.

¹⁰ *The Story of My Heart.* Dutton, 1924.

¹¹ *The Soul's Sincere Desire.* Atlantic Monthly Press, 1925.

¹² *Prayer* and *Far Horizons.*   ¹³ Articles in *The Atlantic Monthly.*

¹⁴ *Some Exponents of Mystical Religion.*

CHAPTER VIII

PERSONALISTS

A SURVEY of prevalent philosophies yields the conviction that of them all the philosophy of personalism is most true to the Christian tradition. While its origins are in the Greek, as well as in the Christian tradition, personalism is a remolding of the contributions of each in the modernistic spirit which has characterized European and American Christianity since the publication in 1859 of *The Origin of Species*. It is therefore obvious that personalism is no mere affirmation of this tradition. The Christian tradition as current in United States when American personalism arose was full of contradictions, ambiguities and diverse currents. The creators of personalism took the tradition, purged it of many of its more flagrant contradictions, clarified some of its ambiguities, gave it coherence, set it before the world as a defensible system of thought.

Some competent scholars have endeavored to show that personalism does not represent the philosophical implications of early Christianity. That may be true. But Christianity has never had a recognized and established philosophy of its own. It has been represented by many different philosophies. This independence of any established philosophy has made it very fluid. It has made it highly adaptable and plastic, but also subject to much confusion and many cross-currents. All this justifies the claim of the personalists that they represent *"par excellence* the Christian philosophy of our day."

Thus speaks one of their own representatives:

It may well be that bondage to philosophical tradition and other contemporary influences prevented the early and medieval Christian thinkers from giving to Christianity the true philosophical expression. Dean Inge and others are no doubt right in pointing out that the traditional doctrines of the Trinity, Incarnation and Atonement do not easily fit into the framework of our current personal idealism. But this may.point to the need of a reformulation of these doctrines rather than to any want of harmony between the personalistic philosophy and the essentials of the Christian faith. That the personality of God and the sacredness of human personality express the true genius of the Christian religion, whatever may be said of its theology, is hardly open to question; and that these beliefs have received their complete philosophical justification in modern personalistic metaphysics, would seem equally clear.[1]

That the personality of God and the sacredness of human personality express the true genius of the Christian religion as it is held in America today is true, whatever may have been true of it a thousand or nineteen hundred years ago.

Personalism had its beginnings in the last hundred years and is probably symptomatic of the era through which we have been passing.[2] Lotze in Germany, Renouvier in France, McTaggart in England all began to teach it in the nineteenth century. The American formulation of it differs from all of these, although it draws most heavily from Lotze. B. P. Bowne and G. P. Howison are the creators of the American version of it. Of these two, Bowne is by all odds the most thorough, the most systematic and the most influential. His thinking has probably reached the minds of more professing Christian people than any other philosophy of religion in the United States. Brightman, Knudson, McConnell, Flewelling, Buckham and Wilson are among its chief proponents today.

Personalism begins with self-experience. The experience of one's own selfhood is the ultimate basis on which the entire structure of its thought is reared. Here, and nowhere else, we have deepest insight into ultimate reality. In this experience of our own selves we find solution of all the basic problems of philosophy, such as permanence and change, unity and multiplicity, causality, time and space, the real and the phenomenal, value, knowledge and the nature of God. What we find in our own personalities affords a basis to interpret everything in terms of personality. Hence the characterizing name of this philosophy.

Since personality is the foundation of all else, and everything is interpreted in terms of it, it is difficult to state just what personality is. But this difficulty of stating the nature of the ultimate reality which is held to be the ground and interpretation of all else, is not peculiar to personalism. It is true of any philosophy and, after all, the basic hypotheses can be defined. While these thinkers differ somewhat in their statement of what personality is, a common formula is the following: Personality is an individual that is conscious of itself and determines itself. But the personalists admit that personality is the dwelling place of the greatest mysteries, although they maintain that it is less mysterious than any other proposed principle of explanation.

Personalism differs from absolute idealism in its theory of knowledge. The latter claims that reality is idea. Hence when we know reality, what we know is the idea itself. Personalism holds that the reality known is not idea. (It is either personality or physical or some universal.) What we know — whether physical things or universals or values or consciousness — is some aspect or aspects of a personality, human, subhuman or superhuman. These entities are always some combination of will, feeling, thought, purpose. In any case they are not merely idea or knowledge. Even when I know myself it is not mere idea that I know. A personality is never merely an idea, although it has ideas. A physical thing also is not idea, but neither does it have ideas; it is an objective energy which the personalists identify with God's will acting under whatever conditions that will may be subject to, such as " The Given." We can have true knowledge of things and persons by way of ideas. We use ideas to know reality which is not itself idea. What things and persons are apart from ideas we cannot say; but we can have true knowledge of them by way of our ideas.

Another characteristic of this theory of knowledge is its voluntarism or rationalized faith, which it relates to the methods of hypothesis and experiment. Faith and the moral will enter into all knowledge. For example, we can know through reason only when we have faith in our own rational nature. But personality has not only a rational nature. It also has an aesthetic, moral and religious nature. Hence faith in our own nature involves faith in all these as truly as in the rational. We know by faith that reality must have the characteristics which our rational nature demands. Faith leads us to try the hypothesis. But so likewise, Bowne at least holds, we are led to try the hypothesis that reality must have the characteristics which our moral and religious nature demands.

Here we have one of the few systematically formulated statements of the nature and function of faith as a way of knowing in addition to the rational and perceptive powers of the mind. The personalists appeal to the authority of Kant for this resort to the practical reason, the moral imperative and faith. Thus it can be said: We know by faith that reality is what the rational, aesthetic, moral and religious nature of personality requires. Bowne was fond of saying that life is much more than logic. This saying he learned from Lotze and William James.

According to some personalists, notably Bowne and Knudson, God is the one absolute personality. Human beings are only imperfect and incomplete personalities. Brightman, however, would deny that God is an absolute personality. According to the latter, God is finite. Most of the personalists would agree that God created all human personalities. Physical nature, on the other hand, is the actual will of God organizing his own experience and communicating it to us.

As we have noted, personalists disagree on whether God is infinite. They who say he is infinite declare, nevertheless, that he limits himself in order that other personalities may have freedom and independence and power to be co-creators with God. If God were not thus able to limit himself he would be something less than absolute and perfect personality. All matter and all material things are but the materials by which God expresses himself. Material things are not merely the ideas of God, as we have already noted. Matter has a genuine existence. But it is not metaphysically real. It has no existence apart from the total experience of God. Matter is a certain kind of willed organization of divine consciousness.

There is no power, no causality, no activity except in personality. We see in nature nothing but the uniformities of co-existence and sequence. We never see any power, any cause, any activity. To find that, we have to look into our own selves. Each experiences in himself the power of causing, of producing effects. But obviously the order of nature with all its manifold ways is not the work of my personality or that of any human. It is the work of God. Everything that happens in nature is due to personality, for the most part due to God, in small part to human beings. " God is indeed in all things, but in some things for their furtherance and in others for their destruction, in some things in love and in other things in wrath and judgment." [3]

Bowne tells the parable of how a wise man demonstrated to a king the reality and presence of God. " See this acorn," said the wise man to the king. " I shall plant it here in the ground, so. Now will you cast your glance into that pool at your side for a moment. Now, turn and look." The king looked and saw that the acorn had become a huge oak. " Indeed," said the king, " God is here." But then he looked down at himself and saw that his beard was long and white, his clothes in tatters. His glance in the pool had been eighty years. He was enraged at the deception played upon him until it was explained that eighty years was nothing to God. Thus everything in nature is directly the work of God. A physical miracle could not reveal God any more than the orderly sequence of nature.

But man is not wholly controlled by God. Just how man can be so dependent on God and yet have such a measure of independence, is cast in mystery. But we have the experience of just such dependence and independence. God knows all we think, but we do our own thinking. It is not God's thinking in us. Also we are free agents and have power to do what God would not do. There must be this relative independence of the human over against the divine, else we could not have that love and obedience toward God which our religious nature requires, nor could we be free to think or to conduct scientific experiments.

All this forces to the front the problem of evil. Since everything that happens is due to God, excepting that small part which is due to the free will of man, how can we account for all the evil in the world, God being perfect in goodness? We have already noted Bowne's statement that God is present in some things for their destruction, and in wrath and judgment. But how did all this evil get into existence, requiring God's destructive power, wrath and judgment? Is the evil will of man the source of all the evil in the world?

Perhaps all of the personalists have recognized this problem of evil in some way or other, but it remained for a modern representative to feel the full force of it and go down to the depths in his struggle to deal with it fully and honestly. Professor Edgar S. Brightman has proposed one of the most original solutions. He teaches that in God are two parts, the holy will and what he calls "the given." This given resists the holy will. Thus the holy will of God struggles and suffers in the heroic and tragic labor of striving to make the best possible world. But the vast evil in the world, other than that caused by man's free will and the self-imposed conditions of reason and goodness, is due to the recalcitrance and perversity of this something in God's own being. Hence we have the cross. The cross of Christ expresses this labor and suffering which God must undergo. But God is slowly mastering this given and thus bringing the world to higher levels of goodness.

This view of Brightman's is not generally accepted by the personalists, but there is nowhere a fuller facing of the problem of evil which lies at the door of personalism.

When one reads the works of Borden P. Bowne today one is amazed to see how fully they express the generally accepted liberal view among Christian people of our time. But in his own time he had to fight to defend and propagate these ideas. This demonstrates how pervasive and mighty has been his influence. However, one can never tell in the case of a great man whether the consequences are the result of his work or the result of powerful currents which shaped him more than being shaped by him. In any case it must be said that the contemporary upholders of personalism have presented this philosophy with clarity and cogency and power. They have kept it fully abreast of the advancing frontier of thought and probably dominate the thinking of the churches more than any other school.

There is probably no more masterly résumé of this philosophy of religion than the statement made by Professor E. S. Brightman. With his permission we shall quote at length from it.

Personalism may be taken to be that philosophical system which holds that the universe is a society of selves, unified by the will and immanent causality of a Supreme Self, and which, therefore, defines matter and the whole system of physical nature in terms of the active, conscious will of that Supreme Self, while it regards human selves (and whatever other selves there may be) as enjoying an existence of their own, dependent, it is true, upon the will of the Supreme Self, yet no part of it.

It is evident that such a philosophy is well adapted to become an interpreter of religion, for the Supreme Self of personalism may be identified with God, the object of religious worship. But personalism is not chiefly, much less exclusively, a philosophy of religion. It is an objective, truth-seeking philosophy, based on the logic of coherence, a synoptic method, an epistemological dualism which (in Kantian fashion) emphasizes the activity of the mind in knowledge, a self psychology, and an activistic metaphysics, closely allied with the monadism of Leibniz — and so is (quantitatively) a pluralism, as opposed to the singularism of a Spinoza,

a Hegel, and a Bradley, although it is qualitatively monistic in its idealism. Its position on these and other controverted points may turn out
to be mistaken; but in every case the position is based on a reasoned
investigation of the problems and not on a desire — conscious or unconscious — to defend religion.

Perhaps the best way to clarify our thought is to set down the main
theses of personalism, in order, so as to present a bird's-eye view of the
system.

1. What we immediately experience is the starting-point of all our
thought and action and the present fact at all times is our own self. All
of our perceptions, feelings, thoughts, desires, volitions — every so-called
state of consciousness — belongs to that complex whole which is the total
fact of experience for each one of us and is called the self. By the self
personalism means a whole of conscious experience, and so rejects any
soul-psychology which would find the true self in some transcendent
entity of substance which underlies and supports consciousness. This
whole is a genuine organic whole, a self-experience, and not a sum of
parts; and so personalism rejects associationalism. Since the self is a
conscious whole, personalism rejects Watsonian behaviorism. It has
closest affinity with purposive, dynamic, and *Gestalt* psychology, and is
usually called self psychology. Many personalists make a distinction between self and person. Any complex whole of consciousness is a self;
but a self capable of reason and value is called a person. The nature of
a person is not evident from the momentary self, but can be known only
through the development of its potentialities. This thesis may be sum-
marized by saying, " The self is the datum." If things themselves were
the datum, as most realists hold, then the same things must be both large
and small, both hot and cold, both at rest and in motion, for they appear
thus to different observers and to the same observer under different conditions. It is much simpler and more reasonable to hold that what we
experience is our own consciousness, which, it is true, interacts with and
seeks to describe and define its world.

2. Within our self we discover a principle of logical coherence. This
principle is, of course, no peculiar property of any philosophical sect;
but personalism makes a peculiar use of it. For, given the self and the
principle of coherence, the problem of thought may be restated in the
terms, " What do I mean? " It should be noted that the formation and
testing of hypotheses is (as Professor Nelson has not long ago pointed out
in these columns) essential to the progress of coherent thought.

3. There are objects other than my ideas of them. This is epistemological dualism, a view until recently rather unpopular in current think-

ing, but brilliantly defended by Professor Arthur O. Lovejoy in his Carus Lectures for 1927. Personalism denies that external things can be given in our immediate experience, but holds that our ideas become utterly incoherent if treated subjectively as referring only to themselves. Our ideas become rational only when they are explained in relation to objects beyond themselves to which they refer.

4. These objects beyond the knowing idea are: my own experiences (any conscious process — past, present or future — may be the object of an idea), other human selves, the world of physical things, universals (mathematical objects, etc.), and values. God is at least an object of thought and perhaps an existing object.

5. Science describes the laws of the appearances of certain selected groups of these objects. Philosophy accepts the results of science, relates the sciences to each other, and raises problems (especially the problems of knowledge and of value) which science does not raise.

6. If these objects are to be thought coherently as belonging in one interacting system, it is more rational to regard them all (even physical things) as of the nature of mind than to adopt any other hypothesis. It is impossible to regard mind as a form of matter — for it does not fill space or move in space. It is even more unintelligible to regard mind as a form of some *tertium quid* or a collection of neutral entities, for then the problems of interaction and of the specific properties of mind are pushed into the outer darkness. On the other hand, what we call material objects may without any confusion or inconsistency be regarded as the conscious experiences of a Supreme Self, deeds of its active will. In other words: matter does not explain mind, but mind does explain matter. Neither view is easy; neither one is without difficulty. But naturalism involves more obscurity and makes more demands on our faith in the miraculous (the turning of matter into mind outstrips the turning of water into wine!) than does idealism. In an idealistic world, universals and values are the universalizing and valuing experiences of selves; as such, they are more at home than they could be in a world in which mind is a secondary product of the non-mental.

7. The many minds, therefore, communicate through a genuinely objective order. That objective order is the active, rational, concretely experienced, will of the Supreme Self.

8. The nature of the Supreme Self is revealed and further defined through the coherent, synoptic interpretation of the facts of self-experience, especially what we call sense-experience and value-experience.

9. Value-experiences, especially moral and religious experience, point to objective features of reality and indicate that the Supreme Self is also

Supreme Value and worthy of worship as God. Notable contributions to this aspect of personalism have been made by W. E. Hocking and W. R. Sorley.

10. The fact of evil indicates that the Supreme Self is achieving value in the temporal order under difficulties. These difficulties are partly to be found in the self-imposed conditions of reason and goodness, and partly in the obstacles caused by human freedom. I have ventured the suggestion elsewhere that within the divine nature there may be a resistant or retarding factor, akin to sensation in man, which, without diminishing divine goodness or wisdom, constitutes a real problem to divine power and explains the " evil " features of the natural world.

11. The belief in God naturally leads to the belief in human immortality, and is, indeed, its only cogent ground. For if God be good, he could not destroy the only intrinsic values there are, namely, persons. . . .

It remains to inquire what personalism has to say about religion. Personalism builds its philosophy of religion on the facts of the history, psychology, and sociology of religion; but (unlike some current points of view) does not believe that philosophy of religion consists in a recital of those facts. Personalistic philosophy of religion is an interpretation of the facts in relation to a total world-view, a world-view which grows out of a critical analytic-synoptic understanding of all accessible facts in all realms of experience. A brief survey of the personalistic position may be gained by regarding it as metaphysical, ethical, co-operatively social, rational, and mystical, and as accepting a developing immortality. The remainder of our study will be devoted to a fuller explanation of this characterization of personalistic philosophy of religion and to a brief consideration of some objections.

First of all, the personalistic position is metaphysical, as opposed to positivism. Positivism holds that knowledge is confined to the immediate objects of human experience, and hence to the objects of the sciences. Science, all schools agree, does not deal with God as its object, or at least does not do so consciously. Hence positivism finds humanity itself to be the only object of religious experience. Humanity is the Supreme Being, the only God there is. So spoke Auguste Comte, and so speaks the voice of contemporary " humanism," when it is self-conscious. But personalism holds that if one is going to confine knowledge to immediate experience, one must be an individualistic solipsist, for " the self is the datum." The positivist talks about humanity; but, the personalist points out, " humanity " is a metaphysical object, which no one ever experienced immediately. The personalist argues that if we can go beyond our immediate experience to the existence and experience of other selves, the same logic which grants us that right also grants us the right to define any other objects which are necessary to the explanation of the facts of experience. The very existence of consciousness and of value experience, especially of moral and religious experience, points to some traits of the rest of the universe which make their existence possible. A real, personal, creative, and active God is, the personalist believes, the only being which possesses traits adequate to explain those experiences. Positivism and humanism are religiously hollow and intellectually unfinished. They simply do not think the problems through. Perhaps no one can think them through in the sense of reaching a point where one is through thinking, and who wants to? But that fact affords no shadow of excuse for getting through before one has fairly begun.

Secondly, personalism is an ethical philosophy of religion. It builds, as we have seen, on value experience; and of all our value experiences the ethical is perhaps the most fundamental. Whether this be true or not, morality is the condition of the realization of all other values in any total and harmonious way. If a man renounces moral obligation, he may have streaks of genius in art, in intellect, or even in religion; but he has abandoned the power which would unify and perpetuate his values. For the personalist, then, the moral will is at the center of personality and hence of religion. Any violation of or disrespect for the moral will is wrong, even if committed in the name of religion. The authoritarian principle is therefore rejected by personalism. No tradition or revelation can be accepted as true because some authority vouches for it. All true religion must commend itself directly to the moral will and reason of man. On the other hand, personalism is equally insistent on the fact that any general philosophy whatever, in order to be true to its task, must take account of the moral facts from the start; and yet we find a contemporary philosopher like Ralph Barton Perry, who banishes every " moral and spiritual ontology," presenting a " philosophy of disillusionment," yet at the same time arriving at " the hazard of faith " and repudiating the " narrow and abstract predictions of astronomy." In the end, he is willing to greet " the residual cosmos " as a " promise of salvation." This is an inspiring hope, but it is difficult to see how it follows from Perry's premises. Personalism finds a basis for the hope in the fact that experience reveals the cosmos to be moral and spiritual.

Thirdly, personalism is a social philosophy of religion of a definite type, which may be called the co-operative. Personalism believes in the genuine separateness of individual minds, such that no mind is a part of or can become a part of any other mind; it is therefore opposed to belief in a "social mind" as any real fact which either includes or transcends the individuals; much more is it opposed to any absolutism or pantheism which includes all individuals with the One Absolute Self. On the other hand, personalism believes in the genuine interaction of the many individuals, and in the presence within all individuals of common laws and common meanings; hence, despite its individualistic emphasis, personalism is opposed to absolute or anarchistic individualism. Its social theory, then, is that of the free co-operation of different and distinct individual persons in the attainment of common purposes. The aim of the universe, then, is not absorption in the Infinite, nor is it the mere assertion of personal liberty; it is, rather, free and moral co-operation. The essence of religion and religious salvation is co-operation with God.

Fourthly, personalism is rational. This does not mean that it regards the universe as an abstract syllogism or that it holds other experiences than thinking in disesteem. Yet in these days when rationalism is a term of reproach in many religious circles and "rationalization" is the byword of psychology, personalism is rational and proud of it. To be rational, as personalism conceives it, means to arrive at conclusions in the light of a coherent interpretation of all the facts. Reason is simply an inclusive and connected view of experience. To be irrational is either to exclude relevant facts or to be satisfied with a disconnected account of things when a connected account could be discovered by more persistent thought. The most inclusive and connected view is the most reasonable and truest which we can attain, although further experience and thought will expand the horizon of reason. Reason is a principle of growth, not of stagnation. Personalism, then, is opposed to every "irrational" philosophy of religion. It must be admitted, however, that the use of that term in much contemporary German philosophy and theology is very misleading; for it is often intended only to confer the idea that experience contains data which cannot be rationally inferred from other experiences, an idea which is true, but compatible with the right and duty of reason to "prove all things" and especially to "prove all spirits." It should be noted that a rational philosophy of religion leaves room for "revelation," just as it leaves room for conversation with other human selves; but it holds that the meaning of any conversation or revelation can only be determined by reason.

Fifthly, personalism is mystical. Its conception of reason as the coherent interpretation of experience makes it empirical in its emphasis. Experience reveals the fact that the relations and persons are mediated by experiences having a peculiarly immediate emotional quality. The consciousness of the presence of a beloved human being elicits our moral nature and our highest rational powers; but it also produces a uniquely satisfactory feeling-tone which suffuses consciousness with a glow which nothing else can equal. Such experiences when ascribed to divine influence are called mystical. They constitute the secret of the joy and rapture of religion; and when they occur in a life which is reasonable and moral, they are a source of great strength and inspiration. Lack of that relation to God which makes mystical experience possible is, in my opinion, one of the chief sources of weakness in contemporary American religion. The personalistic conception of mysticism, it need hardly be said, differs from that of the pantheistic mystics. For the personalist, the mystical experience is one of communion, not of union. Or, if one insists on calling it union, it is union of purpose by feelings which subserve that purpose rather than a union of actual being. Personalism, then, is a philosophy of prayer, laying especial stress on the prayer of communion with God, but also finding room for the prayer of intercession; for a reasonable God will have to respond differently to a situation in which prayer is present than he would to a situation from which it is absent.

Sixthly, from its general conception of religious values and from its belief in a good God, personalism infers that the human person is immortal. A good God could not destroy an intrinsic value, and persons are the only intrinsic values. Personalism does not attempt to speculate, in the lack of evidence, about the details of the future life, and it finds little coherence in the pretended evidence of spiritism. But I venture one suggestion. If the future life is to be good, it must be moral and rational; and if so, it must be developing, if there is any continuity between the life in this world and in the world to come. Too often, orthodoxy has adopted a perfectionistic or rigoristic ethics for this world, and a hedonistic ethics of eternal selfish enjoyment for the other world. If there be immortality, it cannot be one of mere pleasure; it must be work and service, if the values which cause us to believe in immortality are truly valuable.[4]

<hr>

[1] *The Philosophy of Personalism:* Albert C. Knudson. Abingdon Press, 1927. P. 80.

[2] The word *personalism* was first used in English by John Grote and first in German by Goethe and Schleiermacher; but Berkeley and Leibniz, teaching at an earlier date, are held to be pure personalists by the upholders of personalism in our time.

[3] *The Immanence of God:* B. P. Bowne. P. 129.

[4] *The Crozier Quarterly.* Oct. 1928.

PART FOUR

ROOTED IN TRADITION OF ROMANTICISM

CHAPTER IX

ETHICAL INTUITIONISTS: PHILOSOPHICAL GROUP

ALL philosophers who make experience the point of reference in interpreting reality may be said to be empiricists. Thus all except supernaturalists are empiricists. In philosophical circles, the term "empiricism" has been pre-empted by the followers of John Stuart Mill, particularly by those who have followed in the line of the pragmatism of William James and the instrumentalism of John Dewey. In theological circles, however, the term "empiricism" has carried a more particularized theological connotation, applying to ideas and beliefs arising out of religious experience of a distinct and impressive sort. Thus, while one might employ the term "religious empiricism" to designate this method, the term "intuitionism" would seem to be more definitive.

This form of religious thought, grounded in the appeal to experience, goes back to the experiential theology of Schleiermacher. It was given more precise and objective formulation in the theology of Ritschl and his followers, defined still more objectively in the religious thought of Troeltsch, and is being developed further in contemporary German thought by Wobbermin, whose book *The Nature of Religion*,[1] recently translated from the German, undertakes an interesting critical revival of the thought of Schleiermacher.

Schleiermacher lived at a time when Christian doctrines were

149

being steadily discredited at the hands of the rationalists of that period. Unwilling to concur with what he regarded as extreme intellectualizing of religion, he was led to the conviction that religion is more a matter of the emotions, a profound experience in which man is made aware of his dependence upon the mysterious, infinite God of the universe. Accordingly, he felt the source of religious insight and knowledge to be religious experience, and the task of theology the faithful exploration of that experience.

The approach of Schleiermacher had a wide following, particularly in his own country; but it was not until the close of the nineteenth century that this view became current in American thought. Bushnell as early as 1849 had voiced the spirit of this approach in his book, *God in Christ*.[2] But it was not until 1890, when L. F. Stearns published his *Evidence of Christian Experience,* followed by *Present Day Theology* in 1893, that the appeal to experience was given systematic formulation in American theology. In 1898 William Newton Clarke's influential book, *An Outline of Theology,* was published. This book, "perhaps the most influential book of its kind in American religious thinking," as Gerald Birney Smith has characterized it,[3] was the beginning of a series of publications by Clarke, developing the experiential approach to religious belief.[4]

Simultaneous with these developments in American theology, a movement of thought more far-reaching in its influence, even in this country, was taking form in Germany under the leadership of Albrecht Ritschl. Ritschlianism, as it was developed by the two eminent German theologians, Wilhelm Herrmann and Adolf von Harnack, has been easily the most potent single factor in shaping American liberal theology. Its most prominent representatives in this country were A. C. McGiffert, H. C. King, G. B. Foster and W. A. Brown. Ritschlianism went a step beyond the appeal to experience, in the effort to reduce the subjective element in its approach, by narrowing down the criterion of experienced knowledge to a single, historical object: the historical Jesus. This led, of course, to the Christocentric emphasis. In thus narrowing the appeal, Ritschl was impelled to react strenuously against mysticism, metaphysics and other related ventures on the grounds that they detoured the believer from the objective reference in religion. Few of the followers of Ritschl concurred in this reaction, and the American Ritschlians least of all. Rather, there appears early in the American movement a marked tendency to draw upon every possible source that might yield such experiential insight, although the direct experience of the historical Jesus remained the central source. Incidentally it is significant to note that among the more recent representatives of liberal theology, the appeal to Christ, while it has persisted, has gradually diminished, and the eclectic tendency steadily increased.

The theoretical basis for the appeal to experience, as a method for arriving at religious insight, was first formulated by Ritschl in his famous theory of value-judgments as over against existential judgments. Existential judgments, he pointed out, applied to the realm of things and actualities which could be described and measured in the manner employed by the exact sciences. Value-judgments, on the other hand, applied to the realm of persons and ideals, spiritual phenomena about which science could explain little or nothing, and which could be understood only on the basis of higher appeals consonant with the realm of the spirit. This is obviously a theological application of Kant's thought, and has had wide usage in the area of liberal theological thinking. In some form or other, this distinction between the realm of science and the realm of ethics and religion underlies all of the views advanced by the intuitionists, and accounts for their free use of practical experience as a source of convictions, on the one hand, and their rather cavalier way of relating the insights of science to the interests of religion. This appeal to religious experience and its accompanying emphasis upon the practical imperatives, together with a gingerly acceptance of the " facts " of science, may be said to be a characteristic, if not the distinctive, methodological trait of the intuitionists.

The appeal to religious experience in recent liberal religious thought, as we have already noted, tends to become widely inclusive of all varieties of experience that might contribute to an understanding of the divine reality. Accordingly, its procedure is eclectic. It draws from the testimonies of the mystics, from the experiments of the sciences, from the reported experiences of earlier generations, as made known by anthropology, the psychology and history of religions, as well as from evidence that it finds in the moral experience of mankind, both social and individual. On the other hand, its eclecticism is weighted on the side of moral and ethical interests. Consequently, among some of its representatives the appeal to religious experience tends toward an exclusive appeal to the moral experience.

Where the appeal to moral experience appears as the singular criterion for religious belief and certainty, we have what has been characterized as *ethical theism*. Ethical theism grounds the doctrine of God, for example, in the moral imperative. The *sense of ought* provides a criterion which points to a beyond that may be adequately accounted for only by the postulate that a moral being evoked that moral response in man. Such is the nature of the argument set forth by contemporary ethical theists like Baillie in *The Interpretation of Religion*, Sorley in *Moral Values*, and Taylor in *The Faith of a Moralist*. All these are British philosophers of religion. There is no representative philosophy of religion in America at present that can be termed ethical theism in this singular sense. Its echoes are to be heard in the arguments of all eclectic ethical intuitionists, although in no case does the reasoning of ethical theism stand out in pure form.[5] Other than the fact that the eclectics draw upon a number of sources for their insights, and employ a combination of methods to construct their philosophies of religion, they differ from the ethical theists in their use of the moral criteria. They argue, not from the experience of conscience to God, but from the demands of the moral ideal and moral living to their belief in God. Their procedure reflects more the adaptation of the pragmatic method, therefore, than the method of ethical theism.

The ethical emphasis among the ethical intuitionists, however, is clearly characteristic. It was present in the theology of Schleiermacher. It was more pronounced, even exclusively emphasized, in Ritschlianism and later Christocentric theologies. And out of it came one powerful phase of the movement known as Social Christianity, represented earlier in the century by Walter Rauschenbusch, and in contemporary theology by John Bennett, whose recent book *Social Salvation* has been characterized as a continuation of the Rauschenbusch tradition.[6]

In its eclecticism, this mode of thought tends to draw also upon metaphysical sources outside of its historical tradition. It is not unusual to find its representatives voicing sympathy with the views of supernaturalists. One of its contemporary proponents, in implying a certain measure of agreement with one form of neo-supernaturalism, characterized his position as turning politically to the left and theologically to the right. In the same volume, however, this same theologian expressed himself in agreement with certain fundamental views of naturalistic philosophers of religion. Also to a marked degree, all of these philosophies of religion and theologies, dominated by the tradition of romantic liberalism, reflect the spirit of idealism. This aspect of their thought should be examined in more detail since most of this group repudiate any connections with idealism.

Idealism, we have said, is the most complex and diversified system of thought we have. Hence it is very difficult to make any definite statement of what it is. But it is not so difficult to state what in idealism has made it so influential in religious thinking. This feature is its insistence that mind is the only ultimate reality. Most idealists would say that all the " choir of heaven and furniture of earth," the totality of all being which is not mind, is dependent on mind for its being in a sense that mind is not dependent on all of it. Some idealists say that this underlying mind is one; others say it is many. But they agree in saying that mind alone is ultimate reality while all else is appearance only. This is the primary distinguishing characteristic of the tradition of idealism in that respect in which we are here using it.

There is, however, a very large and most influential group of religious thinkers who are under the domination of this tradition yet are not idealists. We wish to emphasize the fact that they are not idealists even though they are influenced more deeply by this system of thought than any other. Most of them have repudiated emphatically and completely the idealistic theory of knowledge. Since the theory of knowledge and not the metaphysics is the most prominent characteristic of idealism in secular philosophy, the rejection of this feature might cause many to think that these men are entirely clear of idealism. But this is not the most important feature of idealism in respect to philosophy of religion, however pre-eminent it may be in general philosophy.

The thinkers we have in mind who have rejected the idealistic theory of knowledge still continue to give cosmic status to mind. While they do not say, as the idealists do, that mind is the only ultimate reality, they do generally say that a Cosmic Mind is the ground and goal of the universe. Most of them say that things, events, forms, have an ultimate reality of their own; but this Cosmic Mind is in control over all. It is the sovereign power.

A number of the leaders who are classified in this group have called themselves religious realists. It may seem, therefore, that we are untrue to their own claims when we say they are under the domination of the tradition of idealism. But this appearance will be removed when we examine their use of the term realism. We shall find that it does not indicate any distinctive system of religious thought.

Realism seems to be used in four different senses by these

men. First, it has some of the meaning it carries in secular philosophy. There it stands for a certain theory of knowledge. But this theory of knowledge does not imply any distinctive philosophy of religion. Also, realism as a theory of knowledge stands for two theories, called respectively neo-realism and critical realism. The religious realists do not always make plain which of the two they support.

There is a second meaning of realism as professed by members of this group. It is the teaching that events, things, forms have being in their own right and do not require to be known by some mind in order to exist or to be. On this point also they depart from idealism.

A third meaning of realism as used by these philosophers of religion makes plain that they wish to give full cognizance to the facts of evil. Some of them have this meaning to the front much more than others when they uphold the position of realism. D. C. Macintosh and E. W. Lyman, for example, would seem to be thinking chiefly of the theory of knowledge and the metaphysical reality of events, when they take the stand of realism. W. M. Horton and John Bennett would seem to be thinking more of facing squarely the facts of evil. This profession of realism among them is rather recent. In turning realistic they mean to repudiate the unfounded optimism that characterized liberalism. A great deal of religious thinking in America has tended to obscure or explain away the magnitude of evil in the world. Christian Science is the extreme example. But much that did not go to the extreme lengths of Christian Science was addicted to the optimistic fallacy. The earnest thinkers in the group we are now considering endeavor to rectify this shallowness and illusion. Realism is the word they use to indicate this goal and endeavor.

Realism in this sense of facing squarely the facts of evil is a very wholesome and worthy aspect of their religious thinking. But it does not suffice to define a system of philosophy. Of course if they meant by realism the philosophy of pessimism, it would. But that is not what they mean. Hence we cannot say that realism in this sense of the word indicates any definable philosophy of religion. Men with utterly diverse philosophies of religion, and men who have vehemently repudiated all religion, have taken pains to set forth the facts of evil in their fullness. Perhaps the extreme example in the United States of a philosophy of religion which has endeavored to do this is the work of Edmund Noble in his *Purposive Evolution*. But the intuitionists we are now considering would hardly consider Noble as one of their number. He belongs to the tradition of naturalism.

A fourth meaning of realism as used by this group brings out what is, perhaps, their chief distinguishing characteristic. It is their practical interest. These men are realists because they are concerned to serve the needs of moral and religious living; and only in the service of such living are they interested in developing a theory or system of thought. This aspect of their work has been neatly expressed by R. L. Calhoun:

> In religious realism an effort is made to deal fairly with all these diverse demands; and a considerable measure of neatness and finality is sacrificed, for the sake of maintaining touch with substantial masses of fact and with urgent practical concerns, though neither present facts nor short-term obligations can be permitted alone to dictate the theologian's view.[7]

In the thinking of all these men " a measure of neatness and finality is sacrificed " for the sake of practicality and for the sake of " dealing fairly with all these diverse demands." Members of this group are more concerned with keeping up " the morale and orientation " of the common man and " dealing with diverse demands " than in setting forth a complete system of thought wherein religion finds a distinctive interpretation. They endeavor to formulate religion in such a way that it will function effectively as an institution and as a way of living; and they regularly sacrifice coherence in their system whenever " diverse demands " and " urgent practical concerns " seem to require it.

It is plain that in such a practical matter as religion a group of thinkers such as these is of the utmost importance. In theory we may develop a neat and consistent system, but in practice we reach out for any principle that may help us get the desired results. So it is with this group.

If the requirements of the most noble living result in a philosophy which does not fit into a neat system, then so much the worse for the neat system. While these men want to achieve a coherent system so far as they can, they will sacrifice it if the best interests of human living seem to require it. Not the theoretical perfection of a system, but the practical requirements of life determine what goes into the philosophy which they develop. In that sense they are pragmatic, or eclectic or intuitive, rather than systematic and consistent.

They might be called pragmatic, but pragmatism is associated with a philosophy which all these men abjure. Hence the term cannot be applied to them.

They might be called the mediating group. They are mediators in several respects. First, they mediate between ways of religious living which are always shaped in chief part by inherited tradition, and the newly developing points of view of science, philosophy and social change. Again, they mediate between the needs of the church and those more radical reformulations of religious thought which are difficult to assimilate by a slowly changing institution and slowly changing loyalties. In the third place, they mediate between the newly emerging moral demands of our changing society and the methods of social action which are perpetuated into our time from an earlier period.

In the recent past, as we have seen, " religious experience " has been one of the chief guides to the thinking of this group, although this category is now falling somewhat into disrepute. When they set up religious experience as a test of the validity of any religious belief or any philosophy of religion they were saying that the practical and emotional requirements for high moral and religious living must determine what goes into a belief or a system of thought. These must determine what direction religious thinking takes and what form is given to it.

The best of these intuitionists or liberals or romanticists or pragmatists or eclectics (whatever term is preferred) keep themselves fully informed on what is occurring in science and philosophy, and what has been thought in the past. They select from all this abundance whatever promises to be helpful for religious living; and they endeavor to organize these selections into whatever system can be made out of them. They are very sensitive to the changing currents of thought and feeling as they bear upon religious living, and they shape their philosophy to absorb or to fend off these veering influences. They are quick to welcome whatever gives promise of aid to the moral, religious enterprise of human living; and they are quick to attack whatever seems to be hurtful to this vocation of man.

In discussing the personalists, we said they were perhaps the most influential among Christian people. Now we are saying the intuitionists hold this place of honor. Perhaps both statements are true in different respects. The personalists seek and achieve more logical coherence. They are more rigorous in applying the tests of rationality. The intuitionists are more sensitive and open to the changing currents of thought and newly emerging problems and needs. Where the one point of view is widely accepted as a systematic formulation of Christian faith, attuned to modern thought, the other is widely followed because of its continuous concern with reconstructing and reformulating Christian beliefs in the light of the changing *winds of doctrine* in related fields of thought.

The ethical intuitionists may be considered in two groups: (a) philosophical intuitionists and (b) theological intuitionists. This division is somewhat arbitrary, but it calls attention to a distinction of emphasis among these men which is important. The members of the first group are pre-eminently philosophers. That is, they are concerned to construct a valid structure of thought that will serve religious devotion. Thus, while they are practical thinkers, their thinking is motivated fully as much by theoretical considerations as by the practical concerns. The members of the second group are theologians; hence their approach to problems of philosophy of religion is clearly determined by the demands of religious living.

DOUGLAS C. MACINTOSH

One of the elders of the ethical intuitionists, a pioneer, and at the same time one of the most clear-headed and outspoken, is D. C. Macintosh. The distinguishing marks of this body of thinkers stand out very clearly in his work. One of his most admirable traits is that he sees so clearly just what he is doing. There is no befuddlement or evasion, and there is no attempt to confuse the issues. He states clearly and reiterates that any adequate philosophy or theology must have two parts: (1) that part based on rational and observable evidence, and (2) that part which cannot be so based, but which must be added to any living faith to meet the requirements of worthful living. He has a succinct term, " moral optimism," with which to express what must go into the making of this second part of any adequate philosophy of religion.

Philosophy of religion, he says, must be solidly founded on empirical evidence. Dr. Macintosh is very insistent on this, and no one has done more than he to establish our faith on such foundations. His great work, *Theology as an Empirical Science,* was a pioneering achievement. But such foundations, however indispensable, are not enough. They are only the substructure of the house of faith. On this groundwork we must rear the beliefs that make for " moral optimism."

This second level of belief is not determined by evidence gathered through use of the scientific method. These beliefs of the second level are determined by what we need to believe in order to live as we ought. On the other hand, however, these beliefs can never be held when they conflict with beliefs that are based on empirical evidence. These beliefs of the second level must be " reasonable." That means they must be consistent with whatever we know to be true by way of observational inquiry. But their real basis is not the rational and perceptual evidence.

This thinker really has three levels in his philosophy of religion. First, and basic to all, are the verified beliefs. Then come the pragmatic beliefs or faith which we have just been describing. Finally are the speculative beliefs or rational surmise. The first might be called the foundation; the second the house in which we live morally and religiously; the third the domes and spires that adorn and ennoble. For example, the belief that there is a reality of some sort upon which we depend for the highest fulfillments of living, is verified belief on the first level. But that this reality is a personality who thinks and loves, is a pragmatic belief on the second level. A God who is a personality is the kind of God we *need*. We *must* have that kind of a God to live as we ought.

A belief that belongs to the third level, which is that of rational surmise, is the belief that God is the creator of all. This is the God that *may be* according to rational conjecture. God at the second level, a supreme personality of intelligence and moral goodness, is the God that *must be,* if we are to have the kind of God we need for moral optimism. The God that surely *is* in the light of verified belief is a power that makes for good in human living, often in spite of man himself, and which responds to right religious adjustment.

Now, are these three Gods, the God that may be, the God that must be and the God that assuredly is, all one and the same God? That these three are one, is not a verified belief. It is not even a pragmatic belief on the second level of certainty. But it is " a permissible surmise and a practically valuable and reasonable faith."

Belief in immortality belongs to the second level of belief. It cannot be verified but it is pragmatically important. Moral optimism requires belief in ultimate conservation of all spiritual values in spite of physical death. Individual personalities can create values indefinitely as long as they exist. Hence highest spiritual value characterizes their continued existence. If persons on whom such absolute values depend are allowed to sink into nothingness, then faith in the conservation of absolute values is mistaken, and moral optimism becomes an illusory dream.

This treatment of God and immortality is altogether typical of this philosophy of religion. Perhaps one more example will make it plainer. Moral optimism requires that ideal possibility be united with reality. But this union must not be by way of a complete and perfect Absolute, such as the absolutists teach, for that would sap the zeal of moral enterprise and aspiration. Thus in the interest of moral optimism we must have a philosophy of religion which avoids two evils: on the one hand, the evil of despair which results when ideal possibility is thought to be unattainable; on the other hand, the evil of complacency which results when ideal possibility is thought to be already completely achieved in the Absolute.

What kind of a God will make us sure of the attainability of ideal possibility and at the same time make us see that we must do our utmost to help attain it? That kind of a God is what we need. That kind of a God we must have for moral optimism. That kind of a God we do have when we believe that God is a personality, completely moral, perfect in holiness and self-giving love. This is so because only a perfect will of mighty power can unite ideal possibility with reality by way of consistent and persistent striving and not by way of actual and completed realization.

The problem of evil also comes up for elaborate treatment in this philosophy. Mr. Macintosh teaches that this present world, in so far as it is the effect of God's causality, is the best possible kind of world for the present stage of man's existence. Here he has a proposition very skillfully stated in the interests of highest moral and religious living. This present world of ours is the best possible, but with two very important qualifications, which guard against the pollyanna complacency so often accompanying such a claim. This world is a long way from being the best possible world in so far as the work of man's free will has made it evil. Also, in the second place, it is a long way from being the best possible world in so far as man's present stage of development requires an evil world. Still other factors enter in to make this a very evil world in some respects, even though it is the best possible.

EUGENE W. LYMAN

One of the most important expositions of this kind of philosophy is found in Lyman's book, *The Meaning and Truth of Religion*. He teaches that religion is made up of three essential components. It is, first, an experience of kinship with the deepest reality in the universe. Second, by virtue of this kinship, one has membership in an infinitely meaningful world; and, third, one shares in an ever unfolding life. Any satisfactory philosophy of religion must be of such a sort as to guard and foster this experience. It is the essential nature of religion to enhance life, to give one enthusiasm, to heighten the vital energies, to engender vision in which larger realities swing into view, to awaken dormant powers and release deadlocked energies and expand the mind and heart to fuller functioning.

Religion is man's experience and belief that the supreme values are in some manner grounded in the deepest reality of the universe. Faith is response to reality in its capacity to produce value. It is response to the potency of the ideal in the actual. Here we see plainly that " moral optimism " is at the focus of interest. These words, however, belong to Macintosh rather than Lyman.

His treatment of the distinction between religion and morality is illuminating and important. Morality is concerned with value, but religion is concerned with the relation between reality and value. Morality works under tension and effort, but religion is marked by devotion and joy. Morality seeks fullest development of every human personality through the co-operative creation of a world-wide community of persons. Religion does that also, but its goes further. It seeks harmonious interaction between personalities of men and the " Deepest Reality of the Universe."

Professor Lyman gives much attention to mysticism. Mysticism, he says, is a sense of a presence that is immediately felt to be divine or an apprehension of truth that is immediately felt to be valid and momentous. Mystical intuition gives us truths that reason itself could never reach; but mystical intuition must be validated by reason.

Perhaps we have here something akin to the second level of religious truth described by Macintosh, the level of pragmatic belief or faith, which is required for moral optimism. The belief gained through mystic apprehension cannot be reached by scientific method. It is not verified as the substructure is. But it must be reasonable. It must be logically permissible and psychologically possible. Mystic intuition makes it psychologically possible or, better, psychologically actual; while reason makes it logically permissible.

This, we believe, is the correct interpretation of Professor Lyman's claim that intuition goes beyond reason and yet must be validated by reason. This claim might be interpreted otherwise. It might mean that scientific inquiry cannot begin nor continue without some proposition to test, and this proposition must get into the mind by way of intuition. This proposition can be called an hypothesis or theory or hunch or clue or insight or intuition or guess or new generalization. But one must have it to carry on any rational inquiry whatsoever. One may get such a proposition from other people, from common sense, from a book. But somewhere, somehow, it must have entered the human mind; and this emergence of the proposition into human thinking can be called intuition. If this were all Professor Lyman meant, he would not be distinguishing mystic intuition from any rational inquiry whatsoever, because always and everywhere the mind must have some proposition with which to carry on any intellectual inquiry. The proposition must always have originated in some way, and one can call that origination " intuition " if one likes. The fact that strong emotion may accompany some cases of intuition, and not others, would not be a distinction of any significance from the standpoint of theory of knowledge, even though it might be a necessary characteristic of anything called *mystical*.

But we do not believe Professor Lyman means anything so commonplace as we have indicated in the previous paragraph. He means to set forth a real distinction between the higher reach of mystical intuition and the lower reach of rational inquiry. What then is this rational validation which mystical intuition must have if it is to be accepted? Manifestly it must be that kind of validation which Professor Macintosh calls making it reasonable. It must be examined in its relations to all other propositions known to be true to see if it is not inconsistent with them. If it should prove to be inconsistent, it would not be validated by reason. If it should prove to be consistent, it would be validated. This is what Professor Macintosh means by the " logically permissible." The contribution of Professor Lyman is to show that mystical experience makes the belief " psychologically possible " or actual.

But there are other ways of gaining truth besides intuition and reason:

But we must bring into relation with intuition and reason that element of moral faithfulness which we previously have found to be vital to religious knowledge. Religion, as we have said, is in its fully developed nature at once mystical, rational, aesthetic and ethical, and each of these aspects of its nature enters into the gaining of religious knowledge. Intuitive apprehension, rational synthesis, imagination, and practical fidelity must all play their part in the knowledge of Divine Reality and of the way of life. And it is no less important that the truths gained by intuition and reflection should be lived out faithfully, if their meaning is to be fully apprehended, than that our practical efforts for the realization of truth should be revivified by fresh intuition and imagination and criticized by reflection.[8]

Thus we see that practical fidelity or faithfulness or faith, in a certain sense of the word, is a further source of religious knowledge. It may be said for all these intuitions that the real test of validity for any belief or practice is what it can contribute to a certain way of living. This way of living must be, first of all, zealously moral. It must also be marked by peace, courage, hope, joy, aspiration. Whatever makes for this kind of living should be accepted and practiced providing it does not contravene what we know to be true on purely scientific and rational grounds. This way of living is the kind of " experience " which is the final test of religious truth for this group and the goal of all their endeavors. It is this emphasis which makes us characterize them as ethical intuitionists.

C. A. Beckwith, who also belongs to this group, has stated this method and point of view very well in the following words:

The ultimate ground of our belief in God is not metaphysical, but moral — the necessity of God for the completion of the meaning of our life — (1) to provide a principle of unity for our intelligence in relation to the world; (2) to guarantee the validity and fulfillment of our ethical and spiritual ideals; (3) to ratify our religious yearnings for redemption and union with God.[9]

Beckwith describes God as Creative Good Will, the same term Professor Lyman has used. Hence all these men are intuitionists in the sense that they make central to all their thinking, and the test of religious truth, a certain kind of experience which is also a certain way of living. Truth for religion is whatever sustains and promotes this kind of living, whether it come from mysticism and intuition, or science or speculative philosophy or common sense or tradition or aesthetic experience or practical fidelity. All sources of human experience are searched and tested to find the gold that will add to the richness and security of this way of living.

[1] Crowell, 1933.

[2] His later books, *Nature and the Supernatural* (1858) and *The Vicarious Sacrifice* (1866) continued this line of thinking.

[3] *Current Christian Thinking.*

[4] His books, *The Use of Scripture in Theology* and *The Doctrine of God* followed later.

[5] All Christocentric theologians have espoused ethical theism with varying degrees of clarity and consistency. The clearest expression of ethical theism in this country is to be found in the theology of A. C. McGiffert. See his essay " The Christian Point of View," and the recent book edited by A. C. McGiffert, Jr., *Christianity as History and Faith.* See also *Reconstruction in Theology and the Social Consciousness:* H. C. King; and *Christianity in its Modern Expression:* G. B. Foster.

[6] We distinguish between romantic liberalism and modernism.

[7] *God and the Common Life:* R. L. Calhoun. Scribner, 1935. P. 78.

[8] *The Meaning and Truth of Religion:* E. W. Lyman. Scribner, 1933. P. 224.

[9] *The Idea of God:* C. A. Beckwith. Macmillan, 1922.

CHAPTER X

ETHICAL INTUITIONISTS: THEOLOGICAL GROUP

THE tradition of romantic liberalism, with its strictures upon reason and its emphasis upon *experience* as the basic source of insight, has had even a wider appeal among theologians than among philosophers. While the interests of the theological eclectics are pre-eminently theological and practical, there is ample justification for including them in a survey of contemporary philosophies of religion. The difference between theologian and philosopher is, of course, one of degree and it is always difficult to know just where to draw the line. Especially in a time of radical reconstruction of religious thought like the present, theologians tend to become philosophical in the sense that they must dig down to the basic structure and try to rear their religious faith on these nether foundations. But this also is a matter of degree.

All that was said concerning the distinguishing characteristics of ethical intuitionists in the preceding chapter applies equally to the theological eclectics. Their theological method is grounded in the appeal to experience. And this appeal to experience tends toward an eclectic use of many sources; although, being practically motivated, their eclecticism tends to be weighted on the moral and ethical side. Being pre-eminently theologians, they are more concerned with belief and action than with concepts and theory. They approach the problems of philosophy of religion from the standpoint of practical imperatives, seeking tenable and usable formulations. This is what gives them their popular appeal. They are nearer to the demands of the common man's experience and therefore better prepared to mediate religious insight. This is the role of the theologian. Among the prominent theological intuitionists we include: William Adams Brown, W. M. Horton, H. P. Van Dusen and John Bennett.

WILLIAM ADAMS BROWN

Of the contemporary theological intuitionists named, William Adams Brown would be recognized as the seer and teacher. All of the others have, at one time or other, been students of his, and have absorbed much of his teaching. Brown's earlier works reflect clearly the Christocentric principle, but like others of his group in recent years he has become increasingly theocentric in emphasis and more eclectic in method. There are two ways of knowing reality, according to Brown: One is logical understanding, made possible through analysis and classification of known facts. The other is by apprehending reality as a whole. The former is attained through reason and experiment; the latter through such practical religious experience as yields the full presence of God in human life. Belief in God, therefore, is felt to be primarily a matter of inner certitude arising from experience. Reason and experiment provide aids for man's reflection about God, and may help in the formulation of legitimate hypotheses for a working faith. But it is out of the working faith and the religious experience that accompanies it that man's conviction of God's reality and the nature of his being arises. The practical test which Brown lays down for the certainty of God's reality is the effect that such a belief has upon those who entertain it as a working hypothesis. Thus he argues that while the persistence of evil in the world makes belief in a good God difficult and theoretical inquiry does little to aid our conviction, the experience of finding our lives transformed through faith in such a God impels us to believe that a good God exists and is present with us. "When we trust our conviction that God is good," he writes, "and that he is in control, we find that this trust transforms our lives as it has already unified our thoughts."[1] Again, "only first-hand evidence of God's power to transform life can give the inward assurance possessed by those who have accepted God's revelation as a fact and who have lived as though God were real."[2]

How, specifically, does God's reality become known to one? "God makes his presence known with irresistible conviction," says Brown, *"in the act of the will by which man surrenders without reserve to the highest he knows."*[3] Such surrender to God brings not only the conviction that God *is,* but understanding as to what God is like as well. Faith finds specific meanings in God:

In their surrender to God, men have found in him beauty, the supreme harmony that resolves all discords. They have found in him righteousness; the unchanging laws that set all standards. They have found in him love, the creative energy that is the spring of all renewal. But the greatest of these is love; for love, and love alone, can bring good out of evil, life out of death, hope out of despair and can make all things new.[4]

To be sure, one might justify such faith in God along rational lines:

Thought may help to remove the obstacles which make faith difficult. . . . God is speaking to us in many ways: through the beauty of nature, through our intuitions of the right, through the teachings of history, through the discipline of suffering, through the appeal of human need . . . but in the last analysis it is the will that must speak the deciding word. . . . It is through what we do even more than what we think that our certainty of God must be won.[5]

Again, "when reason, in balancing the evidence pro and con, leaves us in uncertainty, it is miracle that must speak the final word."[6] By miracle he means the invasion of the natural process by a transcendent power that transforms and makes men new.

Likewise in regard to other religious beliefs such as the efficacy of prayer and the assurance of immortality. Reason may be employed to show their reasonableness and their justification; but belief in the sense of conviction arises only when, acting upon them as valid hypotheses, one finds moral renewal and spiritual transformation taking place in one's life. The legitimacy of a belief rests ultimately upon its practical consequences for moral and religious living.

WALTER MARSHALL HORTON

The most inclusive in method, among the theological group, is W. M. Horton, whose writings have received more popular attention and approval in religious circles than almost any other American theologian of our day. Horton finds affinities with practically every serious venture now current in human thought and experience. He is open to the experimental insights of the sciences as well as to the dogmatic claims of the orthodox believer. He is attentive to the urgent appeals of the social activist as well as to the lure of poet and aesthete. He finds something appealing in humanist and supernaturalist alike. And he accepts the tenets of a realistic theology with all the hope and optimism of a thoroughgoing liberal idealist.

But the guiding track of Horton's thought issues from the appeal to religious experience. His treatment of religious concepts is best revealed in the chapter on " God as a Psychological Fact " in his book, *A Psychological Approach to Theology,* originally published in *The Journal of Religion* under the title " The Objective Element in the Experience of God." [7]

The appeal to " religious experience " as the touchstone for the testing of religious dogmas has been characteristic of modern theology ever since Schleiermacher. The adoption of a thoroughly empirical point of view has been an indispensable means of acclimatizing Christian thought in a scientific age; and the gain in intellectual integrity has been so great that any radical departure from the empirical principle can henceforth only be regarded as a step backward. It is becoming plain, however, that the concept of " experience " needs clarification, to free it from a certain persistent ambiguity.   To say that theology is the science or the philosophy of " religious experience " may mean one of two things, according to the stress laid upon the subjective or the objective element in the concept of experience.   It may mean that theology is simply the study of religious experience as a peculiar group of mental phenomena; or it may mean that theology is the attempt to erect, on the basis of such a study, a verifiable theory concerning the nature of the Object of religious experience — God.[8]

Horton chooses the latter, and proceeds to analyze the objective element in religious experience.   He finds the existence of an object of religious experience to be a *fact of certainty* on the grounds that in worship, man's projected ends are attained only as " he relinquishes his self-sufficiency and reaches out humbly for aid in a genuine Objective Beyond." [9]   Only as man acts on the assumption that such a Being exists, does his venture in worship prove successful.   Here we have the same sort of adaptation of the pragmatic argument as is found in the reasoning of William Adams Brown.

Discovery of the *nature* of the religious Object, he continues, must also proceed along empirical lines.   The criterion which distinguishes between the experience that is religious and that which is not is taken from Rudolf Otto's analysis of " the holy." That which naturally evokes the creature-feeling is to be set down as productive of *religious* experience.   On this basis, Horton finds three approaches to the experience of God: through nature, through society, and through the inner life.   " In each of these three regions," he says, " are to be found realities which naturally evoke the creature-feeling in the candid beholder, and adjustment to which means enhancement of life."   That is, in contact with the world of nature, in association with the life of the community, and in company with one's self in deep communion, one, who has not lost his sensitivity to the sacred, comes upon conditions or events that bear in upon him and evoke in him the sense of deep humility and dependence.   He becomes creature-conscious, which in turn calls up awareness of that of which one is creature. On the basis of these experiences, Horton concludes, *"it is empirically certain that at least three divine Objects exist: the God of nature, the God of society, and the God within."* This is as far as experience can take us. To go further in discovering the *nature* of deity, whether these three divine Objects are one or many, personal or impersonal, one must pass from the realm of fact to the realm of hypothesis, says Horton. For Horton, the hypothesis that "all nature is a unity" motivated by "one great universal cosmic energy" seems assured on observable grounds. Likewise in regard to the *personal* nature of deity. Theistic religion, he asserts, has dared to venture upon the further hypothetical leap of identifying "the God of the heart with the God of society and history and with the ruler of the cosmos, and it has conceived him in personal terms." Note Horton's justification for this hypothesis:

> The difficulties of this colossal concept are obvious; but pantheism and humanism, its chief contemporary rivals, involve difficulties of their own. The problem of evil is more acute for pantheism than for theism; while the humanist buys his solution of the problem at the price of severing man from the cosmos. If the humanist is ready to admit that the inner life of the individual, apparently isolated, is really capable of merging with the larger life of humanity, why may not humanity, in turn, be capable of transcending its apparent isolation and allying itself with some larger cosmic life? Here we run beyond our empirical tether; but we cannot avoid taking sides and *living as though one of these hypotheses* were the true one. Faith can never completely give way to knowledge in these high regions; yet a theology that is thoroughly empirical in its starting-point and candid in its desire to do justice to rival hypotheses may yet lead us nearer to a genuine knowledge of God than we dare hope at present.[10]

Another striking example of Horton's mode of thought, and representative also of other theological eclectics, is given in the passage that follows. We quote it at length because it admirably illustrates the method of deriving beliefs through the appeal to religious experience.

One of the most impressive religious experiences I have ever had came to me, not in church, but — shades of my Puritan ancestors, avert your faces! — in a New York theater, where John Drinkwater's *Abraham Lincoln* was then playing. As scene succeeded scene, and the soul of Lincoln was more and more completely revealed — triumphing over his own misgivings, forsaking ease for the sake of the well-being of all, unflinching in his opposition to evil, but overcoming evil with compassion, giving his life at length as a ransom for many — I found myself at last looking upon the stage with the eyes of a worshiper, and I said to myself: "*This, this is God.*" Nor was I a solitary worshiper. Consciously or unconsciously, each person there worshiped God that evening. I felt it in the applause, and in the still more significant silences; and the fellowship of adoration added greatly to the depth of it for all of us; for it helped us to feel that this was not merely *my* God, but *our* God — yes, the God of all mankind.

Now what do I mean by saying I met God in Drinkwater's *Lincoln?* Well, what did I mean at the time? Let me scrutinize the workings of my mind. I think that Lincoln's divineness in my eyes consisted precisely in the " combination of ideality and final efficacity " which was the criterion of the divine for William James. I got a double impression of moral nobility in the highest degree, and of irresistible power. In the first place, Lincoln humbled me as the ideal always humbles the actual; his human figure, with his homely qualities and obvious limitations, became, as it were, translucent, and through it shone a pure and unwavering light, the light of the ideal, making me long unutterably to be like him — and unlike myself. But this was not all; he was for me the incarnation of irresistible might. This was, if possible, the stronger of the two impressions. " This is the spirit that is bound to win," I said to myself. I saw it triumphing before my eyes — winning the respect of the supercilious Seward and the cantankerous Stanton, turning a condemned youth into a hero and bidding fair to bind a nation into a unity based on justice and mutual forgiveness. I saw it hushing a miscellaneous New York audience into reverence. And then, the theater could not contain it. I looked out beyond the stage into the tangled world, and I saw that spirit, embodied in the message of President Wilson, putting an end to a great war, and arousing fabulous hopes in the hearts of all the peoples — and chaos and despair rushing back upon the scene when that spirit which had governed us in war failed to get incorporated in the treaty of peace. I thought of the triumphs of many folk, ordinary and extraordinary, missionaries, reformers, plain people, in whom this spirit finds more or less imperfect embodiment, and I said to myself: " It's irresistible; it's almighty. No one can stop it. Nail it to a cross and it smiles at you and continues. Sooner or later, it is going to capture the last redoubt, and rule in the hearts of *all*."

If my enthusiasm had permitted me to stop at this point, I should have been affirming, as you see, that the God whom I glimpsed in Lincoln was *a tendency in human history, a growing social entity,* if you will, of such a nature that it was bound to overcome all obstacles and become the organizing principle of human society and the object of each human individual's allegiance. Poeticizing a bit, I should easily have arrived at the conception of an Invisible King or Captain of mankind, growing with the growth of mankind, yet always leading on. . . .

But I did not stop at this point, just on the margin of metaphysics, where all good humanists draw the line. I pressed on — rashly, perhaps — and it began to rain metaphysics, thick and fast. "The spirit of Lincoln," I said in my haste, " *must* triumph. The nature of things is such — human nature, of course, but nature in general too. The universe is built that way; that's why the universe is on his side." "Yes " — and here I took a terrific leap, from an impersonal moral order to an anthropomorphic deity — " there is at the heart of things a spirit like that of Lincoln, a personality like his." Thus did the primitive Christian reason concerning Christ; and thus, I admit, I reasoned concerning Lincoln.[11]

Then Horton goes on to add: " I do not rest my conception of God upon any one experience or any one type of experience." He rests it in part as he says upon the experiences of his Christian predecessors, as crystallized in the words and notions he was taught in childhood; in the experience of the Holy Spirit, the overtone that accompanies group worship; in the experience of ethical insight; and in the more definitely mystical experience. In all of these he finds further insight concerning his conception of God.[12]

I may define the conception of God which seems to emerge spontaneously from such experiences as these [he concludes] by comparing it with the conception of God which Professor Royce defended in his earliest writings. I would agree emphatically with him that God must be conscious that we are; for the conclusion we jump to in our moments of elevation is that there is some mind which always sees things as we see them at these moments. On the other hand, the religious consciousness seems to object strenuously to Royce's conception of a God lifted above time, taking no part in history except to survey it at a glance. The

God of religion belongs in that " World of the Powers " in which Royce could find no God; He is a Power among powers, the Power that is progressively victorious, not by compulsion, but through the gradual impartation of His purpose and outlook to the leaders of mankind.[13]

Yet, Horton is not content to rest his beliefs merely upon the intuitions of religious experience. These ventures and leaps toward hypotheses favoring a conception of a *personal* God, he finds substantiated by psychological reasoning, and by recourse to philosophical arguments that have been persistently entertained. Psychologically, he argues, man's *personal* response to his cosmic environment suggests the existence of an external stimulus that is itself personal in character, for on the basis of our knowledge of social interaction within the social environment, " personal ideas can only be awakened by contact with personalities." And this suggestion he finds supported by philosophical arguments that point to a purposive trend in the evolutionary process. The nature of the process, he argues, is reflected, not in its earliest, but in its latest stages; hence personality in man, the latest to evolve in cosmic growth, points to personality of a more significant order in the process that has produced man. " Hence all my argument tends to prove," he concludes, " is that over the little stream of cosmic history, in which you and I are eddies, there broods the influence of Personality greater than man's."

The insistence that theology become an empirical science and that religious beliefs be grounded upon the combined evidence of experience and rational support, is indeed worthy of earnest consideration. However else liberal theology may have failed in its attempt to reconstruct a receding orthodoxy, it has contributed the inestimable service of rendering religious thought amenable to empirical inquiry and rational testing. How successful these theologians have been in accomplishing their objective, however, and whether or not the objective is possible of attainment along lines they suggest, are by no means assured matters.[14]

The precariousness of "religious experience" as the basic criterion for religious knowledge and belief is, of course, well recognized by these men. The analogy between the appeal to experience in scientific procedure and the appeal to religious experience in theological inquiry can not be taken too seriously. The experience to which the sciences appeal is a body of data that has been verified by tested methods and which continues to be verifiable when those methods are subsequently employed. Religious experience is a far more ambiguous body of data, and it has the further problem of being complicated by subjective emotions which make objective observation practically impossible. One need only consult the varieties of religious experiences that have been reported to discover how utterly unreliable they can be as sources of evidence.

This would be acknowledged by any of the ethical intuitionists. For that reason, effort has been made in all such theologies so to define religious experience that the subjective element is diminished. We noted that the Ritschlians narrowed it down to the experience of the historical Jesus, and that subsequent theologians extended it to comparable data outside of the Christian faith. Rudolf Otto, following somewhat in the tradition of Schleiermacher, undertook to characterize the experience of "the holy" through the analogy of related psychological categories, and Horton, as we have seen, attempts to apply the results of Otto's analysis, describing all experience as religious, however or wherever encountered, which evokes in one the creature-feeling. Yet, while this identifies religious experience with a specific response, there is no assurance that the stimulus that evoked the response is of such a character that one might rightfully apply the term God to it, unless one arbitrarily asserts that all stimuli that evoke such a feeling in man are divine, and then the essential distinctions become lost. Such a solution would advance the problem of religion no further than the situation of early man, where the experience of *mana* might be evoked by any number of strange and uncanny sights or sounds. To say that man's reactions have become more disciplined in modern culture, and therefore more reliable as indications of the nature of the stimuli, suggests a point. But its value as an argument is nullified by the fact that man still responds awesomely, humbly, even loyally and devotedly to stimuli, in the form of objectives, causes, enterprises, and persons, which from other standards of judgment are clearly demonic rather than divine.

To say that the experience of awe and wonder before objects in nature, or the sense of devotion to group or society, or the feeling of inner certitude in mystic communion points to something in environment, worthy of consideration and experimentation, is indeed a suggestive insight. But to say that they make empirically certain that " three divine objects exist: the God of nature, the God of society, and the God within," is to overstate the conclusion, unless, as we have said, one is indifferent to the content of the term " God."

The intuitionists come nearer to a valid interpretation when they assert that the religious element in experience is always to be discovered in the act of the will " by which man surrenders without reserve to the highest he knows." This introduces the element of evaluation, and makes religious experience ethically and morally attentive as well as emotionally submissive. But even here the criterion is ambiguous, unless what one believes to be highest is actually highest. Most of the ethical intuitionists have attempted to make this evaluation objective by identifying " the highest " with what Christian tradition has acknowledged to be highest, namely: the personal values discerned in the figure of Christ. As an ethical commitment, this is a valid and worthy decision. As a philosophical conclusion regarding the nature of ultimate reality, however, it still leaves the burden of proof unlifted.

The intuitionists undertake to go a step further in asserting that if, when one surrenders unreservedly to the highest he knows, he discovers that his life becomes transformed and enhanced, he may be assured that " the highest " to which he has committed himself actually exists as an objective reality. Now this argument is in need of careful scrutiny. Granting that such devotion to projected values, a venture of faith, does result in the enhancement of life, the least that one may conclude is that devotion of the self to a reality or realities beyond the self, or to the more-than-self, integrates and promotes human personality. This is a fact which the findings of modern psychology clearly confirm. That means, then, that religious devotion, when it is directed toward ethically defensible ends, is an aid to personal fulfillment. But does it follow that one may then leap to the most that one may conclude, namely, that such devotion, with its accompanying beneficial results, makes empirically certain the existence of a divine being, consonant with the human values experienced? That it points to the existence of a creative order in the universe which promotes human life when the demands of integrity, justice, and good will are observed, might be reasonably claimed. But to claim more than that would seem to go beyond the logic of the matter.

To say that religious beliefs are legitimate in the sense that they lead to practical results that are psychologically beneficial and morally desirable, is to make an ethical pronouncement. But to infer that this *pragmatic truth* thereby makes empirically certain a *metaphysical truth* is clearly an unwarranted inference.

It becomes obvious, therefore, that the appeal to religious experience, for attaining knowledge and belief, however carefully defined, is open to grave and unavoidable difficulties. And the more ambitious the theological quest, the more serious and multiplied these difficulties become.

Now if the ethical intuitionists were to be content with discovering what is empirically tenable regarding man's relations with environing reality on the basis of observation and reason, instead of undertaking to demonstrate the validity of inherited religious convictions, their task would be fraught with less error and ambiguity. To be sure, their conclusions would be less ambitious and less assuring to the " wishful " popular mind; but their procedure would be more defensible.

But to these theologians such a solution would be an unworthy and unwarranted compromise with science. For " in matters of religion," as one of them asserts,

scientific method can never be cool and impersonal. . . . The religious experimenter must throw himself, heart and soul, into the experiment; he must perhaps live a whole life on unproved assumptions, and appeal to posterity for the verification of these hypotheses. If he abandons his hopes whenever they run against adverse facts, and resigns himself to a drab and constricting view of reality because he fears to play the fool, he may be missing his chance to discover some pathway out of the morass of human misery which will not reveal itself to a less ardent and impetuous investigator.[15]

It is this heroic element, this high romance in the theology of the ethical intuitionists that gives it its wide popular appeal. It is this same heroic element that clearly identifies it with the romantic tradition, and sharply differentiates it from the rationalist tradition of both idealism and naturalism.

[1] *God at Work*, p. 112.   [2] *Ibid.*, p. 113.   [3] *Ibid.*, p. 118.   [4] *Ibid.*, p. 150.
[5] *Pathways to Certainty*, p. 250.   [6] *God at Work*, p. 159.
[7] October 1927. According to the author's own word, the same general line of reasoning is followed in Chapters III and IV of his *Theism and the Modern Mood*.
[8] *A Psychological Approach to Theology*, p. 185.
[9] *Ibid.*, p. 203.   [10] *Op. cit.*, p. 208.   [11] *Ibid.*, pp. 209–12.
[12] *Ibid.*, pp. 212–13.   [13] *Ibid.*, p. 213 f.
[14] See Chapters VI and VII of *Current Christian Thinking* by Gerald Birney Smith for a keen, critical analysis of the appeal to experience and the appeal to Christ as theological methods.
[15] Horton, *op. cit.*, p. 232.

CHAPTER XI

AESTHETIC NATURALISTS

ESTHETIC Naturalism represents religion as being primarily an appreciative response to reality. It accords with the view expressed by Havelock Ellis in *The Dance of Life,* in which he defines religion "in its quintessential core" as *the art of finding our emotional relationship to the world conceived as a whole."* On its theological side, this view goes back to Schleiermacher; but as a religious attitude it is much older. It breathes the spirit of the Greek poets and speaks the language of the *Phaedrus* and of Aristotle's *Ethics.* It finds a sympathetic response also in Shakespeare, Goethe, Rousseau, Wordsworth, Shelley, Keats, Coleridge and Emerson. It bears affinities to the robust spirit of Whitman, Burroughs and Thoreau,[1] and to the temper of thought found in certain contemporary poets.[2]

The underlying *motif* of this type of thought is that art provides the best approach for comprehending the vast relations of life and for entering feelingly into the wealth of its meanings. This gives to aesthetic naturalism a degree of inclusiveness which is not possible in philosophies of religion committed to a rationalistic or purely ethical interpretation of reality. For aesthetic experience seizes in a single grasp what science, labor and morality treat in separate ways. Yet this inclusive quality of the appreciative approach tends toward a quiescence that ignores the moral imperatives. In a thoroughly monistic world-view, such as emerged from Schleiermacher's philosophy, or as is to be found in certain forms of pantheism, this tendency appears legitimate. Existence is bathed in an ocean of Being which in turn permeates all of existence. What is, is good enough, and eternally shall be. The goal of life is to cease from restless striving and to relax joyously into all that is. This gospel appears to some extent in all forms of aesthetic philosophies. When the monistic view of life is dispelled, however, this quiescent gospel no longer carries conviction. Dualistic philosophies of any sort, whether they have the sharp demarcations of supernaturalism, or the relative distinctions of evolutionary conceptions, contrasting what is with what might be, the existent with the possibilities, put a premium upon action and conflict. For contentment in the face of evil or imperfection is an admission of unworthiness. In the experiences of the great mass of human folk, conflict has been more real than quietude; hence action has seemed more respectable than contemplation. For that reason, whether they have been aware of the philosophical choice or not, they have preferred dualisms to monisms. It is this incurable commitment to the need of striving that has led to the repudiation of aesthetic philosophies with their gospel of quietude and contemplation. Yet the repudiation, however justified it may seem in the light of the problem of evil and the day's work, turns out to be purely reactionary. For even in a world where good and evil are clearly in conflict, or where the reach from what is to what might be has become an incurable habit of the people, as in our American commonwealth, a philosophy of life that is purely activistic becomes self-defeating.[3] Sober reflection impels one to return to some degree of contemplative living through which perspective and incentive for life may be recovered. If reflection does not bring one to this decision, then the tragic experience of progressive defeat and ennui inevitably must.

This, then, raises the question as to which ignores the moral imperative most disastrously — the gospel of quietude, or the gospel of incessant striving. The question need not be answered, for the truth is that both are extreme gospels. Life well lived moves in alternating rhythms, and the philosophy of life that will bring men to their highest possibilities as creative creatures is a philosophy that combines contemplation and action.

Aesthetic philosophies have varied in the degree to which they have recognized this basic problem. Some have persisted serenely on their Olympian heights, utterly indifferent to the babble and struggle below, or to the taunts of critics, impatient with their complacency. But there have also been philosophers of this faith who have taken the pick in hand to hew a path from the solitary heights to the valleys where the multitudes labor, confident that their labor would improve and their zest for labor increase were they to ascend that path at intervals.

Aesthetic philosophies have varied also in their metaphysics. Aesthetic naturalism is peculiar in that it views reality in terms of the world of sense, and thus joins with other forms of naturalistic philosophies in undertaking to discern the fundamental meanings of reality through sense experience and reflective study. Within aesthetic naturalism there are further differences in the degree to which correlation with scientific and practical interests are pursued.

GEORGE SANTAYANA

O world, thou choosest not the better part!
It is not wisdom to be only wise,
And on the inward vision close the eyes,
But it is wisdom to believe the heart.

These famous lines by Santayana strike the keynote of romanticism and express with unusual aptitude the motivating sentiment of his own thought. As a philosopher, Santayana would choose to be known as " the only living materialist "; but he is a materialist only in the sense that every aesthete is a

materialist. He is by temperament neither materialistic nor
naturalistic in any exclusive sense. Nor does his preoccupation
with "the realm of essences" signify such leanings. Whatever
sympathies he may profess with other moods and modes of
thought, he is at heart a romanticist of the aesthetic sort. The
"inward vision" is his source of truth, as it is also for him the
end of truth. For Santayana has taken to the contemplative
life to which, in his judgment, the maturing of a disciplined
life of reason inevitably leads. Professor Dewey, in commenting upon this standpoint, says:

> The road to freedom by escape into the inner life is no modern dis-
> covery; it was taken by savages, by the oppressed, by children, long
> before it was formulated in philosophical romanticism. The generalized
> awareness of the fact is new, however, and it added a new dimension to
> characteristically modern experience. It created new forms of art and
> new theories of aesthetics, often promulgated by literary artists who have
> nothing but contempt for philosophical theories as such. Mr. Santayana
> is a thinker whose intent and basis are at one with classic thought. But
> if we note the importance assumed in his thinking by the "inward land-
> scape," there is before us a measure of the pervasive influence of the
> kind of experience that was seized upon by Romanticism as the exclusive
> truth of experience.[4]

Viewed from this vantage ground, life is seen to move in response to two realms: the realm of existence and the realm of
essence. To the former Santayana ascribes the world of action.
Hence, to it, he would say, belong science, labor, and such pur-
suits as promote the activities of existence. To the latter he
assigns the life of reason — that life which seeks to translate
human experience into terms of ideal and rational appreciation. To this realm, then, belongs religion, for religion is that
pursuit of the imagination which lifts men from the level of
drab and harsh existence to the impelling heights of the ideal
good. Religion, therefore, is essentially an art. From the point
of view of poetic form, in fact, Santayana believes no creative
art has achieved its perfection and expressiveness. Thus he
writes in *The Sense of Beauty:*

The greatest of these creations have not been the work of any one man. They have been the slow product of the pious and poetic imagination. Starting from some personification of nature or some memory of a great man, the popular and priestly tradition has refined and developed the ideal; it has made it an expression of men's aspiration and a counterpart of their need. The devotion of each tribe, shrine, and psalmist has added some attribute to the god or some parable to his legend; and thus, around the kernel of some original divine function, the imagination of a people has gathered every possible expression of it, creating a complete and beautiful personality, with its history, its character, and its gifts. No poet has ever equaled the perfection or significance of these religious creations. The greatest characters of fiction are uninteresting and unreal compared with the conceptions of the gods; so much so that men have believed that their gods have objective reality.[5]

Religion, then, according to Santayana, is a symbolical rendering of the experiences of life. Its approach is always imaginative. Its language is poetic. When man seeks to explain the events of life in the terms of religion, he creates myth. When through the approach of religion he undertakes the celebration of life, he resorts to dramatic ritual and pageantry. When he would employ the method of religion to discipline his life and to project the deep aspirings of his soul, he takes to prayer. Thus religion in its simplest terms is the symbolical expression of man's knowledge, emotions and aspirations. "Religions thus," says Santayana, "will be better or worse, never true or false." They will be better or worse according as they succeed in depicting men's imaginative envisagement of life's meanings with insight and persuasive appeal, in giving expression to the deep-surging emotions of the soul, and in impelling men's minds and wills toward new frontiers of human achievement through projected dreams in contemplation of the ideal. But to speak of religion as true or false, says Santayana, is to read into religious interpretations literal meanings that simply do not belong to it:

Religion pursues rationality through the imagination. When it explains events or assigns causes, it is an imaginative substitute for science. When it gives precepts, insinuates ideals, or remoulds aspiration, it is an imaginative substitute for wisdom — I mean for the deliberate and impartial pursuit of all good.[6]

Hence:

The only truth of religion comes from its interpretation of life, from its symbolic rendering of that moral experience which it springs out of and which it seeks to elucidate. Its falsehood comes from the insidious misunderstanding which clings to it, to the effect that these poetic conceptions are not merely representations of experience as it is or should be, but are rather information about experience or reality elsewhere — an experience and reality which, strangely enough, supply just the defects betrayed by reality and experience here.[7]

The idea that religion contains a literal, not a symbolic representation of truth and life is simply an impossible idea. Whoever entertains it has not come within the region of profitable philosophizing on that subject.[8]

This persistent tendency in religion to confuse symbolic interpretations for scientific truth has been its great defect, Santayana believes. And where it has become a basic emphasis, as in Protestantism, it has been the undoing of religion and the destruction of its worth.[9] Were it not for this "insidious error," he thinks, religion could have far greater value than poetry itself for it deals with higher and more practical themes.

Now the real value of religion, Santayana maintains, lies in its ideal enhancement of the world. "Like poetry, it improves the world only by imagining it improved." But in so doing, it gives to existence, otherwise drab and unbearable, a warmth and lure to which the human heart can respond. In this sense, he concludes, religion has a very noble function.

This function of religion is made more explicit in his interpretation of prayer:

Prayer is a soliloquy; but being a soliloquy expressing need, and being furthermore, like sacrifice, a desperate expedient which men fly to in their impotence, it looks for an effect: to cry aloud, to make vows, to contrast eloquently the given with the ideal situation, is certainly as likely a way of bringing about a change for the better as it would be to chastise one's self severely, or to destroy what one loves best, or to perform acts altogether trivial and arbitrary. Prayer is also magic, and as such it is expected to do work. The answer looked for, or one which may be accepted instead, very often ensues; and it is then that mythology begins to enter in and seeks to explain by what machinery of divine passions and purposes that answering effect was produced. (*Reason in Religion*, p. 40.)

The mythology that pretends to justify prayer by giving it a material efficacy misunderstands prayer completely and makes it ridiculous, for it turns away from the heart, which prayer expresses pathetically, to a fabulous cosmos where aspirations have been turned into things and have completely thereby stifled their own voices. (P. 42.)

What successful religion really should pass into is contemplation, ideality, poetry, in the sense in which poetry includes all imaginative moral life. That this is what religion looks to is very clear in prayer and in the efficacy which prayer consistently can have. In rational prayer the soul may be said to accomplish three things important to its welfare: it withdraws within itself and defines its good; it accommodates itself to destiny, and it grows like the ideal which it conceives. (P. 43.)

Prayer, in fine, though it accomplishes nothing material, constitutes something spiritual. It will not bring rain, but until rain comes it may cultivate hope and resignation and may prepare the heart for any issue, opening up a vista in which human prosperity will appear in its conditional existence and conditional value. A candle wasting itself before an image will prevent no misfortune, but it may bear witness to some silent hope or relieve some sorrow by expressing it; it may soften a little the bitter sense of impotence which would consume a mind aware of physical dependence but not of spiritual dominion. Worship, supplication, reliance on the gods, express both these things in an appropriate parable. Physical impotence is expressed by man's appeal for help; moral dominion by belief in God's omnipotence. This belief may afterwards seem to be contradicted by events. It would be so in truth if God's omnipotence stood for a material magical control of events by the values they were to generate. But the believer knows in his heart, in spite of the confused explanations he may give of his feelings, that a material efficacy is not the test of his faith. His faith will survive any outward disappointment. In fact, it will grow by that discipline and not become truly religious until it ceases to be a foolish expectation of improbable things and rises on stepping-stones of its material disappointments into a spiritual peace. (Pp. 47–48.)

Expressed in this manner, Santayana would seem to encourage the pursuit of illusion and ideality for the sheer consolation and support that such contemplation affords. Doubtless much of life is lived on this basis. As children we are born into a make-believe world. As youth we climb to maturity, lured on by what might be. And many there are who come to the trailing years of life, still seeking the might-have-beens, hardly aware that all life for them has been but a *lovely dream*.

> Ah lovely must their visions seem
> Who only sit and play
> With rosy gleam and fairy dream
> And tenderness and Fey!

Yet this view has difficulties which not a few have been quick to point out, none more piquantly, perhaps, than Walter Lippmann when he writes:

When the truths of religion have lost their connection with a superhuman order, the cord of their life is cut. What remains is a somewhat archaic, a somewhat questionable, although a very touching, quaint medley of poetry, rhetoric, fable, exhortation, and insight into human travail. When Mr. Santayana says that "matters of religion should never be matters of controversy" because "we never argue with a lover about his taste, nor condemn him, if we are just, for knowing so human a passion," he expresses an ultimate unbelief. For what would be the plight of a lover, if we told him that his passion was charming? — though, of course, there might be no such lady as the one he loved.[10]

Man can be content with his "heart-warming beliefs" and ideals so long as there is the assurance that they are, in some genuine fashion, correlated with a reality about which there is no illusion. This is as true of the artist as it is of the religious man. Sherwood Anderson has expressed this in these lines:

The life of the imagination will always remain separated from the life of reality. It feeds upon the life of reality, but it is not that life — cannot be. . . . For some reason I myself have never understood very clearly . . . the imagination must constantly feed upon reality or starve. Separate yourself too much from life and you may at moments be a lyrical poet, but you are not an artist. Something within dries up, starved for the want of food.[11]

So it is with the religious man in relation to the environing reality with which he would find adjustment. His idealizations and poetic prayers, however imaginative, must feed upon reality else they become haunting illusions which no honest mind can endure.

This, I believe, is acknowledged by Santayana in some of his statements, which suggest that he holds a deeper view of reality than his description of religion implies. In discussing the matter of prayer, for example, he writes:

There is such an order in experience that we find our desires doubly dependent on something which, because it disregards our will, we call an external power. Sometimes it overwhelms us with scourges and wonders, so that we must marvel at it and fear; sometimes it removes, or after removing restores, a support necessary to our existence and happiness, so that we must cling to it, hope for it, and love it. Whatever is serious in religion, whatever is bound up with morality and fate, is contained in those plain experiences of dependence and of affinity to that on which we depend. . . . A man who studies for himself the ominous and the friendly aspects of reality and gives them the truest and most adequate expression he can is repeating what the founders of religion did in the beginning.[12]

From this he is led to say that

Religion is not essentially an imposture, though it might seem so if we consider it as its defenders present it to us rather than as its discoverers and original spokesmen uttered it in the presence of nature and face to face with unsophisticated men. Religion is an interpretation of experience honestly made, and made in view of man's happiness and its empirical conditions. That this interpretation is poetical goes without saying, since natural and moral science, even today, are inadequate for the task. But the mythical form into which men cast their wisdom was not chosen by them because they preferred to be imaginative; it was not embraced as its survivals are now defended, out of sentimental attachment to grandiloquent but inaccurate thought. Mythical forms were adopted because none other were available, nor could the primitive mind discriminate at all between the mythical and the scientific. Whether it is the myth or the wisdom it expresses that we call religion is a matter of words. Certain it is that the wisdom is alone what gives the myth its dignity, and what originally suggested it. *God's majesty lies in his operation,* not in his definition or his image.[13]

Does Santayana mean to imply by this statement that what early man missed because of his inadequate powers of thought and expression, modern man, with his refined methods and improved discernment, may attain? This deduction would only partially please Santayana. For it overlooks the nature of man's conceptualizing about religion and points to a literalizing which Santayana abhors. This is made clear, I believe, in what he has to say about God. Here Santayana's insistence upon the instrumental motive and symbolical character of religious language comes to the fore. In the passage quoted below, he means to interpret St. Augustine's view, but it is apparent that he is expressing his own thoughts on God as well. Commenting upon St. Augustine's statement that "God is the good and the beautiful," he continues:

He was never tired of telling us that God is not true but the truth (i.e., the ideal object of thought in any sphere), not good but the good (i.e., the ideal object of will in all its rational manifestations). In other words, whenever a man, reflecting on his experience, conceived the better or the best, the perfect and the eternal, he conceived God, inadequately, of course, yet essentially, because God signified the comprehensive ideal of all the perfections which the human spirit could behold in itself or in its objects. Of this divine essence, accordingly, every interesting thing was a manifestation; all virtue and beauty were parcels of it, tokens of its superabundant grace. Hence the inexhaustible passion of Saint Augustine toward his God; hence the sweetness of that endless colloquy in prayer into which he was continually relapsing, a passion and a sweetness which no one will understand to whom God is primarily a natural power and only accidentally a moral ideal.[14]

The obvious comment here would be, of course, that for Santayana religion is simply an inward and intimate expression of man's evaluations, arising as with wings in contemplative imagination and aspiration. And that the objects of faith which have generally been ascribed to an objective reality are in actuality the projections of man's own aspiring soul. Santayana's retort to this expected comment is very significant, not only for what it implies as a judgment upon more literal metaphysical interpretations, but chiefly for what it reveals concerning the deeper side of Santayana's own philosophizing. Speaking further regarding the contrast between St. Augustine's awareness of God and the views of those "to whom God is primarily a natural power," he says:

Herein lies the chief difference between those in whom religion is spontaneous and primary — a very few — and those in whom it is imitative and secondary. To the former, divine things are inward values, projected by chance into images furnished by poetic tradition or by external nature, while to the latter, divine things are in the first instance objective factors of nature or of social tradition, although they have come, perhaps, to possess some point of contact with the interests of the inner life on account of the supposed physical influence which those superhuman entities have over human fortunes. In a word, theology, for those whose religion is secondary, is simply a false physics, a doctrine about eventual experience not founded on the experience of the past. Such a false physics, however, is soon discredited by events; it does not require much experience or much shrewdness to discover that supernatural beings and laws are without the empirical efficacy which was attributed to them. True physics and true history must always tend, in enlightened minds, to supplant those misinterpreted religious traditions. Therefore, those whose reflection or sentiment does not furnish them with a key to the moral symbolism and poetic validity underlying theological ideas, if they apply their intelligence to the subject at all, and care to be sincere, will very soon come to regard religion as a delusion. Where religion is primary, however, all that worldly dread of fraud and illusion becomes irrelevant, as it is irrelevant to an artist's pleasure to be warned that the beauty he expresses has no objective existence, or as it would be irrelevant to a mathematician's reasoning to suspect that Pythagoras was a myth and his supposed philosophy an abracadabra. To the religious man religion is inwardly justified. God has no need of natural or logical witnesses, but speaks himself within the heart, being indeed that ineffable attraction which dwells in whatever is good and beautiful, and that persuasive visitation of the soul by the eternal and incorruptible by which she feels herself purified, rescued from mortality, and given an inheritance in the truth.[15]

Proofs of the existence of God are therefore not needed, since his existence is in one sense obvious and in another of no religious interest. It is obvious in the sense that the ideal is a term of moral experience, and that truth, goodness, and beauty are inevitably envisaged by any one whose life has in some measure a rational quality. It is of no religious interest in the sense that perhaps some physical or dynamic absolute might be scientifically discoverable in the dark entrails of nature or of mind. The great difference between religion and metaphysics is that religion looks for God at the top of life and metaphysics at the bottom; a fact which explains why metaphysics has such difficulty in finding God, while religion has never lost him.[16]

He continues with his reply to this protest by contrasting what he calls *cosmic piety* and *spirituality*. Cosmic piety, he points out, is pre-eminently concerned with reverence for the sources of life. But " in honoring the sources of life, piety is retrospective. There is a higher side to religion which looks to the end toward which we move. This aspiring side of religion may be called Spirituality."

Spirituality is nobler than piety, because what would fulfill our being and make it worth having is what alone lends value to that being's source. Nothing can be lower or more wholly instrumental than the substance and cause of all things. The gift of existence would be worthless unless existence was good and supported at least a possible happiness. A man is spiritual when he lives in the presence of the ideal, and whether he eat or drink does so for the sake of a true and ultimate good. He is spiritual when he envisages his goal so frankly that his whole material life becomes a transparent and transitive vehicle, an instrument which scarcely arrests attention but allows the spirit to use it economically and with perfect detachment and freedom.[17]

This ideal synthesis of all that is good, this consciousness that over earth floats its congenial heaven, this vision of perfection which gilds beauty and sanctifies grief, has taken form, for the most part, in such grossly material images, in a mythology so opaque and pseudo-physical, that its ideal and moral essence has been sadly obscured; nevertheless, every religion worthy of the name has put into its gods some element of real goodness, something by which they become representative of those scattered excellences and self-justifying bits of experience in which the Life of Reason consists.[18]

Now these passages seem to cast an entirely different light upon Santayana's thought on religion. There can be no doubt but that he encourages idealization as a legitimate illusion. I can make nothing else of his lines:

A candle wasting itself before an image will prevent no misfortune, but it may bear witness to some silent hope or relieve some sorrow by expressing it; it may soften a little the bitter sense of impotence which would consume a mind aware of physical dependence but not of spiritual dominion.

But the illusory function of religion is not the whole of Santayana's thought, nor its most important truth. In saying that in religion man improves the world by imagining it improved, he certainly means to include the active implications of imagination — projecting men's will as well as their thoughts toward the idealized, thereby impelling them to move toward the ideal. This would seem to be implied in what he says of the accomplishments of prayer: In prayer the soul *defines its good,* it *accommodates itself to destiny,* and it *grows like the ideal which it conceives.* This is equal to saying that it makes articulate what is most needed and desired; it enables one to face the inevitable and to make what adjustments that confrontation demands, evoking, it may be, the reverent and profound utterance, "Thy will be done." And through patient and faithful devotion, man may bring to pass the end to which he aspired.

Looked at from this angle there would seem to be some similarity between Santayana's view and those expressed by Dewey and Ames, particularly where Santayana stresses the instrumental function of religious concepts for envisaging the ideal. This may seem surprising, for in popular opinion two men could hardly be selected to illustrate more decisively the opposite poles of philosophical thought than George Santayana and John Dewey. Yet it is not surprising when one recognizes that both of them, and Ames as well, proceed from the common thesis that religious language is a symbolical rendering of reality and that religion itself is basically the idealization of the experienced values of life.

We should not, however, lose sight of the basic difference that divides them in their philosophies. For Dewey, the locus of religious imagination is what Santayana terms the realm of existence. And the religious use of imagination is directed toward the actualization of ideal ends that are essentially utilitarian in character. For Santayana, on the other hand, religious imagination is projected, not toward existential realities, but toward the realm of essences, the pure ideal, that which transcends the world of action, and therefore which yields only to contemplative envisagement. Accordingly, there is this further difference between them: Santayana would seem to urge religious contemplation of the ideal without sole regard to the measured consequences of such imaginative procedure. As with the poet and the artist, it becomes an act worthy in its own right, in which case the consequences appear to be secondary. In Dewey's thought, however, such imaginative effort is purposive, directed toward the actualization of ends, specifically defined and pursued. Accordingly Dewey's ideals are more selective with regard to felt needs and intended ends, together with the possibility of their realization. They are therefore better described as *objectives* rather than as ideals. I would not say that this purposive element is not present in Santayana's view; that would be to unsay what has just been pointed out in relating his thought to that of Dewey and Ames. I simply wish to re-emphasize what is commonly acknowledged, that Santayana is essentially aesthetic and contemplative, rather than activistic in approach. And this marks the difference between his philosophy of idealization and the one set forth by Dewey in *A Common Faith*. The counter fact is also important, however: namely, that the aesthetic interpretation of religion which Santayana sets forth does not exclude the purposive, creative function of such idealization, so explicit in Dewey's position. In fact, it would seem that Santayana's thought had been only partially evaluated were this element to be overlooked in his interpretation.

JOHN CROWE RANSOM

A persuasive presentation of the aesthetic view of religion has been set forth in a more recent book, *God Without Thunder,* by John Crowe Ransom, a man of letters rather than a philosopher. Less serene and objective in his manner, he nevertheless defends the symbolical interpretation of religion with the same suggestive insight that one finds in Santayana's writings. Myth, says Ransom, is inevitable in religion, for religion, contrary to the procedure of science, undertakes in its utterances to bring into focus a more-than-historical history. It " attempts to imply the whole of history " whereas science never goes out of its natural history, and " uses only an abstract or part of that history." A case in point is the concept " God."

The myth-maker sets him up a God. Why a God? I am sure that there are, at one time or another, two motives for a God as the explanation of the universe. First, to represent its indefiniteness in extent of time or of space. For here is the visible portion of the universe in space, but we are constantly going a little farther out, and evidently the universe flows on beyond the bounds of observation. And here is the universe as it has had its successive states within the limits of historic time, but each new day has added another state, and we desire a universe that had states before history began and will go on having states to-morrow and thereafter. Let us have an entity to represent this out-and-beyond and this before-and-after universe, let it be God, and let his name mean when we pronounce it: A universe of a magnitude exceeding its own natural history. Few can resist, even among the regular scientists, the need of that entity.

But there is another motive for having a God that is quite imperious, especially perhaps among Orientals and people with a powerful aesthetic sense. The universe might be defined in the terms of its own natural history, and yet no item within it was ever fully explored by natural history; while still less, of course, did its fullness get into that abstract of natural history which is the scientific generalization. The universe in every local detail is evidently of inexhaustible fullness or particularity. The universe is not therefore a simple cosmos, or the sum of its constants and cores-of-repetition. Let the universe then be the body and manifestation of an inscrutable God, whose name shall mean: Of a fullness of being that exceeds formulation. These are two Gods, an extensive and an intensive. Sometimes they merge, in the thought of the expert mythmaker, into one very great God. (Pp. 69–70.)

Religion, then, in Ransom's view, is not simply a function of poetic imagination for improving the appearances of reality, as in Santayana, but a legitimate way of envisaging the larger reaches of reality which in the nature of the case cannot be designated in any manner other than symbolical portrayal. Their difference is merely one of motive, however, not of method.

This necessity of employing the imaginative language of the myth in religion is a fact of prime importance, Ransom holds. When men lack the imagination to grasp this insight, there generally arises a destructive rationalizing tendency that turns religion more and more into an impetuous concern for literal facts and practices. Dogma and social creeds then replace the religious celebration of life. This, he finds, is what has been occurring with increasing momentum in our western world ever since the Protestant reform. And the modernists have carried it to its extreme stage.

The present movement away from Fundamentalism [he writes] is simply the form which the destructive tendency of Protestantism takes for this age. . . . It is the movement of the people who have not the imagination and the courage to enjoy the excellent Gods they have inherited. (P. 101.)

Ransom has in mind here, not the Fundamentalism of the Tennessee trial, but rather the view of those who intelligently conceive the dogmas in their traditional aesthetic sense, as representations of truths, deep and far-flung in scope and implication. That is, "the best of the Fundamentalists" as he calls them.

That religion has to do with the imaginative grasp of reality, using imaginative in the sense of pictorial, no one who has really thought about the matter can fail to apprehend. This assertion becomes dangerous, however, unless it is balanced by the other half of the truth, namely, that for that very reason religion needs to be tempered by science, lest it soar away into dreams and myths of illusion and sheer fantasy. Religion must relate itself to reality of the empirical sort, else "something within dries up," to repeat Sherwood Anderson's caution. The same difficulty that applies to Santayana's view would seem to apply to Ransom's statements also, though with less emphasis perhaps. The chief limitation of Ransom's interpretation is the short range of his aesthetic perspective when applied to religion. He seems to assume that the appreciative response to reality is bound up with the emotive appeals of traditional religion. Hence "the only contribution" which he sees fit to offer, as a concluding word, is the caution: "With whatever religious institution a modern man may be connected, let him try to turn it back toward orthodoxy." But it does not follow that because religion must employ symbolical or poetical language to envisage its realities, one must employ the myths and symbols of old, or that one is justified in adhering to them. When, in the course of several centuries of growth in the culture of a people as well as in their intellectual outlook, the symbols of tradition cease to convey the same wealth of suggestive meaning and significance, it would seem that new symbols, more suggestive and evocative of genuine emotional response, would be in order. That, exactly, is what has been occurring in our modern world. The reaction of the modernist against the old forms of thought and ritual are not simply confessions of his impoverished imagination, not simply the culmination of the blindness of Protestant rationalism; that is too simple an account of it. The basic fact is that realities which the older symbols portrayed have become illusive. Something deeper than the recovery of aesthetic appreciation is needed, therefore. There must come a reorientation of soul in the new milieu. If the sciences have compelled us to become more realistic about the universe in which we live, then our emotional life as well has been deeply affected, and the symbols through which we establish our emotional relationship to reality must be adjusted accordingly. When the religion symbolized by the Gothic cathedral ceases to arouse men to high devotion, the solution will lie, not in improving their aesthetic appreciation of Gothic architecture, but in reconstructing the patterns of faith, which, in turn, may impel men to create a new architecture to house man's spirit.

The discovery that religion is an aesthetic approach to reality, therefore, does not of necessity lead to the conclusion that modern religion must turn back. It argues even more imperatively, it would seem, that religion must create new patterns of religious response, consonant with man's experience in modern culture and in the new universe that environs him. A more mystical naturalism may be the better way out.

BAKER BROWNELL

In his two books, *The New Universe* and *Earth Is Enough,* Baker Brownell has made a lunge in this direction. Religion, says Brownell, is conceived in three ways: religion as salvation, religion as the integrative moment of living, religion as the deep identity of being. Of the three, religion as salvation is the least appealing to Brownell, for it involves the admission that life is no longer religious. Therefore some sort of escape is sought. It may take the course of world-fleeing, escaping from evil through eschatological deliverance, or through the inner way of the mystic. It may take the route that leads to a heaven within or beyond present space and time, or it may take the course of reconstruction and reform in which the creating of new values, to supersede present and immediate existence, is incessantly pursued. All of these several routes toward salvation "repudiate the native integrity of things." Religion of this sort, says Brownell, "belongs to the sparrows, America, and those who cannot dwell in the intimate stuff of living."

Religion as the *integrative moment of living,* although more difficult to describe, is more worthy to achieve:

> A moment of living, an integrative moment of living, is living. It is unique. It is vital, whole; words cannot capture its significance. In its own terms religion is thus rather beyond discussion. (P. 278.)

But were one to attempt to discuss it, he would be led to say that

> Religion is vitality in things. Moments of living that hold thus within themselves their value and significance are hardly temporal moments. They are poured full of life like empty vases, and they differ from other moments less in space or time location than in immeasurable quality and being. They have no reference beyond themselves to other moments past or future. They are subject to no order or procession. They are unique, as life is unique, and religion, in this sense, belongs to no other system. In three ways, more logical than temporal, religion of this sort may be located: It is a primitive integrity first of all, as in children or Tahitians, before salvation is needed. It is a moment, second, found many times through life amid the fragments and abstractions of a mature world. It is a fusion, third, of mature diversities and fragments into a life, so called, of spirit. In these places and times this religious life is found. (P. 279.)

The following quotation will suggest the thought more vividly:

> The faint grass of Spring has come around the edges of the ground where the boys will play scrub this afternoon with a dozen others. The faint grass comes from the ground in a haze of green. It rises from the soil under the sun, and the black earth around the edges of the field is grass, green under the living sun. Through old leaves, a broken branch or so from the elm tree, the grass boils up in a green froth. The earth steams and simmers into the air, smells of the grass and the steaming. The earth lives; earth is enough, warm with spring, warm, a luminescent lamp; lights of green and bronze gleam there. (P. 289.)

This integrative moment of living lies below defining marks and conceptions. At best one can define it as " the appreciative integrity of living " that is discerned or experienced in such moments of growing grass, the child at play, or the man at work.

There come rare moments, Brownell continues, when this integrity of living intensifies into a fulsome identity with being, as in the experience that follows:

It was a fine day. The water was almost calm, the sky blue, a few clouds. I was lying on my back, my arms outstretched beyond my head. I was looking upward, just doing nothing. I could see nothing of the town or the boats or people, only the sky, a few clouds. The water was in my ears. Sometimes it splashed a little. I could feel, or seem to feel, the slight pressure of the ripples. A gull was above me, a great bird flying, flying without motion. He was planing against the breeze, still, fixed by some strange tension there in space. Then I let go, somehow. I relaxed, settled down a little in the water. And I felt I was not anywhere. I was everywhere; I was always. I looked at the gull, at the clouds. I felt myself one with them as I imagined the gull felt himself to be. I made no separation. I was nowhere. I made no distinctions between myself and them. There was no distinction. We were the same. I cannot tell you how it possessed me. I was somehow drowned in them; drowned, or shall I say awakened from the particular dreams of life? Drowned in being; awakened to being? I do not know. I lay there forever, which I suppose was a few minutes. (P. 249.)

The full force of this view of religion can be grasped only as one enters sympathetically into the mystical realism of Brownell's *new universe.* To the degree that one approaches his conviction that *earth is enough,* that, along with man's vivid awareness, to be growing creatures of earth like the trees, the fish of the sea, and the cattle upon a thousand hills, is an end worthy in itself, this view takes on meaning and significance.

HARTLEY BURR ALEXANDER

The impulse to find a satisfying emotional relationship to the world may go beyond the mere enhancement of life through poetic imagination or the simple search for appreciative zest in each integrative moment of living to the more ambitious and precarious venture of discovering whether there be something about the cosmic environment that renders it congenial to man's deepest longings and highest aspirations. When this venture is undertaken, the quest becomes charged with a religious earnestness that carries the mood beyond what is generally understood as *aesthetic appreciation*. The aesthetic response merges with both mystical and ethical feeling. Religion, while it continues to be aesthetic and mystical in approach, becomes a life of devotion to what in the nature of things demands adjustment and loyalty.[19]

Of such a temper is the philosophy of religion of Hartley Burr Alexander. More prophetic and mystical than any of the philosophers considered in this group, he nevertheless approaches philosophy and religion with the method characteristic of aesthetic naturalists. Like Santayana he finds the subjective symbols of drama and the myth the most adequate instruments of thought for expressing philosophic and religious truths. Philosophy, in fact, is best conceived as an art — in Alexander's estimate, *the Great Art*.

In naming philosophy art rather than science [he writes in his autobiographical statement] I have no notion that I am in any wise detracting from its dignity as a quest for truth, but am adding thereto, for I conceive that I am ascribing to it a range and subtlety of expression such as no science may be found to possess, yet without which all communication of truth must be feeble and mutilated. Historically science is the offspring of philosophy, and is participant with it in the pursuit of understanding; yet science is not a capable heir in the sense in which philosophy inherits power from its own parent, which is the whole of that art whereby mankind has sought, and still seeks, to create intelligible images of meaning of our human life, upwelling from chaos. Such imaged meanings are truth, and for truth no measures may suffice that employ less than the total resources of our intelligence, which richness of resource is the mark of art, and it is also the mark of philosophy, for where truth is the stake philosophy is of all modes of understanding the subtlest and the most penetrating. Therefore it is first of all with reference to the gift of truth-speaking that I name philosophy an art, although surely it is an art also with respect to its purpose and its wisdom.[20]

In his *Truth and the Faith*, which, as an interpretation of Christianity, bears striking resemblance to the symbolical depiction of the Hebrew and Christian religions in Santayana's *Reason in Religion*, Alexander sets forth his theory of religious insight, distinguishing its understanding of reality from that derived from scientific and speculative inquiry. The prime assessor of human understanding, he says, regardless of the level of intelligence, is the sense of sight. It is true of all sense-perception; of all rational insight, whether in the form of a systematic science or of common observation. And it is true also of imaginative intelligence, applied either to aesthetic interpretations or to such readings of the world's life wherein " men have sought to convey that which is least utterable of all understandings, the inward and spiritual." But the *seeing* that reports to the understanding in each case varies enormously. Consider for example scientific truth:

In the end all our science is reduced to readings: if it be space, there are meters; if it be time, there are dials, if it be weights and pulls, there are scales and levels; for every motion there are arcs and trajectories, minutes and seconds of space, and for every computation of events there is a graph; the denominations of the stars are spectroscopic and the patterns of atoms are orbital; sound itself is given physical reality by an image of visible waves, and the world's energies by spaced paths or a motion which the mind can see.[21]

Scientific truth, then, is concerned only for the " shaped world "; yet a world whose shapes are abstract and quantitative, destitute of " the emotions and contours of the sculptor's art." It cares nothing for quality and color. " The pages of scientific truth know no rubrics: they are all in black and white." But life, says Alexander, is " written with many rubrics, and of its truths there are many that can be conveyed only by some art of illumination." Thus adjacent to the stony world of fact and the grayed world of thought, Alexander sets a third world *which is consciously image and myth and consciously truth.* This he calls man's Cosmos of imagination. For the world of the imagination, he holds, is an ordered world no less than that of science. Where the abstractions of science are directed toward movement and action, the selections of the imaginative world are directed to quiescent and contemplative ends which,

he adds, " in its lighter phases we call appreciation and which
in its more commanding form is absorption."

Thus while scientific thinking "thins and pales the object
of its study," imaginative thinking causes this object to flush
and glow with qualities of color, sound and emotion. This
Cosmos of imagination which illuminates life's meanings
through the arts, drama and music, floods the world also with
the spiritual hues that issue from the inner experiences of man's
life.

> Thus the world of imaginative understanding is built into continuities
> of time and space which while they have elements in common with the
> analogous forms of sense-perception and of mathematico-physical think-
> ing, are none the less, and in themselves a " transcendental aesthetic " of
> a cosmos all theirs to shape. It is not a cosmos that begins with the outer
> senses, and it is not one which is product of number and division; but
> it is one which embodies in its moments and its particularities, all the hue
> and stir of our inner natures — melody along with sound, glory along
> with color — and in the breadth of its comprehensions grasps all that
> makes life spirited or nature dramatic. . . . In the end, all our greatness
> in art is recognition of such truth; it is faith in beauty, and it is the con-
> viction that the ideal alone can impart reality to our experience of life.
> This is what we mean when we say that life is out-written with rubrics,
> and that its dearest truths are spiritual illuminations.[22]

These spiritual illuminations, like the discernment of beauty,
are intimate revelations that come to one who has eyes to see.
Thus for Alexander, as with Santayana, religion, in the last
analysis, is always a personal evaluation of reality. I do not
take this conclusion in Alexander's thought to imply that religion, accordingly, is illusory. For while he seems to be in
accord with Santayana and Parker in regarding the imaginative truths of art and religion as subjective evaluations, he appears to reach beyond their premise with regard to the essential
import of the religious vision. Both Santayana and Parker
seem to suggest that man's imaginative envisagement of life's
objects and events must issue only in idealization of the drab
world. Like poetic imagination, the religious vision creates a

legitimate illusion that warms the heart and inspirits man with noble thoughts and dreams. But Alexander goes beyond contemplation to hearty participation. He is no mere spectator. Nor is religion for him a mere avenue of escape leading to Olympian heights from which to view the world's turmoil in tranquillity. Rather, the religious vision brings to light the full-orbed drama of life — a drama of tragic conflict between the good and the evil. It is not a drama to be observed only, but one to engage men's loyalty and devotion. For it is a fight to the death between forces that bring light and forces that turn the world into darkness. This impassioned moral spirit in Alexander's philosophy sets him apart from other aesthetic naturalists who view religion solely as an appreciative response. The passage that follows is expressive of his view:

> I see nothing that is indifferent, except chaos, and nothing that can be called true that is not either good or bad in its honest essence. Therefore I have schooled myself to face even shudderingly the black realities of cruelty and bestiality and senseless monstrosity and pitiful affliction and the leprous destruction of innocence and beauty; I have looked down into the reek of hell as well as upwards towards the Bow of Promise; and I have refused to praise God or to idolize Nature for the presence in their world of what I abhor. I believe this to be Christian truth, though it is perhaps beyond the pale of accredited theology. Certainly it is taught by the Drama, which is so vastly more convincing than any dogma can be; but even if the Drama were peculiarly *my* image of its revelation, still I should believe it to be the truth. Dualism is the old name for this belief, and metaphysically dualism means war at the core of being. I assent to this.[23]

Again, in his lecture on " God and Philosophical Thinking," he declares:

> I shall not deny the facts of evil, nor its worst realities. I cannot: there they stand, malignant in Nature and glaring in History; no softness of speech can expunge them, no folly of persuasion exorcise. It is true that more than one theology has sought to cleanse creation and to save the face of divinity by denying the reality of evil, maintaining that the Bad is but appearance and due to the frailty of human comprehension:

viewed from the altitudes, they say, all will be seen as fair, all as beautiful and good, even as from the lookout height the blistering trails and
alkali wastes of Death's Valley take on glamors, remote and serene, —
but for the bones bleaching there, is this their comfort? Nay, it is small
wonder that the Great Negation has seemed to the tough-minded but
the pathetic folly of self-dupes, unwilling to face the hard facts, who
make of God and religion their compensatory illusion for mangled
lives.[24]

Yet the fact of these evils impels Alexander to affirm God
rather than to deny him or to doubt him. Unlike Santayana,
behind whose majestic lines there lurks a stoic skepticism, Alexander is confident and jubilant. God as "the greatness of
human experience" is for him an inescapable fact, more uni-
versally acknowledged than denied — not as one all-powerful
in the midst of conflict, but as one struggling to bring victory
out of the conflict. For God, as man's heart has discovered him,
says Alexander,

has been actor and worker and maker in the midst of time; he has been
a laborer, mighty in travail; a champion, contending with huge forces
and facing difficulties which only the patient aeons can resolve; a lord
and leader, encompassed by glooms which his shattering bolts do but
transiently dispel; a slow builder, laying the foundations of his house
upon the abyss and securing it only by an eternal vigilance: and who
shall know that some vast Twilight of Divinity shall not yet engulf it?
Such have been the images that have expressed the convictions of peoples:
God their Hero, their Noble, the great Protagonist of their cause! [25]

Nevertheless there is assurance, Alexander believes, that the
cause will conquer — an assurance born not of illusion, but of
the accumulative certitude which the experience of life lays
upon us. For man's life, as seemingly Nature's, is *oriented to
the Good,* even as a flower to its sun. "Whatever our ter-
rors, our disasters, none the less we will and can follow no
other standard — we, who are the company of the Good and
strugglers after the light."

If with me you hold that such facts are elementary in experience, then
assuredly you will join in the understanding that by *God* we mean that

power which out of old blindnesses has opened and is opening our eyes, physical and spiritual, to a light that can illumine and a vision that can exalt. This is a fact of human experience, and so far as we can read, it is also a truth of Nature, and it is in this fact that we take our stand. God is the lord of righteousness and the power that makes for the Good, and for our souls and for Nature's being He is more tremendous than any massy center of gravitation.[26]

In this noble utterance Alexander passes from aesthetic naturalism, although not beyond the pale of romanticism. If our presentation of his philosophy of religion is representative, he would seem to combine the methods of both aesthetic naturalism and ethical intuitionism. In the basic approach to his constructive philosophy, he is clearly an aesthetic naturalist, making aesthetic experience the channel to religious insight and the symbols of drama and myth the medium for interpreting its truths. Alexander's preoccupation with myths and symbols is by no means incidental to his philosophizing.[27] If, in fact, one were to designate the key to his thoughts on philosophy and religion, it would be his thesis regarding the symbolical meanings of life.

But he does not stop where most aesthetic interpretations of religion conclude. Rather, he goes on to affirm a moral optimism as the corollary of the religious vision. This allies his thought in part, therefore, with that of the ethical intuitionists; not only because of his moral passion, but also because of his appeal to individual experience as the ground for his religious certitude.

No writer among contemporary philosophers has combined the imagery of aesthetic expression and the appeal of religious passion with greater beauty and power than he. This passage from his Scripps College Lecture singularly illustrates that fact:

Ringing down through the centuries unstilled and unstillable, with overtones a-many but with fundamental unchanging, like a deep, commanding chime, into human experience has entered and been sustained, love, and with it the sense of divinity. I do not say that love is the whole of being, for life has not taught me that this is fact; and even though it be love — love of truth and cleanness and rectitude — which gives structure to reason and power to science, still, with the impurpled Empedocles of old, I shall own that though love govern the citadel yet hate tears at the walls of the world. I do not say that love is wholly pure, nor never led awry; rather with the unflinching poet of the Purgatorio I see it slothful, perverted, and passion-cleft, with such stains as only the harsh climbs of the hill of purification can take away. I do not say that love is forever the conqueror; for there are deeps of futurity beyond any vision, and love unblinded is love defective, even as God's love can be infinite only as it becomes oblivious of all that He must forgive. I do not say that love suffers no wrong; but rather that all things are suffered for love, and that this is the meaning of that image of the Great Sufferer which has branded its crucifixions into the very substance of the stars and has brought awe and adoration into the hearts of all peoples. I cannot say, then, that love has no need of its Christs; but I do affirm that in human life the part of love is the beautiful and heroic and noble part, and that no instinct of our being is less to be denied than this which commands that it is for us to live unto love's nobility. Love is a world's fact, as blindingly real as the sun; and in the life of man love is an untaught experience, which mankind, with one avowal, have named their experience of God.

At the last, unto each of us, falls the question, not of belief, but of life's realities. Beneath thinking stands experience, mine and yours and all mankind's, and it is this that gives the final answer and the abiding conviction. If within our lives there be found any invincible certitude that the Good lays upon us a command and that the Nobler Way is for us to search out, and if within our lives there be any felt surety of an evadeless love, which is the soul's magnet and would save us if it could, then we are in the presence of God, before whom all argument is meaningless. We shall not then ask what is God's nature; we shall only hail Him as our Greater Comrade, whose being is the impulse of life itself, such that so long as we *are* God also *is,* breath of our breath and lodestar of our days.

There is a moment when speech is no further of avail and the fleeting plausibilities of words break and shatter like the spray from the last wave of a receding tide, fallen futile against the granite. Man turning from the glamors of sense and the confusions of thought stands upon the brink of being, in his own naked solitude face to face with the last reality. Remote are the noises of the market-place, and his own days are as dust and as a wind-blown dust are the stars in their ages. Before him, alone, is the still form of the eternal, but whether it be empty and a nothing or whether it be full, it is for him who hath seen to say, even in the chambers of his own soul and before the Truth that there he knows. Which if he hath found it full, and not to be forsworn for that he hath beheld it — he, alone, with his own life,— he will answer it with a quieted heart, and he will name it the presence of God.

The measures of heaven and hell, of stars and dominions, are in our own souls. . . . Comrades in life, ye have known love! ye have seen God! [28]

[1] See *The New Spirit:* Havelock Ellis.

[2] See "Kinsmen of the Wild ": A Study of Religious Moods in Modern American Poetry: Bernard E. Meland. *Sewanee Review,* October 1933.

[3] See Hocking's important discussion of this point in *The Meaning of God in Human Experience,* Chapter XXVIII.

[4] *Experience and Nature,* p. 230.   [5] *The Sense of Beauty,* pp. 186–187.

[6] *Reason in Religion,* p. 10.   [7] *Ibid.,* p. 11.   [8] *Ibid.,* p. 98.

[9] Santayana's estimate of the rationalizing element in Protestantism is vigorously set forth in his *Winds of Doctrine,* Chapter II.

[10] *A Preface to Morals,* p. 36.

[11] Sherwood Anderson's *Notebook,* pp. 72–73.   Quoted by DeWitt Parker in *Human Values.*

[12] *Reason in Religion,* p. 30.   [13] *Ibid.,* p. 31.   [14] *Ibid.,* p. 156.

[15] *Ibid.,* pp. 156–158.   [16] *Ibid.,* p. 158.   [17] *Ibid.,* pp. 193–194.

[18] *Ibid.,* p. 212.

[19] When aesthetic naturalism of this sort takes up with a thoroughly naturalistic world-view, it becomes *mystical naturalism.* As a philosophy of religion, its tenets then point in the direction of naturalistic theism. See the discussion on mystical naturalism in Chapter XV.

[20] "The Great Art Which is Philosophy," in *Contemporary American Philosophy,* Vol. I, edited by G. P. Adams and W. P. Montague. Macmillan, 1930. P. 89.

[21] *Truth and the Faith.* Holt, 1929. Pp. 27–28.

[22] *Ibid.,* pp. 34–36.

[23] *Contemporary American Philosophy,* p. 102.

[24] In *Lectures on the Meaning of God in Modern Life,* Scripps College Papers Number Five, 1933. P. 67.

[25] *Ibid.,* p. 68.   [26] *Ibid.*

[27] H. B. Alexander has achieved distinction as an authoritative interpreter of the myths of American Indians and as a scholar in the field of mythology. See his *L'Art et la Philosophie des Indiens de l'Amérique du Nord:* Serie de Conferences faites à la Sorbonne aux mois d'avril et de mai, 1925, Paris 1926, and his contributions to *Mythology of All Races,* Vol. X (North American) and Vol. XI (Latin American). Marshall Jones Co., 1920.

[28] From "God and Philosophical Thinking," in *Lectures on The Meaning of God in Modern Life.* Pp. 70–71.

PART FIVE

ROOTED IN TRADITION OF NATURALISM

CHAPTER XII

EVOLUTIONARY THEISTS

NATURALISM in religious thought has developed along three lines: one, motivated by a theological concern to discover evidence in nature for a theistic cosmology; another by a philosophical interest in formulating a metaphysics in the light of facts made available by the experimental and mathematical sciences; and a third, by the endeavor to formulate a philosophy of life based on the method and findings of the sciences which can guide and inspire the strivings of men. Out of the one have come various forms of natural theology, theistic evolution, and evolutionary theism. Out of the second have developed realistic formulations of cosmic theism. Out of the third have arisen the more strictly empirical philosophies of religion such as religious humanism.

Evolutionary theism is the contemporary successor to theistic evolution. During the eighties of the last century, idealistic philosophy began to make inroads upon American thought, with the result that theologians, who had been reluctant to take up with the theory of evolution, began to adapt evolutionary thinking to the essential postulates of Christian theology. Idealism had furnished the key to conceiving evolution in terms more amenable to religious faith than was possible with the philosophical formulations of the seventies, dominated by the materialism of Spencer and others. Scientists such as Le

Conte and Agassiz, and the philosopher John Fiske, gave vigorous support to this undertaking. Before the new century had dawned, it had become thoroughly respectable in liberal theological circles to affirm both God and evolution. Thus theistic evolution had bridged the gap between science and theology.

Within recent years, with the far-reaching discoveries in astro-physics, the focus of popular attention has shifted from the field of biology to astronomy and physics. These revolutionary developments in physics have led to radical changes in our concept of fundamental reality. The static concepts of the mechanistic outlook have been displaced by *operational concepts*.[1] Matter, once thought to consist of infinitely small, solid particles, has come to be described by the new physics in terms of wave-particles. The atom is a merry-go-round of electrons, moving within a field distinctive to their level of activity. Accordingly, the physical world described by Eddington, Jeans and Millikan is a world of process, a vast complex of related behavior. This concept of *activities within a field* has had development also in modern psychology in the concept of the *gestalt* or the pattern, and to a less extent in modern biology in the new conception of environment. Since the publication of Bergson's *Creative Evolution* in 1911 and Boodin's *A Realistic Universe* in 1916, modern philosophy has been turning more and more to an organic conception of reality. Within the last decade, a pronounced trend of thought emphasizing this organic character of the world has come into prominence, and has been designated *organismic philosophy*. Among the important contributions to this trend are: Sellars' *Evolutionary Naturalism*, Alexander's *Space, Time, and Deity*, Lloyd Morgan's *Emergent Evolution* and *Life, Mind, and Spirit*, Smut's *Holism and Evolution*, Boodin's *Cosmic Evolution* and his recent work on *God*, Noble's *Purposive Evolution*, and Whitehead's great work, *Process and Reality*.

Organismic philosophy, in so far as it undertakes to expound the evolutionary process, makes no religious commitments.

Each of the several systems, with varying divergences, describes cosmic evolution as proceeding along a course that involves levels of being. In some this hierarchy of levels is more pronounced than in others.[2] The religious aspect appears when they undertake to point out what, in the total process, is worthy of religious devotion. At this point these philosophers diverge in two directions: one group affirms the controlling operation of a Cosmic Mind and seeks in the evolutionary process for evidence to support this religious affirmation; the other group searches the cosmic process for whatever it may yield of highest worth without directing the search to any prior affirmation derived from religious convictions arising independently of naturalistic inquiry. The first of these groups we call evolutionary theists, and include, as contemporary representatives, J. E. Boodin, W. P. Montague, R. L. Calhoun, W. K. Wright and H. W. Wright.

JOHN ELOF BOODIN

The most complete and systematic metaphysics based upon cosmic evolution has been formulated by John Elof Boodin. In his series of studies beginning with *A Realistic Universe* (1916) and culminating in the recent volume, *God* (1935), he has contributed an impressive solution to the problems of religion. In the effort to account for the wonders of the evolutionary process, "the appearance of life as a new synthesis of energies, the appearance of new characters, new species and individuals in the life process, and for the order and adaptiveness of the evolutionary series," Boodin posits an eternal hierarchy of levels in the universe, each level being what it is and acting as it does because of interaction with higher levels.[3] In his latest book, *God,* he speaks of the cosmos as "a hierarchy of fields."

We may think of the structure of the cosmos as a hierarchy of fields. We are familiar with such a hierarchy in the human organism. There are the fields of the lower centers of the nervous system; there are also the cerebral fields and the psychological fields. The cerebral fields give definiteness and organization to the lower neural fields. . . . The cerebrum with its habits in turn is controlled by dominant interests which give direction and purpose to our activity as contrasted with the chaotic reveries when psychological control is weak. In the cosmos we must suppose a far greater range of fields — electro-magnetic fields, gravitational fields, chemical fields, organic fields, psychological fields, and, over and above them all, the supreme spiritual field which prescribes the architecture of all the subordinate fields, which in turn make their variant individual adjustments according to their own relativity. (P. 69.)

This " supreme spiritual field " is the field of life and mind, within which the " Genius " of the cosmos works, controlling, shaping and directing the course of evolution and events. This controlling and directing force is by no means arbitrary, but is conditioned by the degree to which *matter* can respond to the organizational or form-giving impetus. Furthermore, the control and interrelatedness within the whole is not merely mechanical communication from part to part in space and time. It is more psychological, as in living organisms, involving mutual adaptation and selection; but, as in the human organism, such interactions are determined by the unitary life of the cosmic organism and are in subservience to the genius of the organism as a whole. All intercommunication within the cosmos, then, is regulated by this spiritual field for the maintenance and health of the life of the whole.

This conception of the cosmos as a " superorganism " is reminiscent of Fechner's suggestive theory of cosmic organism. But Boodin's cosmology goes beyond the anthropomorphism of Fechner's view. He recognizes the inadequacy of his analogy in likening the cosmos to the human organism, pointing out that there are pluralistic conditions in the universe that are not dominated by life and mind and in which life and mind are not manifest. Boodin's insistence upon the universe as a living whole is based upon insight which he gleans from the recent findings of the physical and biological sciences, bearing upon the new conception of environment. In contrast to the old mechanistic conception of atoms, which makes them independent in character and relations, the new physics views the electron as a wave or cosmic field extending through the whole of space. Thus the electron cannot possibly be understood when taken as an abstract individual entity. And furthermore, as Schrödinger has pointed out, the relations between groups of electrons can be understood only by conceiving them as wholes. As groups, they have a pattern or Gestalt.

"Now this structure or pattern within the atom," says Boodin, "is immanent in nature. The relations within the atom are not merely external and accidental, but they are due to the structure of the atom which is intrinsic or immanent in the atom itself and conditions the relations of atoms to one another in various compounds. The more complex structures like molecules and molar masses likewise have their immanent structures which determine their characteristic properties. Reality at the material level, then, is not a fortuitous combination of separate elements, but the individual includes the field. There must, therefore, be a structure of the whole which prescribes the relations, as well as the character of the parts."

If matter with its patterns can be understood only within the control of the cosmic field, argues Boodin, how ridiculous to suppose that, in the far more complicated matrix of life, nature falls back on chance. Accordingly, Boodin continues, in the light of the new physics we must postulate for life a universal field.

Thus the picture of the universe which we get from Boodin's metaphysics is a vast ongoing configuration, a community of activities, all integrated within fields peculiar to their level, which in turn are integrated within the vast community of fields that find their unity in the spiritual field of life and mind that dominates, controls and shapes the total process.

Yet Boodin would not have the cosmos viewed as a vast collective society in which the individual is so completely subordinated to the controlling field as to be shorn of individual freedom.

> We are not mere functions of the spirit of the whole [he writes], any more than an electron is a mere function of its relations within the atom. There is the factor of individual willingness and individual capacity. But in the spiritual field the participation in the whole becomes true freedom. The health of the individual soul can be maintained only by its creative co-operation within the spiritual whole of which it is a part, though, of course, we may court disease and suicide by refusing to enter into rapport with the whole. The spirit of the whole does not prescribe to the individual finite spirit what it must do, though the viable structure of spiritual life (as well as the structure of matter) is prescribed by the structure of the whole. Throughout nature, from matter to spirit, the individual retains the power of initiative and choice. . . . (*God*, pp. 93–94.)

Now what is it that integrates these many fields into an organic whole? What is it that has kept this total organic whole pulsating with ever new emergent activity throughout the aeons of time? What is it that has shaped the course of this emergent evolution toward ever higher and higher synthesis? It is God, the Genius that works within the whole, says Boodin.

> We cannot account for advance in evolution without assuming a cosmic guiding genius. Everything moves within the field of divinity and each part responds by creative adaptation as it is prepared to respond. (P. 35.)

The nature of God cannot be comprehended, says Boodin. Yet by analogy we may aesthetically depict him. In some such sense as we speak of the " soul of man," God may be conceived as the " soul of the cosmos." But we are not to think of the material world as the body of God in the sense that we think of the emergent human soul and its body. " The world," writes Boodin, " is rather the body of God as sound is the body of music or as the instrumentation gives body to the harmony. But the ultimate harmony is in the medium of God."

Yet Boodin is not content with identifying God wholly with

space or with the spiritual field. Real being is more than a field, he writes. It must have its individual aspect.

God, to be a creative artist and the Savior of those who seek, must be more than an impersonal field. He must be in some sense personal as well as omnipresent. But how this can be, our limited minds cannot fathom. (P. 128.)

In some sense, then, according to Boodin, God is a personal being. More than that, he is a being who shares in the tragedy and pain of the world. He is conceived

as incarnating himself in space and time, laboring, suffering, dying in the tragic struggle to overcome the indifference of nature, within man and outside; yet he is ever eternal and, therefore, the resurrection of spirit in new and higher ideals. . . . Instead of an awful picture of calm power, a stony image of gray, who beholds indifferently the course of a fated world . . . I think of God as the infinitely sensitive poet who suffers in the death of the beauty which he has created — in the destruction of material beauty, in the death of the flowers, in the death of the helpless animals, but above all in the death of the incarnations of spiritual beauty, because these, having required the greatest pain and having most of the quality of God, must be infinitely dear to him. Shall Socrates drink the hemlock and Jesus be nailed to the cross in divine devotion, and God not suffer? A God who does not feel pain could feel no compassion, the most precious attribute of God. . . . And if his love suffers with ours to stain in beauty the mosaic of our life in the spirit, shall he not retain the mystic pattern? We must abandon our attempts to picture God, and accept the mystery of an eternal God living the tragic life of time, just as science accepts the mystery of light as being both a particle and a wave — though it cannot picture such duality — because experience requires both. . . . We must confess with humility that we cannot understand how God can be eternal and perfect, and yet be immanent in the temporal striving of history, incarnating himself in mortality. But if we must think of God in terms of our highest human experience, can we deny to him the things which make human experience significant?

This daring and devout portrayal of cosmic reality by Boodin stands in its own right as an achievement of high order. In constructing his metaphysics, he has employed the method common to the tradition of idealism, namely, that of positing imaginative hypotheses and then weaving his postulates into a consistent whole. Yet Boodin is an idealist only in the Platonic sense. He will have none of that form of modern idealism that makes only mental phenomena real. The ultimate unity of existence for Boodin is an " activity system " — individual systems of activity in action, reaction and interaction with one another. And in this he is in accord with the new physics. At this point he clearly distinguishes himself from both the Absolutist and the Personalist. He further diverges from the Absolute Idealist by insisting, with the Personalist, that God, persons, and the world of nature are distinct and separate realities, although unlike the Personalists he achieves an organic world unity through his concept of the controlling cosmic field.

Boodin's distinctive idealistic trait, however, is that he posits Mind as the pervading and controlling guide of cosmic evolution.[4] Thus while the " activity-system " is the ultimate unit in analysis, the ultimate reality in synthesis, according to his view, is mind, which is a basic idealistic postulate. It is to be noted that in this fundamental observation Boodin is supported by the modern physicists.[5] There is a suggestive note, therefore, in the insistent theme of Boodin's recent book that our age is destined to move on toward a renascent idealism, an idealism that portrays cosmic life as purposive, and that inspires men with the call to " recreate the world into a better world, with the assurance that a power, greater than ourselves, is on the side of the creators."

WILLIAM PEPPERELL MONTAGUE

The philosophy of religion developed by Montague has all the characteristics which distinguish the evolutionary theists. Like them he is very attentive to the teachings of modern science and approaches the subject of religion with the scientific view of the world well fixed in his mind. Like them his problem is first to establish the fact of God on the solid basis of natural knowledge. To this extent all in this group are naturalistic.

But what we can thus know with assurance, says Montague, is entirely insufficient to make a religion worth having. A religion that makes no claim concerning the nature of reality beyond what any informed and reasonable person would admit, is not worth discussing. The only kind of religion that he would consider is one " that is neither certainly and obviously true nor certainly and obviously false, but possibly true, and, if true, tremendously exciting. The question of its truth or falsity is exciting and momentous because it is a question, not of the validity of this or that theory as to the nature of the physical world or as to the origin and destiny of the human race, but because it is the question whether the things we care for most are at the mercy of the things we care for least." [6]

This attitude toward religion would lead us to put Montague's philosophy of religion under the tradition of romanticism. But all the evolutionary theists are on the borderline between the two traditions of romanticism and naturalism. They are moving toward naturalism after the fashion we have indicated, but they retain most of the traits which we have seen in the ethical intuitionists. In respect to all of them it is difficult to say on which side of the line they should be placed. They are somewhat more naturalistic than the others so we place them at the beginning of the group that moves deeper and deeper into naturalism as the book proceeds.

The fact of God, which could never give the exciting kind of religion which is the only kind that interests Montague, but is so well established by his reasoning that no informed and educated mind could reject it, is stated by him thus:

Material nature makes altogether too many winning throws for us not to suspect that she is playing with dice that are loaded, loaded with life and mind and purpose. This is the solution that seems to me the almost inevitable solution of the problem which, for want of a better name, I have called the Problem of Good.

And so we are confronted with a God, or something very like a God, that exists, not as an omnipotent monarch, a giver of laws and punishments, but as an ascending force, a nisus, a thrust toward concentration, organization and life. This power appears to labor slowly and under difficulties. We can liken it to a yeast that, through the aeons, pervades the chaos of matter and slowly leavens it with spirit.

This thrust toward organization is known with such measure of certainty that Montague can say it is the "almost inevitable solution" of the Problem of the Good. That is to say, the facts of value which we find in the world practically demonstrate the reality of God in this sense. But if you stopped with such an idea of God you would have a religion which Montague scorns as one of platitudes and truisms.

So, after getting this purely naturalistic idea of God, Montague develops it into "an exciting possibility" by showing how it might be a Cosmic Mind. But this Cosmic Mind must have a will that is finite in power. The facts of evil show this. The will of this Cosmic Mind is laboring against great obstacles which prevent it from making a better world than what we have.

Montague notes that advancing civilization is giving the mind of man more and more power. Man is destined to overcome the evils of life so completely that a religion which cherished belief in God because of the help which God can give in time of trouble and perplexity will be outgrown. What then would be the value of God for a triumphant humanity that is subjecting nature to the service of its needs? The answer is that man craves infinity yet never can be infinite, no matter how completely he masters the ills of existence and magnifies the goods. This craving for infinity can never be satisfied except by mystic union with the Cosmic Mind of God. That there is such a Cosmic Mind we do not know. One can scarcely even say it is a probability. But it is a possibility.

To those who say there is no such Mind, Montague replies:

Perhaps you are right, but there is a chance that you are not. There is at least a chance that there is an upward-tending power in nature to account for such adaptations as we find. There is at least a chance that the cosmos as a whole has a unitary life and consciousness and that the evolutionary nisus is its will which, though not omnipotent, is omnipresent.[7]

In the statement just quoted Montague has combined two propositions which are very different in respect to the probability of their truth. That there is an upward-tending power in nature has all the surety of an almost inevitable solution of the problem of the good. But that this power has a consciousness and will that is omnipresent is the tremendously exciting possibility which, if true, would make " one's world . . . radiant, and one's life become a high romance."

ROBERT L. CALHOUN

A brilliant contribution has been made to the thinking of this group by Professor Calhoun of Yale. Belief in God, says Calhoun, does not come from authority and revelation, as the supernaturalists claim; nor from response, observation and reason directed to the process of nature in which we live, as the naturalists say. It comes from deeper levels, from something that is deeper than thinking.

My own belief in God, and I suspect that of many others who believe, has been generated painfully enough, not by argument but by the concrete ebb and flow of living, in ways that I do not fully understand and cannot control.[8]

Our own belief in God arises in the first instance not out of our thinking about the world and man, but as response more primal than thinking to impacts of unfathomable reach.[9]

Of course it could be said that our belief in everything that exists, such as stones, dirt, trees, houses, mountains, originates in something deeper than thought, namely, reactions of organism to physical environment. But Professor Calhoun does not mean anything so commonplace as that. He means that there is something unique about the source of this belief in God. Therefore he is not a naturalist. But neither is he a supernaturalist. He is not clearly a mystic; and he is not an idealist. But he holds that there is in the universe a cosmic mind which is God.

The chief support which modern science and philosophy offer for this belief in Cosmic Mind is emergent evolution, says Calhoun. According to this doctrine there emerges from purely physical existence that kind of existing thing which we call a living organism. Then, after some time, there emerges from the order of existence which is purely biological that higher order called psychological. Later on emerge the rational and moral, making that creative, ordering kind of existence called the human mind. The human mind has one striking characteristic. It strives to bring forth higher and higher orders of existence. Here we have clue, according to Calhoun, for believing God is a cosmic mind. The fact of emergence of higher orders out of lower supports this belief.

Now a physical system has in it nothing which would render probable the emergence of a living organism. Yet, according to the theory of emergence, living organisms did emerge out of a prior state of existence in which there was the physical only. How could this highly improbable event occur? It might occur once by chance. But out of living organisms still higher orders emerge which are equally improbable, and this keeps on to higher and higher levels. While the evidence is not conclusive all this would seem to indicate that there is something operating over and above the physical system, to give rise to the living organism which would otherwise be so improbable. The same is true when mind emerges from a system that is purely biological.

But what is this Something which is operating over and above the physical, over and above the biological? Whatever it may be in addition, it is Mind. We believe it is mind because it seems that the only thing in existence which works to achieve higher orders of being is mind. The human mind does this, and nothing else in existence does, except this Something, so far as we have discovered to date. Since this Something has this characteristic of mind, we can reasonably assume, on the principle of analogy, that it is mind.

Thus faith in Cosmic Mind, concludes Calhoun, which is so essential to moral and religious living, is supported by the teachings of emergent evolution and finds itself at home in the modern world of thought.

HENRY W. WRIGHT

Professor Wright of Canada has not received the attention in the United States which the merit of his work deserves. *The Religious Response* opens the way for new developments in religious thinking that have not been followed as they might.

He shows that things and events in the world have characters and possibilities by virtue of which they progressively form an objective order of value. Value is not found in things as such, but is found (1) in the way things are so related by identities and differences as to exemplify a coherent rational order, (2) in the way they can be functionally connected for utilitarian purposes and (3) in the way qualities are so related to one another as to mutually vivify and enrich and form an aesthetic whole. Thus value consists of an order or system of relations by which things and events and possibilities are made meaningful, useful and beautiful. It is this order that constitutes value, and not the world otherwise. Of course this order pertains to the world only when sensitive, appreciative and intelligent minds deal with it. But it is there, relative to minds, as truly as anything else is there in the objective world of reality.

This order is not finished. It grows. It develops chiefly through the intercommunication of minds, by which the meaningful relations, the useful devices and the aesthetic qualities discovered by one individual are communicated to others. Each individual has access, more or less, to this order which is brought to light by the intercommunication going on among all.

Such is the organized system of valuable objects or, as it has sometimes been called to distinguish it from the system of physical objects, the *realm of ends*. The realm of ends is a developing system, a diversified

unity, which is constantly revealing new possibilities of expansion and enrichment. This it does in all three types of relation by which it is organized. Suppose that an object is understood in terms of its relation
to the intelligible system. This does not exhaust its intellectual interest.
On the contrary, it offers to attentive thought greater and more varied
possibilities of meaning to be explored and appreciated. Since the living
organism has been understood by evolutionary science in its wider and
cosmic relations, its processes have become an ever more fascinating and
fruitful subject of study. The same is true of the fossil as understood
by the geologist, the relics of earlier civilizations as interpreted by the
archaeologist, and of similar objects in every field of investigation. The
evocation of new and useful properties in existing materials and forces
by inventive skill has not diminished but increased their possibilities of
adaptation to rational purposes. This is well illustrated by the recent
remarkable progress in mechanical invention and control. The invention
of the telegraph and telephone with the discovery of electro-magnetic
waves led to the invention of the wireless telegraph, the broadcasting of
speech and music, and television. In the same way, the beauty of the
sunset sky, the cultivated countryside, the surging waves, grow as we
contemplate them. Because of the new intimations of meaning which
a great work of art is constantly suggesting to our attentive scrutiny, it
is a constantly increasing source of enjoyment.

Our activities of appreciation are responses to the real value of existing
objects. This value consists in their possibilities or potencies or original
contribution to the organized system to which all by virtue of their distinctive characteristics belong. In our appreciations we respond to the
infinitely diversified, continually growing unity of the real world, the
cosmic reality — and to objects in their relation to this universal
system.[10]

This growing order of value thus discovered and known is
the rightful object of religious response. But it is only the
irreducible minimum. For a fully developed and powerful
religion one must have more. One must have a Cosmic Mind
and Purpose which sustains this order of value and holds the
completed and perfect form of it eternally in mind. This
Cosmic Mind we cannot know with the certitude we know the
developing order of value. The order of value we can know
by scientific method, says Wright. The characters and relations which make things intelligible is precisely what scien-

tific investigation brings to light. But the Cosmic Mind is an object of faith.

Why must we have the Cosmic Mind for full-orbed religious living? For several reasons. For one thing, suppose this earth should be destroyed or suppose, through some catastrophe, the human race would be reduced to a few roving savages. What would become of the order of value? It would sink to small proportions or disappear entirely unless there is a Cosmic Mind which holds it forever in reality. Still again, where was this order of value before men existed or any living thing existed? Professor Wright considers various attempts to meet this difficulty but thinks none are satisfactory except the postulate of a Cosmic Mind.

Finally, religion requires a Cosmic Mind in its distinction from morality. Morality seeks to explore and develop the order of value to its highest fulfillment. But it does this by seeking out and developing one part after another of the order of value. Religion, on the contrary, reveres and seeks access to the whole, perfect and completed order of value. But there is no completed order of value unless there is a Cosmic Mind which can hold it forever in ideal perfection while it is being partially achieved in this imperfect world.

Here is the tendency toward realism, but insistent retention of the Cosmic Mind of idealism. Here is the rigorous use of all the methods of intellectual inquiry to discover the realities that concern religion; but after thus establishing a solid substructure, there is added the further beliefs that are needed for moral optimism. Here is a coherent system of thought carried as far as it will go, but finally sacrificing the neatness of a system to meet the practical demands of religious living. Here is mediation between the best findings of modern thought and the religious tradition. All these are traits which characterize the romantic intuitionists described in a previous section. The only reason we cannot classify Boodin, Montague, Calhoun and Wright with the romanticists is that they base their philosophy of religion much more solidly on the findings of the sciences then do the thinkers who make religious experience the foundation stone. The men we are now considering also keep an eye on religious experience and draw upon it. But they expend most of their intellectual labor in searching the knowledge brought forth by science to discover what there is in all this scientific teaching which can be turned to religious purposes and made to support religious convictions. The romanticists will turn their back on science if it seems to conflict with the requirements of religious experience. The theistic evolutionists would not do this.

This concept of Cosmic Mind, controlling and directing the evolutionary process in the universe, is developed to some extent also in the philosophy of W. K. Wright, as revealed in his book, *A Student's Philosophy of Religion,* and in an essay, "God and Emergent Evolution" (in *Religious Realism,* Chap. XIII). W. K. Wright is insistent upon the evidence of teleology in the cosmic course, but prefers to identify "the third level" or dominating level of reality with the characterization of "person" rather than "mind." Yet his logic carries him to the conclusion that it is Mind in the Cosmic Person that ultimately controls and provides purpose in the process.

This point of view has the double advantage of being grounded in a thoroughgoing scientific cosmology, yet metaphysically constructed to satisfy the life of the heart. In setting up their metaphysics, these philosophers readily acknowledge that what they affirm regarding the purposive control of the cosmos is affirmed as a venture of faith. Says one of their representatives:

Life always turns out to be a venture of faith. The question is: Does the conviction of the divine illumine the world of which we are a part, does it give a new quality to life? One does not prove the existence of music or poetry or love to those that have the experience. . . . The quality of divinity is present everywhere to him who is qualified to experience it — as the quality of the artist is present in his work, as the quality of the soul is present in the behavior of the organism.

These philosophies of religion, based upon the teleology of cosmic evolution, provide the contemporary expression of one of the foremost arguments for theism. Their systems of thought, for the most part, give evidence of being more intelligently grounded in the insights of the physical sciences and more sensitive to the wider area of data affecting the religious synthesis than any of the earlier systems of natural theology. Consequently, there is promise that this line of reasoning may become increasingly fruitful in its contributions to the metaphysical problem.

[1] See Bridgman's *Logic of Modern Physics*.

[2] This theory of a hierarchy of levels is developed in the works of Sellars, Boodin and Morgan.   [3] *Cosmic Evolution*.

[4] In this he differs from such organismic philosophies as that of Smuts, Sellars and Whitehead and approximates the views of Alexander and Morgan.

[5] See for example, Jeans' *The Mysterious Universe* in which he concludes that the universe looks more and more like a " big thought."

[6] *Belief Unbound*, by W. P. Montague, p. 66.   [7] *Ibid.*, pp. 97–99.

[8] *God and the Common Life*: R. L. Calhoun. Scribner, 1935. P. 3.

[9] *Ibid.*, p. 206.

[10] *The Religious Response*: H. W. Wright. Harper, 1925. Pp. 155–57.

CHAPTER XIII

COSMIC THEISTS

THE significant developments in astro-physics and related sciences have given rise to another group, more realistic in temperament and approach than the evolutionary theists. As compared with the views thus far considered, these philosophers have been more thoroughgoing in their effort to reconstruct religion in terms of the scientific world-view, and more consistent in applying the scientific method to its concepts. As contrasted with the humanists, who also lay claim to a thoroughly scientific outlook, these cosmic theists are dominated more by the physical than by the social sciences. Humanism, being essentially shaped by pragmatic interests, has kept within the purview of the social sciences; hence its preoccupation with the social process.

However, the chief difference between the humanists and the cosmic theists can be seen if we take a clear statement of the humanistic position and compare it with the outlook and purpose of the cosmic theists. Professor Haydon has stated the position of the humanist very clearly in the following words: " Taken thus naturalistically, the religions of the world may be understood as the manifold ways in which human life has sought to mold a cosmic process to the service of man's growing ideal."[1]

Now the cosmic theists are diametrically opposed to this position in one particular. While the humanists consider religion the way human life seeks to mold a cosmic process to the service of man's growing ideal, the cosmic theists regard religion as the endeavor of human life to mold man's growing ideal to the service of a cosmic process. The humanists make the growing ideal of man the supreme guide and sovereign over human life, while the cosmic theists put some cosmic process or order in this place of sovereignty.

Nevertheless the cosmic theists, the humanists, the humanistic theists and the empirical theists are all united on one principle and so stand as a group over against all the other philosophies of religion we have been considering up to this point. This principle which distinguishes them from all the others is stricter adherence to the scientific method in developing their view of the supreme reality which concerns religion.

The evolutionary theists, discussed in the section preceding, make large use of the findings of science. They use these findings to support a belief in God which has its basis elsewhere than in these findings or in the method of science. Professor Calhoun, as we have noted, makes this very plain.

The cosmic theists, on the other hand, do not start with a belief in God which they try to defend by using the findings of science to support the concept of a divine ground and goal of the process of nature. Rather they seek to find something in the process itself which they can hail as the reality demanding our supreme devotion.

The cosmic theists are represented by Whitehead, Northrop, Conger, Noble and Overstreet.

ALFRED N. WHITEHEAD

Whitehead has written a powerful defense of rational speculation.[2] But he makes it abundantly plain that it can never reach truth by itself alone. Its great value, he declares, is to direct and test future observations. These finespun and farflung speculations are like a great gossamer net which will catch many a fleeting observation and make it significant when it would otherwise sink into oblivion with nothing to indicate it had ever occurred. These speculations are of value only as they provide a network to be filled in with observations. Until they are filled in, they give us no knowledge of existing reality.

Also Whitehead insists on the importance of intuition. But his treatment of the matter seems to indicate that he means either or both of two things. He seems to mean at times the emergence into the mind of a new speculative proposition, to be used in guiding, inspiring and giving meaning to observations. At other times, he means new observations which arise because of some highly sensitized state of the psycho-physical organism or because of some strategic situation in which it is placed.

Thus his emphasis upon the importance of rational speculation on the one hand, and on intuition on the other, would not seem to depart from the canons of scientific method as we have been using that term. This method can be exemplified in his inquiry concerning the nature of God.

Whitehead discusses God under two aspects. One he calls the primordial nature of God. Almost the whole of his philosophy is pervaded with the idea of God in this aspect. The other aspect of God he calls the consequent nature. This he introduces only very briefly in a few pages in his great work, *Process and Reality*. We shall consider first the primordial nature of God.

For Whitehead, God is a character to be found in the natural process of existence. God is not for him, as with most philosophies of religion, a reality to be reached by some speculative venture. In Whitehead's philosophy we do not find God in any other way than we find anything else in the natural world that is all about us. God is one factor in this natural world that is open to our daily observation. God has his being there and is to be sought and found there in the same way that we come to know other features of this natural world.

For Whitehead, God is not even *the* ultimate reality. If any-thing in nature can be called ultimate as over against all else, it is what he calls the creative advance into novelty or, more simply, creativity.

"Neither God, nor the World, reaches static completion. Both are in the grip of the ultimate metaphysical ground, the creative advance into novelty."[3]

God clings to this process of creativity. He is to be found as an order in this process. He does not make this process go. He is not the power back of it. Why does this process keep going on and on and on without end? For no reason at all. It keeps on going and always will because it is the ultimate nature of things to go and go and go. Whatever meaning and value is brought forth out of this process is due to God, but the process itself is not due to God. Rather, if one is to speak in such terms, God is due to it. That is to say, without this process of creativity there could be no world, God could not create a world. There would be no ordering power making for value. But to speak of what would be left, were this process of creativity wiped out, is to speak in meaningless terms, be-cause everything we can mention presupposes this process. Per-haps it makes more sense to say there are three kinds of ultimate reality — this process, God and the eternal forms or possibilities which come into existence and pass out of existence.

But we must first get some understanding of this creative process if we would have any grasp of Whitehead's idea of God. This ongoing process consists of an infinity of tiny units of existence forming themselves and then perishing, followed by others coming into existence and passing out and so on and on. They are the ultimate units, call them atoms or electrons or whatever. But they are not inert pellets of matter as people once thought atoms to be. They are minute organisms. They begin, they strive and grow, they reach maturity and perish; and all this occurs in a volume of space so tiny and during a period of time so brief, that we can scarcely imagine it. The process of creativity is just the continuous emergence of these innumerable droplets of existence, beginning, growing and perishing, beginning, growing and perishing without end. That the process of existence is made up of such tiny organic units is not mere speculation on the part of Whitehead. Modern science indicates that all matter is made up of something like this.

These tiny organisms may be progressively organized into living cells, into multi-cellular organisms, into human personalities, into social groups, into huge societies, into epochs of history. Any such unit of existence, whether it be a single tiny droplet or a living cell or an epoch of history, Whitehead calls an epochal occasion. Also he has called them events. Doubtless he does this to get away from such common words as " thing," because " thing " always suggests something static. These events or epochal occasions are not inert things. Nothing that exists is an inert thing. Always it is going on, striving, reaching forth, perishing and giving rise to some further event that also grows to maturity and dies.

This constant coming into existence, growing and perishing of events is not the work of God. It simply goes on because it is the ultimate nature of the universe to go on without end. But God has very important work to do in this process. This work of God must be made plain.

Each of these tiny droplets of existence strives to organize itself. It does not strive to organize the universe. The tendency of each droplet is to work for itself in disregard of all others. That is to say, it would do so were it not for God. Each droplet works to preserve itself and complete itself by gathering up all the influences emanating from other droplets and organizing them in such a way as to reach its own fulfillment. Now it is plain that if each operates in this way they must all frustrate and destroy one another and the world fall into chaos, unless, over and above all these innumerable organisms, there is some organizing power which regulates their interactions in such a manner that each can find fulfillment without being destructive of the others.

Observation makes plain that while these droplets or epochal occasions do work in this self-centered way, yet the world does not fall into complete chaos. There is mutual frustration and destructiveness aplenty, to be sure, yet at the same time there is an amazing amount of mutual support and mutual helpfulness in reaching fulfillments. But this mutual helpfulness does not come from anything in the nature of epochal occasions themselves. It does not come from the process of creativity. Yet it is present. It is an observable fact. Now this observable fact is, for Whitehead, the reality of God. God is this mutual adjustment, mutual helpfulness, the mutual support that all epochal occasions find in attaining their several fulfillments respectively.

It is very plain, however, that God is not almighty because the obvious fact stares us in the face constantly that there is a vast amount of mutual frustration and destruction along with mutual support. Of course if one claims that God is a power outside this process of existence working upon it to bring about just so much mutual support and no more, then one might accuse God of responsibility for not exercising himself more to achieve a greater measure of mutual support and stop this ghastly destructiveness which is so widely present throughout the cosmos.

But this hypothesization of a power back of the process working upon it from the outside is exactly what Whitehead does not do. It is this kind of postulation which most philosophies of religion perpetrate and which Whitehead constantly condemns. It is just this kind of postulation which makes these other philosophies less scientific than that of Whitehead. Whitehead stops with the observable facts. He formulates whatever theory is required to account for observable facts, and no more. He finds this fact of mutual support in the creative process. This fact is something more than the bare creative process taken by itself alone. When he finds this fact he stops there and does not claim that God in his primordial nature is anything more than just this fact. He takes the same attitude toward the creative process. When he finds that it goes on and on and on, he does not hypothesize a power back of it to make it go. He simply stops with the fact that it goes. Apparently the very nature of it is to go. Why then claim that there is anything back of it to make it go, until observable evidence indicates there is?

This, we say, is the scientific method or, if one prefers not to call it that, it is one method as distinguished from others. The same difference in method can be noted in explaining simpler things, such as a flowing stream. When early man found the stream flowing he was not content to analyze the process of the flowing. Rather he imagined a God that made the stream flow. But scientific method said that all this talk about gods making the stream go is the lyric exuberance of human fancy. Let us stop with the fact that the stream does go and simply analyze this " go " of the stream. After we have analyzed it, we can synthesize it again into the total concept of the flow. There may be no limit to this process of analyzing and synthesizing, but at any rate such procedure is different from the method of postulating a power back of the stream to make it go and then assume we have reached the final explanation. So it is with the whole flowing process of nature.

But why does Whitehead give the name of God to this fact of mutual support in the creative process? He does so because this reality is the most precious reality there is. It is the greatest value that is or ever can be. It is itself the supreme value. Therefore it rightly demands the supreme devotion of all human living. What does that, is God; because the basic perennial use of the word God by all devout people has been to designate the reality which has this rightful place of sovereignty over human life and over the heart's highest loyalty. Not what all men serve supremely, but what they ought to serve supremely, is God. But what is that which they should serve supremely? Plainly it can only be what is supremely worthful. This fact of mutual support is precisely that.

This fact of mutual support, when taken simply as a fact and not used as a springboard from which to leap out into speculative realms, is an order. That is what Whitehead calls it. He calls it the primordial order. It is primordial because it must be the one order that always was and always will be as long as there is any world at all. Without it there would be only chaos. It is the primordial order that gives to the world whatever mutual support can be found there. This order of mutual adjustment is what makes it possible for each epochal occasion to fulfill itself instead of destroying itself in interaction with other epochal occasions. Hence it is the sustainer and maker of all value.

But an order is not a physical force. It cannot exert power over the process of existence. How then can an order, even a primordial order, do anything to make the creative process move in one direction rather than another? A power working on the creative process from the outside might deflect it toward mutual support and away from mutual destruction of epochal occasions. But this primordial order which is God is not a power outside the process. How then can it make any difference? The answer to this question reveals one further important fact about God.

This primordial order does not exercise physical force on the creative process from the outside. It could not, for to do that would be a self-contradiction. Physical force, force of any kind, can be nothing else than some process of existence. Hence to speak of a force working on the process of existence from the outside is to talk nonsense. But the primordial order of God does something more important than exert physical force or force of any kind.

What the primordial order of God does to give value to the creative process is to hold over it forever all the different forms of order which might enter into it. If we may speak in crude figurative language, God presses against creative process all these forms of order so that they can slip into the process whenever circumstances permit. Of course, speaking literally, you cannot exert the force of pressure with abstract, disembodied forms, and the primordial nature of God does not exert physical force in any case. Expressing the matter more literally we should say that the primordial order of God is that order by virtue of which all these forms are forever relevant to existence, so that as existence passes through its endless transformations some of these orders enter into the process and thus the process becomes ordered more or less. One order in the process tends to make way for more order, and so on and on. But all these forms of order, that is to say, all these different ways in which epochal occasions can be adjusted to one another in mutual support, constitute an infinite system of orders. This infinite system is comprehended by the primordial nature of God and is eternally relevant to the process of creativity by virtue of this primordial order which is God. Over the ceaseless turmoil of existence forever looms this ethereal dome of eternal forms of order ready to enter existence, bringing truth, beauty and goodness whenever the flux of events opens the way.

With this interpretation we see the meaning of such statements as the following by Whitehead: " God's role is not the combat of productive force with productive force, of destructive force with destructive force; it lies in the patient operation of the overpowering rationality of his conceptual harmonization. He does not create the world, he saves it; or, more accurately, he is the poet of the world with tender patience leading it by his vision of truth, beauty and goodness." His phrase " conceptual harmonization " means the comprehension of all the forms of order in serried rank within the all-inclusive primordial order.

The work of God is always to bring more harmony into the world. But simple words like harmony are dangerous. They suggest a simplicity that falsifies reality. This harmony in fact is very complex. It means that each epochal occasion, as it comes into existence and grows to fulfillment, shall receive all the influences from all other epochal occasions in such a way that, (1) these influences shall not neutralize one another and, (2) the epochal occasion that receives the influences shall not be destroyed by them, but (3) shall be brought to most complete fulfillment by them. Of course all this is a matter of degree. Influences always do neutralize one another more or less; and often they impair or destroy the epochal occasion that is influenced. Absolutely complete fulfillment may be never attained. It is always more or less; but God forever works to make it more.

This receiving of influences by an epochal occasion so that they do not neutralize and do not destroy one another, is not a conscious experience except in the case of the higher animals. Throughout most of the universe it is unconscious. But when human beings experience it consciously to any high degree, they call it aesthetic experience. Aesthetic experience is experience in which many influences vivify instead of neutralize one another and at the same time do not impair or destroy the clarity of consciousness. Thus, when the primordial order of God reaches human consciousness with any degree of fullness, we have what we call aesthetic experience. That is the reason Whitehead calls God the aesthetic order of the universe.

Thus far we have been considering the primordial nature of God. We must examine briefly the other aspect of God called his consequent nature. This side of God's being is not nearly so basic in Whitehead's philosophy as is the primordial. Whitehead's system could not stand without the primordial nature. It enters into the essential structure. The consequent nature, on the other hand, is added on like dome and spire. It seems to be set forth to meet an insistent demand of high religion. Therefore we feel that Whitehead is reverting from the scientific to the pragmatic method when he sets forth this idea. However, as we said before, the scientific method is an ideal which no one fully attains. Thinkers differ only in the degree to which they approximate it. We believe Whitehead comes closer to it than almost any other thinker in the field of religion.

The consequent nature of God is added to meet the awful fact of evil which Whitehead sees and feels so keenly.

The ultimate evil in the temporal world is deeper than any specific evil. It lies in the fact that the past fades, that time is a perpetual perishing. . . . The present fact has not the past fact with it in any full immediacy. The process of time veils the past below distinctive feeling. There is a unison of becoming among things in the present. Why should there not be novelty without loss of this immediacy among things? [4]

Then a little later he adds:

The evil of the world is that those elements which are translucent so far as transmission is concerned, in themselves are of slight weight; and that those elements with individual weight, by their discord impose upon vivid immediacy the obligation that it fade into night. "He giveth his beloved sleep." [5]

Heroism, sacrifice, tragedy, beauty, the vision of truth, the exquisite perfection of an hour, all these perish. They sink into oblivion. At least so it seems when we view the process of creativity. Relentlessly, forever, this process drives on and everything is engulfed in the fading past. Not utterly, to be sure. All living things retain some of the past. There could be no development, no increase of value, if some of the value of the past could not be retained and built on in the present and handed on to enrich the future. If every moment had to commence again at zero, time would yield no gain of any sort. Living organisms, especially highly developed organisms, could not exist. But living organisms do exist. Growth does occur. Therefore we know the past is not utterly lost. All living things retain some of the past in some mysterious way, otherwise life could not advance from embryo to maturity and species could not rise to higher levels. Pre-eminently in human life

we see this accumulation of the values of the past in the form
of a growing culture. Indeed this seems to be the supreme
endowment of human life lifting it above the existence of all
other animals. Even when great cultures perish, there can be
hope that some future culture will recover some of its values
through archaeological and historical research. We see just
that going on before our eyes.

Yet with full acknowledgment of this accumulation of value
through time, there is a terrific loss. The sacrifice and striving
that comes to naught in the long last is a ghastly fact when one
considers it. Finally we must note that those powers of consciousness, memory, mentality, and the eternal forms by which
values are conserved, have little power. The brutish masses of
existence that hurtle through time with scarcely any conservation of the past have most of the physical force, while "those
elements that are translucent so far as transmission is concerned,
in themselves are of slight weight."

Is there any deliverance from this awful wastage? How can
the values of the past be conserved that good may grow? It is
conserved and it does grow to some degree. We see that. But
the conservation is so pitiably small compared to the wastage
and so precarious amidst the brutal masses that do not conserve
and do not foster the growth of good.

Now the consequent nature of God is the way of deliverance
from this wastage. The consequent nature of God is the gathering up of all the values as they arise and their conservation
in an everlasting consciousness that grows from more to more
as each epoch rises and perishes and delivers up the value which
it has achieved to this cosmic consciousness.

Is there such an all-conserving Cosmic Consciousness? We
believe that here Whitehead has indulged in a speculation,
driven to it by the awful tragedy of life. If he had proceeded
here as he did in treating the primordial nature of God, he
would have stopped with the observable fact that values are
conserved and do grow to some degree. This, he would have

said, is the consequent nature of God. But the human heart cries for more, as it views the continuous perishing of so much that is superbly precious. It cries for more and Whitehead yields to the appeal. " Religious experience " demands a God that will conserve all, and insure the inevitable growth of good in some realm beyond the evils of this world where moth and rust corrupt and the thief of time forever breaks through to steal. So in the face of this ultimate tragedy Whitehead yields and builds a dome of glory and perfection above this world which we know by observation and reason. How does he rear this dome? By analogical reasoning? By rational speculation? By intuition? By aesthetic experience? By faith? By revelation? It is not clear how he attains it, but there it is for the student to accept or reject as he will. The actual world as we know it is a very long way from the perfect aesthetic order achieved by this Cosmic Consciousness. But over this world, with all its destructive forces and perishings, hovers this perfect consciousness which shows a " tender care that nothing be lost." It is heaven:

What is done in the world is transformed into a reality in heaven, and the reality in heaven passes back into the world. By reason of this reciprocal relation, the love in the world passes into the love in heaven, and floods back again into the world. In this sense, God is the great companion — the fellow-sufferer who understands.

This consequent nature of God prehends every actuality for what it can be in such a perfected system — its sufferings, its sorrows, its failures, its triumphs, its immediacies of joy — woven by rightness of feeling into the harmony of the universal feeling, which is always immediate, always many, always one, always with novel advance, moving onward and never perishing. The revolts of destructive evil, purely self-regarding, are dismissed into their triviality of merely individual facts; and yet the good they did achieve in individual joy, in individual sorrow, in the introduction of needed contrast, is yet saved by its relation to the completed whole.

Such is " the patience of God, tenderly saving the turmoil of the intermediate world by the completion of his own nature."

This is the consequent nature of God. A glorious dream, some will say. A vision of reality, others will declare.

F. S. C. NORTHROP

In respect to their approach to the cosmic problem, in respect to the basic facts which they accept and the basic problem with which they struggle, Whitehead and Northrop corroborate one another. They reach very different conclusions, but the fact with which they begin and the problem which haunts them is the same. Both have achieved high mastery of modern science and so are able to see the universe as modern science reveals it. It seems that all the men who have attained this eminence encounter this basic fact and this fundamental problem, although many make no attempt to find a solution to it. But Whitehead and Northrop have that kind of restless, inquiring, dauntless mind which cannot let such a problem alone until something is done about it. Einstein, Jeans, Eddington, Bavink, each in his own way, have done something about it. The fact that all these men seem to see the same basic fact and the same cosmic problem would indicate that the fact and the problem is genuine, no matter how diverse the outcome of their several efforts to find a solution.

The fact seems to be this: The universe is made up of units which are highly active, call them atoms or what you will. The activities of these units are highly independent, one of the other. There is nothing in the nature of these units to keep them from frustrating and destroying one another and producing a hopeless confusion. Yet as matter of fact they do not fall into such confusion. Doubtless there is plenty of confusion and frustration, but at the same time there is a very high degree of order, of mutual adjustment and mutual support between all these seemingly diverse and relatively independent activities. How can we account for this mutual support and mutual adjustment? Whence does it come? It does not come from the atomic units. It cannot come from the higher organization of these units, such as animals and men and societies, for these latter could never have arisen if the microscopic units were not adjusted and organized sufficiently for these more complex bodies to arise.

Whence then comes this mutual adjustment and order?

That is the problem with which these men struggle. We have already seen the answer which Whitehead offers. Northrop suggests a different answer. He says that this order must come either from some abstract, disembodied order or else it must come from some physical force. There is no other alternative. But abstract, disembodied order has no power. It cannot do anything. Therefore this order must be due to some physical thing which exerts pressure upon all the innumerable diverse and thronging activities of the atoms. What can be the nature of this physical thing? Northrop concludes it must be a macroscopic atom which is a field of force encircling completely all the microscopic units and so forcing them together into some order of mutual adjustment. God, then, is this macroscopic atom enclosing all the universe in a perfect sphere which congests and orders all activities.

Why call this macroscopic atom God? For the same reason that anything has ever been called God. It is the source of all value and therefore the supremely worthful reality, demanding our highest devotion.

This idea of Northrop has many complexities which we cannot here discuss and such a brief statement can scarcely do it justice, but space forbids a fuller treatment. It would seem that Whitehead offers a solution in his primordial nature of God which requires less rational speculation and therefore is more scientific. But Northrop has rendered the high service required of all great thinkers, and that is to develop one answer to the scope and fullness necessary to appraise it and thus either eliminate it or follow it on to further inquiries.

GEORGE P. CONGER

Professor Conger, in his *World of Epitomizations* and his *The Horizons of Thought,* reveals the emerging outlines of a cosmic theism. But his work on philosophy of religion is yet to appear. He has promised that it will come forth, but it would be rash to attempt to set forth his interpretation of religion and the meaning of God before he himself had made his own statement. Therefore we cannot attempt a formulation of his thought here, although his writing makes plain that he is a thinker belonging to this group of cosmic theists.

EDMUND NOBLE

Another important contribution to modern metaphysics is Edmund Noble's *Purposive Evolution.* Noble bears some affinities with the evolutionary theists in that he bases his philosophy upon teleology and the evolutionary process; yet the temper of his thought allies him properly with the cosmic theists.

According to Noble, the universe is purposive, but he interprets purpose in a manner peculiar to his thought. The universe he believes to be one vast system of power which forever works to keep all stresses equalized. The power is enormous, overwhelming. Whenever any inequality of stress occurs, the whole universe operates to restore equality of tension. Just how differentiation of stresses ever began is not known. But now that it has occurred, all change, all motion, all growth, all thinking, all evolution is the purposive work of this universal system of power constantly to recover equilibrium of stresses and strains. All the diverse configurations which we find in the universe are due to this.

Motion and change of motion are ways through which differential stresses automatically eliminate themselves by finding their goal in configurations and forms that endure. And it is these forms which we know as teleological, purposive, intelligent. The sign of their teleology, simple and complex, incipient and complete, is equalized stress — the endurance which, relative as it may be, results from the automatic elimination of differential stress. They seem designed, put together for a purpose, display the character of intelligent adaptations, because they are so many goals of conservation reached by a self-maintaining universe engaged in converting differences into likenesses.[6]

The electrons form atoms, the atoms molecules, the molecules aggregate by a process which culminates for the inorganic in suns and planetary families; where conditions favor the higher kind of collectivism there arise the wonderfully complex combinations which make vital phenomena possible. . . . Chance may continue between systems ununified with each other, but within systems it is reduced by collectivization to a minimum. The whole drift of things from absolutism to relatedness is a drift toward purposiveness away from fortuity. Nor does the process differ when organisms gather into animal and human societies. Here also the unit, while remaining an individual organism, comes under the determination of its system. That man's subjection to his own society takes effect, not by a series of pushes and pulls, but through mental states involving consciousness, memory and will, neither makes the control less effective nor differentiates it in any fundamental way from the like process in the physical realm.[7]

All intelligence and purpose are found to be this working of the universe to achieve and preserve equilibrium. Thus the universe as a total system is purposive and intelligent. Thus it presents itself as the rightful object of religious concern.

The naturalistic approach to God and to religion, represented in part by the evolutionary theists, but much more clearly and fully by the theists we are now discussing, is the most distinctive expression of our times in the field of philosophy of religion. In so far as our age has made an original contribution to these ancient problems, it would seem to be here.

HARRY A. OVERSTREET

H. A. Overstreet has hoisted a sail that has caught the winds which are sweeping toward an idealistic and religious naturalism. He has discerned and brought to lucid expression the religious significance of such thinkers as Whitehead, Lloyd Morgan, S. Alexander and some of the philosophical scientists who see the religious possibilities of the cosmic view which modern science discloses. Since all these men, and Overstreet with them, base their philosophy of religion upon a view of the cosmos, they are properly called cosmic theists. No one has stated this cosmic theism with such deftness, clarity and simplicity as Overstreet. So we believe there is no better way to close the discussion of these thinkers than to give a series of quotations from his *Enduring Quest,* which is to date the most simplified statement of cosmic theism that we know. He first makes clear that it is a form of naturalism, but a *religious* naturalism that is diametrically opposed to the old materialism which once pre-empted this title.

Sometimes we are made to think that man fights nature. For example he builds up ethical codes which he does not find in nature. Nature is grim, bloody. Man, so we are told, tries to overcome nature and builds a life of mutual give and take that succeeds despite nature's difficult processes. Sometimes, again, we are made to think that nature fights man. There are tornadoes, thunder and lightning, earthquakes, invading hosts of insects, sudden climatic changes. Thus man, we are taught, is a creature apart. He belongs to another order.

But this, when one thinks about it critically, can surely not be true. Is it not a left-over of the old dualism that produced, among other things, the religion of supernatural magic? There were supposed to be two spheres — the natural and the supernatural — and man was supposed to belong by kinship to the supernatural.

All our later thinking, however, tends to go counter to this. The trend of modern science has been in the direction of making man a creature of nature. If, then, we find certain qualities in man, we must apparently conclude that they are qualities which, to that extent, belong to nature. Man, in short, is nature on one of nature's levels.

Man, therefore, does not fight nature. On the contrary, what we call "fighting nature" is merely man's refusal to remain within the narrow areas in which he first finds himself. He struggles to release himself into wider areas. His ethical codes, for example, mark the development of more adequate ways of functioning. Thus he fights his limited nature, not Nature.

In point of fact, creatures which we ordinarily regard as so intimately parts of nature that we always think of them when we use the word

" nature " are largely isolated from wide relationship with nature. They move within exceedingly limited fields. They have only the smallest contact with the nature around them. Man, on the other hand, has the power to make contact with nature far more widely. When, for example, he discovers the movements of the planets, the laws of chemical combination, the sequences of the seasons, the principles of organic growth and decay, it is not an exaggeration to say that he is far more intimately and understandingly a child of nature than the armadillo that noses about ignorant of all these matters.

It seems that we need to impress upon ourselves this rather novel idea, for the reverse one has too long held sway. *Man is far more a child of nature than any of the animals or plants around him.* And he is increasingly a child of nature as the growth of his intelligence makes him able to make contact with nature more widely.[8]

Thus far we have caught a glimpse of one quality or process which seems fundamental and persistent in human life. It is the process of integrating more of reality into one's functioning self, of becoming, in short, a more widely adequate whole.

It is in this drive toward more widely functioning life that something deeply essential in nature seems to be revealed. If human beings have this drive, then nature, the source and continuer of us, must *to that extent* be credited with the same drive. But then nature is apparently not meaningless or directionless. In one aspect of its being, at least, it is a progressive achievement of increasingly significant wholes.[9]

He examines the assertion that life has no meaning and the universe is indifferent to man, and makes this reply:

It is a view that bears investigating. At the very outset, however, we are arrested on our course. *We ourselves, the accusers of the universe, are then greater than the universe?* For we, at least, have justice in our hearts. . . . But let us apply our test. Let us take the first possibility that the universe is utterly irrational. By that we mean that irrationality is the fundamental reality, and rationality is an illusion. Let us try, now, to act out irrationality by being in every possible circumstance utterly irrational. One can predict the outcome. To act irrationally is almost instantly to court disaster. . . .

Or suppose, to take the second possibility, that we regard the scheme of things as incredibly cruel. Let us try to act out cruelty. We quickly note that it is a type of behavior which can maintain itself only with the greatest difficulty. Even when one is, with some success, extremely cruel one must make exceptions. One cannot be cruel to those upon whose protection one depends in order to carry out one's cruelty. As soon, in short, as one universalizes cruel behavior — is cruel to everyone under all circumstances — cruelty brings defeat. Cruelty, in other words, is another type of behavior that will not bear acting out. Apparently there is that in the nature of things which rejects it. Thus, if our test is a veritable one, cruelty is not, in an ultimate and enduring sense, a reality, but rather, in that same enduring sense, an unreality.[10]

Human life, in brief, grows more adequate as it grows increasingly competent in the linking of itself with the various realities of its environment. If this is true, then the basic education of life should be training in unification or integration. . . .

So, in various ways, we make him (the child) into a creature linked in wider scope with his world. That unquestionably is the true course which education must take. We do it clumsily and ineffectively as yet, and it is for this reason, doubtless, that, after an average course or schooling, men still do tragic things to each other, and women can still sentimentally bind up the wounds. But unsuccessful as we still are, the direction of life would seem clear. The way to truth is the way of fundamental integration. We achieve the thoroughly good life when we learn in all possible ways how to link our behaviors with reality around us in such measure that an enduring coherence results. Thus Truth and Beauty come together on the human level, in the Good.[11]

Thus even on our average plane we recognize that the true direction of life is toward living into a larger wholeness of life. We sometimes express it as the progress from the egocentric (the child's normal condition), to the increasingly socio-economic life — love, home, community, nation, world. The level of conscious life which Bucke describes is then simply a further stage in this progression. It is the stage in which the individual becomes vividly one with the universe. And because he becomes one with the universe he is transformed in all his being so that he becomes vividly one with his fellows. . . .

The foundation principle of the world, then, would indeed seem to be love, if we mean by love the urge to identify oneself with that which is beyond oneself and alluringly greater than oneself. Whether it be in the quest of the True, or the Beautiful, or the Good, in the creative passion of personal love, or in those high heroisms in which man yields himself in an utter devotion, the authentic movement is toward a oneness with what is loved. And whenever that movement is strong in him, there is no sense of deadness; there is a sense, rather, of kinship with what is far more living. Thus the most significant movement of man's experience would seem to be away from relative death to that which is more enduringly and veritably alive.[12]

God is, in infinite degree, the everlasting creative life that moves toward wholeness.

Obviously, everything that is of significance has come out of this quickening vitality of the universe. In the upthrust of centuries, life, mind, and personality have come. It would be strange, then, to accord to this cosmic *élan* less than that which has emerged from its own being. However, we shall err if we say that God is mind and personality. That, again, would be patterning upon the human. But may we not say that mind and personality are in this quickening vitality just as truly as we can say that this quickening vitality is in mind and personality? This that we see as the ektropic power of the universe is indeed personality, but is as far more than personality as the cosmic is beyond the merely human. Since, however, personality is the highest form of reality which we can contemplate, may we not be permitted, in our inadequate and metaphorical human way, to speak of this cosmic *élan* in personal terms?

There is, however, an immediate danger in this, for we shall at once be tempted to set this Person over against ourselves. We must keep to the difficult task of conceiving of this vitality not as an individual over against ourselves, but as a life in which we live and which itself lives in us.

If the divine is the quickening life in us, then we devote ourselves to that life in the degree that we respond to the deep impulse within us toward creative integration. This is far different from the traditional meaning of devoting ourselves by prayer and ceremony to a Deity who is afar in the heavens. On the contrary, this God is a life within ourselves. Again, we love this God in the degree that we love the life that is creatively uniting. This is very different from loving a Father in the heavens and at the same time, on earth, exploiting or killing our fellows. To love God is to love the processes of bringing life into a more vital integration. The scientist, in this sense, loves God as he ranges out into the universe to unite his mind with the yet unknown realities. In similar sense, the teacher loves God, as, standing before his class, he seeks to unite his hearers and himself in a oneness of understanding. The mother loves to integrate her life with the life of her child. Wherever, in short, there is the process of vital integration, there is God. Wherever there is a passionate love of integrating, there is the passionate love of God.[13]

There is much to indicate that the prevailing winds of human discovery and thinking are driving us toward a kind of naturalism that is ardently religious and loftily idealistic. The evolutionary theists discussed in the previous chapter show the beginning of the movement in this direction. They have not gone very far. They show it more in the pains they take to keep close to the findings of modern science when constructing the foundations of their faith, but not so much in the superstructure which is reared for the living of the religious life. The cosmic theists treated in this chapter are farther along the way toward a religious naturalism or, if one prefers, a naturalistic religion. The cosmic theists not only keep close to the *findings* of the sciences but they make more effort to use the method of science in rearing the superstructure of their living faith.

The religious humanists that follow seem to represent a sort of transitional stage of thought between the evolutionary and cosmic theists on the one hand, and the more extreme religious naturalists which we call the empirical theists, to be discussed later.

The characteristic of the religious humanists is that they rear their house of faith almost entirely out of the material consisting of the findings of the sciences, especially the social sciences. The reason they are transitional and have not gone all the way in constructing a naturalistic religion is that they have not made any effort to develop a form of scientific method fitted to religious inquiry. Instead they have depended on the teachings of the sciences. That is transitional to a fully developed naturalistic religion in the same way that a biology which depended on the teaching of physics for its subject matter would be transitional to a fully developed science of biology. Before we can have a naturalistic religion, the special field of inquiry that is peculiar to religion must be defined, just as each science or group of sciences has its special field. The basic principles of its subject matter must be clarified and its special method of inquiry must be formulated. The groups which we discuss after the religious humanists have made attempts to do this. The humanists tend, rather, to rest religion on the sciences without any attempt to give religion itself a distinctive naturalistic form and structure.

The cosmic theists discussed in this chapter are more naturalistic in their formulation of religion than were the evolutionary theists. The religious humanists are still more so, and as we move toward the end of the book we find thinkers moving outward farther and farther in this direction.

[1] *The Quest of the Ages:* A. Eustace Haydon. Harper, 1929. P. xiii.
[2] *The Function of Reason:* A. N. Whitehead. Princeton University Press.
[3] *Process and Reality.* Macmillan, 1929. P. 529.
[4] *Ibid.,* p. 517.
[5] *Ibid.,* pp. 517–18.
[6] *Purposive Evolution:* Edmund Noble. Holt, 1926. Pp. 205–6.
[7] *Ibid.,* p. 212.
[8] *The Enduring Quest:* H. A. Overstreet. Pp. 76–77.
[9] *Ibid.,* p. 81.   [10] *Ibid.,* pp. 142–143.   [11] *Ibid.,* pp. 169–170.
[12] *Ibid.,* pp. 246–247.   [13] *Ibid.,* pp. 264–265.

CHAPTER XIV

RELIGIOUS HUMANISTS

WHERE the impulse to bring philosophy and religion into conformity with scientific insight has been expressed in terms of the social sciences, the outcome has been some form of religious humanism. Two rather distinctive types may be distinguished: one arising from the psychological approach to religion, which takes the form of subjective theories of religion; the other from the sociological approach and the historical study of religious cultures, which is the more common form of religious humanism.

From the standpoint of supernaturalists and other theists outside of the tradition of naturalism, the total effect of this impulse to define religion in terms of the sciences has been to trim down its scope and dimension and to reduce its claims to interests well within the bounds of the human world. Naturalism has thus been regarded as a *secularizing* influence. The implication of this characterization is that philosophies of religion that undertake to come to terms with the sciences, taken as a tendency, represent simply a tendency to *naturalize the supernatural,* hence a negative procedure. While this tendency is certainly present in naturalism, it should not be regarded as its basic trait, nor as its primary objective. Naturalism stands for a constructive venture in religious interpretation. Its stand appears negative only when its views are categorically contrasted with the views of the supernaturalists, the idealists and the romanticists, which is but a way of saying that its dominant, affirming gospel is not discerned by such superficial contrasts.

Another fact to note is that naturalistic philosophies of religion have varied in the degree to which they have reflected the *iconoclastic* tendency, that is, the tendency to discard traditional concepts and to slough off their emotional garbs. The naturalistic theists, whose views we have just considered, leave the fabric of faith least tattered. Only to the degree that they make rigid application of the scientific method in constructing their philosophy of religion, do they diverge radically from the views of supernaturalists and these other philosophical theists. The basic concepts of the older structure remain unimpaired. Their divergence consists mainly in the qualifying attributes that are associated with the concepts: for example, the manner in which they deal with the character of God, whether it is personal or impersonal, infinite or finite.

Religious humanism goes further in relinquishing traditional concepts. Although not committed to an antitheistic position in every case the humanists purposely minimize the "Godward" side with a view to focusing sharply the human interest. Accordingly, the God-concept is entirely secondary in the thinking of humanists and among those who carry the humanistic principle to an extreme conclusion, the God-concept is excluded altogether. In minimizing the significance of the objective dimension in religion, humanism is led to abandon also interest in concepts and practices that concern man's relations with objective reality. Consequently prayer, worship, or any other concept that implies adjustment or devotion to objective reality, are of secondary interest in humanism, if, in fact, they are included at all. Thus, from the standpoint of one who views religion in terms of the traditional categories, humanism is a *truncated supernaturalism*.

This negation of objective reality in religion has been carried even further among humanists who hold to subjectivist theories of religion. Motivated by a psychological analysis of religious behavior, they sever religious practice entirely from objective reality, and thus represent religion in its conventional forms as purely illusory.

It does not follow from this cursory survey of the humanistic procedure that the humanists are entirely negative in matters of religion. They are negative simply in relation to the claims of traditional religion and philosophical theism. Whether or not this actually does amount to negation of all religious value is, of course, a matter of point of view. An important fact to keep in mind, however, is that from the humanistic standpoint there is a positive and affirming aspect, even when the objective dimension is relinquished. Even the subjectivism of Feuerbach issued in an ardent plea to recognize the divine qualities, erroneously ascribed to deity, as genuine expressions of personal life and therefore highly significant. And in Comte's religion of humanity, worship of a supernatural deity was sublimated in the worship of humanity. Likewise in contemporary religious humanism, there is a positive outreach in the form of a passionate social idealism that looks toward the high fulfillment of man's possibilities through wise and sacrificial devotion to the end that he might control sub-human forces both in society and in the world of nature, and release the potential spiritual forces in man, himself. In considering the contemporary forms of religious humanism, it is important to keep these negative and positive aspects in balance.

SUBJECTIVISTIC THEORIES

The subjectivist form of humanism arising from the psychological approach to religion is represented in the writings of Everett Dean Martin,[1] James H. Leuba,[2] and W. K. Wallace.[3] This type of analysis was first advanced by Ludwig Feuerbach in his *Wesen des Christentums* (1841), later translated as *The Meaning of Christianity*. Feuerbach was concerned to " pierce to the living human needs which lie behind the ideas of religion." He sought to discover the source of dogmas in human feelings and impulses, fears and hopes, longings and wishes. His point of view is clearly expressed in his famous dictum, "All theology is psychology." He believed that feeling itself produces its object. The wish, then, according to Feuerbach, is the fundamental phenomenon in religion. He establishes his position in the following manner:

Man can never get beyond his own nature: all his conceptions and thoughts bear his own stamp. Hence we may learn to know his nature from the objects to which he relates himself. At the very beginning man has no reason to mark out limits to his nature. He quietly surrenders himself to all ideas, and attributes to them unlimited validity. It is especially characteristic of the nature of feeling that it is inclined to infinitise its object, to regard it as real. Doubt, then, can only arise when man learns to know his limits, and when understanding begins to distinguish between the subjective and objective, a distinction which is unknown from the standpoint of faith. For faith is nothing else than belief in the absolute reality of subjectivity. Not everything subjective of course becomes an object of religious faith. Religion arises in a separation, an estimation of worth; man does not regard as divine that to which he is indifferent, but only that to which he attributes the greatest value. Every man who has a highest aim has a god. That which a man praises and treasures is his god; God is the book in which man has inscribed his highest feelings and thoughts.

In the divine qualities we have the qualities which man, at that particular stage, estimates most highly. That God is personality means that personal life is the highest; that God is love means that there is nothing more excellent than a loving disposition. In the Christian religion God suffers; this means, to suffer for others is divine. If we are to understand religion, we must everywhere take as subject what it takes as predicate and *vice versa.*

The positive worth of religion, then, according to Feuerbach, is that it values these qualities of personal life so highly. And it is because Feuerbach values them so highly that he objects to having them attributed to a Divine Being, outside of man, instead of identified with man, out of whose feelings they have arisen.

"The true atheist," says Feuerbach, "is not he who denies the existence of the Divine Being, but he to whom these qualities are nothing. There is nothing of real value lost by the abandonment of religious faith. We merely cease to project. We no longer cross the stream to fetch water because we have discovered that the water which we fetched comes out of the stream itself." (Taken from Höffding's *History of Modern Philosophy,* Volume II).

The critical issue determining the validity of this approach turns upon the soundness of Feuerbach's saying that " all theology is psychology." From Feuerbach to Freud this dictum has implied the sheer subjectiveness of religion and theology. This problem is part of a larger problem: Is human experience and knowledge shut up within the walls of the human ego (the solipsism into which the early forms of idealism fell) or do human experience and knowledge, because of their social nature, have an objective aspect? Modern philosophies, while recognizing the subjective limitations of human thought, have come to striking agreement in the assumption that in thinking, man does interact with facts and forces beyond his ego, and where the test of observation and reason can be applied, he is justified in claiming an objectivity to his knowledge. Psychology, too, has gone beyond the subjectivist standpoint, where mind, the self, and human behavior are seen to be part of a configuration, not an isolated entity acting within itself. Once one begins to consider this configuration, and the activities that constitute it, he is compelled to ponder the more extended aspects of the pattern which are not readily observed or discerned. Social interaction then takes on a cosmic aspect. And one is led to adopt, at least, a sort of social symbolism to describe these larger reaches of social phenomena. Yet, underneath that symbolism are the processes of the world that shape our being, however defined or described. Theology thus goes beyond psychology, even social psychology, and is returned again to philosophy, or, more particularly, to the realm relating worshiper and the metaphysical realities with which he is concerned.

A more recent exposition of this viewpoint is found in the writings of the New Psychologists, of which Freud is the distinguished exponent. A typical analysis of this sort is *The*

Mystery of Religion, by Everett Dean Martin. Martin sees religion as a process of wish-fulfillment, starting in the small child as a normal behavior of infancy, and continuing in adult life, where maturity has been arrested, as a compensatory illusion. Two examples of his reasoning will suggest the nature of his analysis. One relates to the development of the " Father Image." Religion, says Martin, speaks in symbols, the most characteristic of which is the term *Father*. The child in his love for his father and mother, says Martin, at first thinks of their love as centering wholly about himself. He deeply resents their loving each other in ways that necessarily exclude him. Throughout his infancy he may remain under the illusion that he is the sole recipient of their devotion. But there comes a time, beginning at puberty, when he awakens to the shocking fact that they do have relations together in which he does not and cannot share. The realization of this fact thrusts him from his Garden of Eden. The child may develop secret aversion to his parents; yet he cannot endure the loss which accompanies this aversion. He must have the security of love and the sense of self-importance which such devotion gives one. Thus it is that, at the time of adolescence, many boys and girls turn to religion. Cast from his family paradise, he must find a place in the large world outside of the family circle. He naturally conceives this larger world in terms of his family relations. Thus he compensates for the loss of the father and mother, whose devotion has come under suspicion, by the unfailing love of the Unseen Father. The adjustment made, new confidence is gained. The maturing youth may thus enter into adult experience and continue his life with the same sense of security and importance that characterized his days of infancy.

The second typical analysis traces the rise of religious experience as a protest against the feeling of inferiority. The conditions of human nature which the infantile egoism was unable to tolerate in the father are later discovered in the subject himself. This gives rise to a depressing sense of sin. Religion is the route by which he escapes this sense of sin. The Father Image is found to be forgiving toward those facts of human nature. Accordingly, the subject learns to forgive his own sins and those of the father. Hence in forgiveness, the solution for the problem of tension between the infantile ego and the demands of the mature organism is found.

It will not be denied, perhaps, that a vast amount of religious faith has arisen out of adjustments to pathological conditions arising in human experience. To say that all religious faith has developed in the maturing youth in the manner described by Martin, however, seems a gross overstatement. It is, of course, a piece with the Freudian hypothesis that all human impulses are basically derivatives of the sex impulse, an assumption that is seriously questioned, if not thoroughly refuted, today.[4] A more important consideration, however, is the nature of the religious response. Is it always pathological? Martin's analysis implies that it is. Here we would disagree most emphatically. It is one thing to say that much religion is pathological; it is quite another thing to dispose of all religion as pathological. Here the inadequacy of the method so commonly employed in the psychological studies of religion, of interpreting all religious phenomena on the basis of pathological behavior, becomes apparent. Religion appears in salutary forms as well as in pathological behavior. It may not come as a resolution of an inner tension, but as a healthy outreach toward objective realities that claim one's devotion on the basis of clear observation and reason. But to recognize this would mean to pass beyond the thesis of the subjectivists, to the point of view maintained by the objectivist theories of naturalism. A discussion of this viewpoint will follow later.

This psychological approach to religion may not be dismissed too casually, however, for it has penetrated the truth concerning a certain area of religious belief and behavior. Both Martin's and Leuba's studies have brought clarity of a sort to our understanding of religion. Now Martin's *Mystery of Religion* becomes a very inadequate guide to the understanding of religion if one shares his supposition that all religion is a compensatory illusion; for that assumption overlooks the fact that religion, like every other important human interest, manifests itself both in pathological and in salutary forms. Martin has ignored the normal, healthy expressions of religion and has restricted his analysis to pathological behavior, identifying it with religion as a whole. This is his inadequacy. Yet it must be admitted that he has presented a strikingly clear analysis of pathological religion. However invalid the psychological basis of his analysis, he has called attention to the important fact of the pathological expression of religion. The importance of this is that it opens the way to clearing up the ambiguities that have accumulated in theologies and philosophies of religion concerning the nature and function of religion. Strange to say, there has been little or no conscious distinction among theologians and philosophers, in determining religious values and their criteria, between the sources issuing from pathological experience and those growing out of normal healthy religious living. Before religion can become a dependable spiritual quest, its objectives and insights must be extricated from the realm of the pathological.[5]

RELIGIOUS HUMANISM

The form of religious humanism, arising out of the broader socio-historical field, is best represented in philosophic literature by M. C. Otto, R. W. Sellars and A. E. Haydon. As a religious movement, its prominent representatives are John H. Dietrich, Curtis W. Reese, John Haynes Holmes, Charles F. Potter, J. A. C. F. Auer, L. M. Birkhead, Burdette Backus, Oliver Reiser, Harold Buschman, R. B. Bragg, Edwin H. Wilson, and a host of others whose names appear as signatures to the Humanist Manifesto.

As a theory of religion, religious humanism may be said to be the culmination of the gradual shift in theological and philosophical thinking from the God-ward to the man-ward side of religious thought.[6] This shift has come about under the stimulus of two lines of reasoning: One group of thinkers has insisted that the objective, or God-ward side, being simply the projection of man's own wish and idealization, is non-existent, except as it exists in man's own consciousness. Another group, believing that the objective aspect has been stressed to the point of obscuring, if not eclipsing utterly, the vital interests of the human enterprise, has urged a concerted emphasis upon the human aspect. Humanists who have held to the first point of view have been antitheistic. Those who have taken the second stand have varied in the degree of their acceptance of a belief in God, but their views have not been necessarily hostile to theism in theory. In most cases they have chosen simply to ignore the theistic aspect so as to see clearly the full implications and possibilities of man and his powers.

In considering the subjectivist theories of religion, particularly the view advanced by Feuerbach, we came upon a mode of thought leading to the first type of humanism. A more directly contributive forerunner to the contemporary movement of religious humanism is the philosophy of Positivism, developed by the French philosophers Saint-Simon and Auguste Comte in the nineteenth century. Contemporary religious humanism is not to be viewed as a direct outgrowth of Positivism, however. It is more than a philosophical movement. At the core, it is a social passion, arising from two convictions: one, that within the world of nature itself there is no guarantor of human values, and second, that the control of nature through the technological sciences is fraught with both blessedness and peril, but that to date its efforts, as evidenced in the rise of our machine civilization, the development of instruments of war, and the economic structure that promote both, is heavily weighted on the side of peril. In the face of this growing catastrophe, the religious humanists have turned from philosophical speculation and religious worship, as they formerly knew it, to deal as directly and as realistically as possible with the contemporary situation. To this end they have abandoned the metaphysical quest. To this end, also, they have forsaken the altars of worship that turn human devotion away from the present human scene to the adoration of a cosmic deity. We must rally our spiritual resources for the urgent social task at hand, is the gospel they preach. At heart, then, the religious humanists are social idealists, stripping their philosophical bulk to fighting weight.

MAX CARL OTTO

This note in humanism has been urgently voiced in the stirring book, *Things and Ideals,* by M. C. Otto. Take this passage:

What is it men want? They want to live the most liveable life. This fact at once gives science a commanding status. The most liveable life must be sought and found in the physical environment which conditions our efforts and which, as far as we can see, is indifferent to our success or failure. Lacking acquaintance with this environment we cannot utilize it, and unless we can utilize it we are helpless. . . . But to utilize nature, we must study nature, and scientific method is the best means so far discovered for that task.

But it gives the higher life a commanding status too. Science, knowing no more of better or worse than nature does, cannot supply us with a program of life. And without that program science may be our undoing. This is frankly recognized by scientists themselves, or at any rate by the more thoughtful of them. The " results of Natural Science," says E. W. Hobson, in his recent Gifford Lectures, " in its persistent efforts to dominate physical nature, have furnished us with the mechanical means of securing an indefinite improvement in the welfare of mankind, if a wise use is made of the power with which they endow us. They have also provided our civilization with the material means of committing suicide, if the increased mechanical powers which they afford are not accompanied by a corresponding rise in the ethical standards which actuate nations in their dealings with one another."

This conviction, that the so-called mastery of nature is in itself inadequate to the needs of life, is bound to become more deep and general as the conditions are appreciated. Indeed it may soon be the one, all-absorbing question of the ages. (Pp. 209–12.)

What, more than the scientific control of nature, is necessary to assure the furtherance of the human cause? Professor Otto's reply is that there must develop a " higher life " that goes beyond the accomplishments of formal religion which will consciously direct the scientific method toward human ends.

The man in whom this change has become a living fact will find it impossible to reduce the higher life to conventional religion or to some form of trance induced by sitting on a peak of mystical abstraction gazing into the face of a oneness that is everything though nothing.

He will rather identify it with active concern for the most liveable, joyous common life; with *dedication to the human venture.*

He will not look upon the life of the spirit as a matter of revelation or immediate intuition delivered once for all to certain holy or wise men, and then forever striven after, but a life progressively discovered and progressively achieved by dedicated souls.

He will endeavor to employ in his own way the disciplined intelligence best exemplified by the scientist; that is, he will try to conform to what may be termed the moral attributes of the scientific attitude: loyalty to fact, insistence upon rigorous, non-subjective standards of evidence, faith in the unbounded possibilities of co-operative achievement. In that high sense he will be scientific.

But he will not make reality as pictured by natural science the model for human life.

He will not reduce to nothingness the attributes which in the course of evolution have distinguished man from the animals, nor will he aim to submit human destiny to the blinder processes of his own nature.

He will free life where he can from the sodden routine, the meaningless rush and scramble and defeat to which machine philosophy has already degraded it.

He will set his face against the conception of life where every knee shall bow and every tongue confess the Great God Hum.

Below all theories and creeds and faiths he will hold to the conviction that neither science nor religion nor art nor commerce nor any of the specialized forms of human activity is the end of man's endeavor, but a satisfying life for all who may have a life to live. (Pp. 222–23.)

If science is to be controlled and directed in the interest of human values, religion must also be bent to aid the human quest. And the first step in this direction, thinks Otto, is to rid the world of the illusion that there is any power beyond man himself to promote his cause.

> What noble things might be accomplished [he writes] if we recognized in our insistence upon cosmic companionship a deflection of the desire for fellowship with our kind, and in the craving for transcendental support of our ideals a distortion of our deep interest in human well-being and progress! . . . One tragic result of our diverted aspiration is that the conditions of life are fixed by those who have no concern for human destiny, either in this world or any other. . . .
>
> It is thus a constructive social suggestion that we endeavor to give up, as the basis of our desire to win a satisfactory life, the quest for the companionship with a being behind or within the fleeting aspect of nature; that we assume the universe to be indifferent towards the human venture that means everything to us; that we acknowledge ourselves to be adrift in infinite space on our little earth, the sole custodians of our ideals. There need be no spirit of defiance in this, no bitterness. . . . No; accept the stern condition of being psychically alone in all the reach of space and time, that we may then, with new zest, enter the warm valley of earthly existence — warm with human impulse, aspiration, and affection, warm with the unconquerable thing called life; turn from the recognition of our cosmic isolation to a new sense of human togetherness, and so discover in a growing human solidarity, in a progressively ennobled humanity, in an increasing joy in living, the goal we have all along sought, and build on earth the fair city we have looked for in a compensatory world beyond. (Pp. 287–90.)

ROY W. SELLARS

An equally unequivocal view of religion is set forth by Roy Wood Sellars in his two volumes, *The Next Step in Religion* and *Religion Coming of Age,* and in his several articles in *The New Humanist.* Sellars has come to his humanistic convictions through arduous inquiry into the problems of the natural order. He was one of the first to develop the view now known as " emergent evolution " and an early exponent of the view that philosophy should be enticed away from its mathematical alliances to take up seriously with the organic sciences. In his *Evolutionary Naturalism* he undertook to cut under the conventional dualism that had led philosophy to affirm either a supernaturalism or a materialistic naturalism. He advocated a thoroughgoing scientific philosophy of nature, viewing it from the standpoint of the evolutionary sciences rather than that of mathematics. So considered, he found process and growth replacing formulations of equations. The outcome of such investigation of nature revealed a hierarchy of levels with new unities emerging at each level to produce higher orders of existence — atom to crystal to organic life, etc. These levels of development were found observable all along the line. Now all of this growth toward higher forms, Sellars pointed out, occurs in a *natural* world. There is no need of introducing supernatural causes to account for it, for this is just the way natural phenomena occur. And man, he continued, is one outcome of this evolutionary naturalism. He is, in fact, the planet-come-to-consciousness. He is the highest of the hierarchy of levels, and as such represents the natural order in its spiritual aspect. Accordingly, the purpose of religion is to promote this high product of the natural forces, to fulfill its ends and to extend its power and influence throughout the rest of nature. This, of course, leads him to his stand for religious humanism. Religion must point its emphasis, not backward to the sources less than spiritual man, but forward to the further evolving of this earth-creature and the order of life that he may progressively create.

His book, *The Next Step in Religion,* is given over largely to pointing out the untenableness of conventional Christian beliefs and the supernatural world-view underlying them, concluding with a vigorous plea to abandon the religion of the past, which is " world-fleeing " and take up the man-centered faith of religious humanism. Contrasting the negative appeal of traditional religions with the affirming note of the new gospel, he writes:

The humanist's religion is the religion of one who says yea to life here and now, of one who is self-reliant and fearless, intelligent and creative. It is the religion of the will to power, of one who is hard on himself and yet joyous in himself. It is the religion of courage and purpose and transforming energy. . . . Its goal is the mastery of things that they may become servants and instrumentalities of man's spiritual comradeship. Whatever mixture of magic, fear, ritual and adoration religion may have been in man's early days, it is now, and henceforth must be, that which concerns man's nobilities, his discovery of, and loyalty to the pervasive values of life. The religious man will now be he who seeks out causes to be loyal to, social mistakes to correct, wounds to heal, achievements to further. He will be constructive, fearless, loyal, sensitive to the good wherever found, a believer in mankind, a fighter for things worth while. . . .

The center of gravity and endeavor of such a religion will lie in society. It will be, to all intents and purposes, a humanist's religion. (Pp. 212–13.)

On the problem of theism, Sellars is clear and outspoken:

Upon this I think all naturalists are agreed, [he writes in *The New Humanist*] that between naturalism and theism it is a case of either — or. Either a reality corresponding to the God-idea is at the center of reality in a directing, planning way or there is no such reality. In the latter case man is left to work out his own salvation as best he can with a fairly stable planet underneath his feet. His is the adventure and the goal.

It has always been my thesis that naturalism has today the logical priority. Nature is under observation in a way that God is not. It is difficult to put the contrast without paradox. For, of course, if God does not exist, he cannot be known. God does not exist means that the God-idea does not have application to what exists.

It is not my intention to brush aside all the arguments which have been used by Christians and other theists to show that the God-idea does have application. I must content myself with saying that none of these arguments have seemed to philosophers very convincing.[7]

In these two presentations by Otto and Sellars, we have representative expressions of the early stage of religious humanism, the temper of which still persists among some humanists. There is something reminiscent in this of Bertrand Russell's " A Free Man's Worship." [8]

A. EUSTACE HAYDON

In recent years there has been a noticeable shift from this stern, stoic temper to a more meliorative mood, relating man more agreeably to the world of nature. This development in humanism is revealed in *The Quest of the Ages* by A. Eustace Haydon and in several of the *Humanist Sermons* edited by Curtis W. Reese. The humanism of Haydon, while it concurs with the anti-theistic emphasis of Otto and Sellars, does not rule out the cosmic support of human values with the same degree of finality. In *The Quest of the Ages,* in fact, Haydon has laid the groundwork of what might be termed *the new theism.* This passage is particularly expressive of his emphasis:

The elements of support and security of hope and promise, which come to man from his cosmic and social environment, are real and effective. . . . First of all is the support of the stable balance of the natural world. . . . Man himself is one phase of the natural order, the result of aeons of cosmic development — an earth-child, molded and trained in body and mind, by constant interaction with environment. The human races have been so thoroughly adjusted to the nature of which they are a part, that man may justly claim to be the form of life most capable, not only of survival, but of mastery on the planet. He has achieved sufficient harmony with the forces of nature to feel secure. He is indeed the planet itself, come to consciousness and capacity for intelligent self-direction. For modern man the physical world has become for the most part a kindly or controllable environment. Man's being is so attuned to the nature from which he sprang, and which has nursed his long racial infancy, that some of the finest emotional experiences he has are rooted in the unconscious past. . . . A modern understanding of our relation to all the manifold phases of the patterns of life borne by the great Earth Mother may add to the mystic feel of oneness. . . . A mystical naturalism has its roots here. (Pp. 111–12.)

In man's secure biological heritage Haydon sees a second element of support for the human quest. But it is in " the enfolding social environment " that he finds " the more important phase of cosmic structure." " This is," he concludes, " *in the final analysis, his real support, master, guide and guarantor."*

And this conviction returns Haydon to the social emphasis, so characteristic of the religious humanist. It should be recognized that Haydon views this social environment as a genuine phase of the natural process. Therefore, from his point of view, in emphasizing the social setting, he is still retaining the cosmic perspective. Actually, however, his emphasis tends to eclipse the cosmic aspect. And he justifies his stand on two bases: first, as we have seen, that the essential phase of the cosmic structure is the social environment; and second, that to pursue any other emphasis would be to divert thought and aspiration from the main line of religious interest, namely, the human venture toward the higher life.

It is this venture toward the higher life that preoccupies the religious humanist. What salvation from sin was to the medieval theologian, the progressive fulfillment of men's desires in their outreach for the good life is to the humanist. And it is in their constructive effort to interpret religion in these terms that the affirming side of religious humanism becomes most apparent. Religion, according to the humanist, is not theology, belief or truth; neither is it any form of devotion to something or someone beyond, or more than, the human realm. Religion, to be sure, has involved these interests, for in its historical practice, regardless of the culture that is examined, religion is seen to involve an ideal, a technique, and a theology, or a world-view. But " the creative thing " has been " the drive of man, man's outreach for satisfying values, man's determination that he must somehow get the things that satisfy the hungering of his body and his social hungering." [9] Only because of man's frustrations and defeats did he fall back upon the gods for help, says the humanist. And, thinking that solution to their problems lay in their dependence upon the gods, men flung themselves with full weight upon the gods. Thus religion became supernatural and other-worldly. But today man is beginning to recover his natural perspective. Today, reinforced with the insights of the sciences, and with the tools which science has made possible, man may venture once again as a son of earth, really to wrestle with the problems that lie in the path of the good life, with vigor and insight. And this is what gives him confidence. He is, himself, maker of his destiny. It is the humanist's dream that he shall become master of it as well.

Interpreting religious humanism on the basis of these three eminent exponents would lead one to the conclusion that its dominant philosophical trait is the conviction that man is alone in his venture toward the higher life. And this attitude ranges from a confirmed sense of being at odds with a hostile universe to the meliorative view that, to a large degree, *earth is for us,* though, in the last analysis, only in the sense that *we* are for ourselves.

Turning to the pulpit interpretations of religious humanism, one finds more readiness to affirm the co-operation of the cosmic aspect. Thus Curtis W. Reese, in "The Faith of Humanism," writes:

> Humanism has faith in the ability of man increasingly to achieve the possibilities inherent in the nature of man and the universe. . . . As man learns more and more about nature's processes — both physical and psychological — he learns that human intelligence is a co-worker with nature.

And John Haynes Holmes:

> Religion remains what it has always been — man's reaction upon this great universe of the infinite and eternal. But this reaction is altogether different in character from what it used to be. Today we accept the universe, instead of fearing and hating it. We run to welcome and receive it, instead of running away and hiding from it. We gather life up into our embrace, that it may become a part of us, and we a part of it. Our desire is the desire of the poet, to be " at one with the perfect whole." [10]

Among the younger generation of religious humanists, this turning toward the cosmic side is becoming even more marked; and there is ample evidence that the younger humanists are seeking to increase in humanism the mystical appreciation of the wider than human realm of nature as an objective phase beyond, yet correlative with, the human scene.[11] This development gives promise of a significant advance in the philosophy of religious humanism. For it points to the likelihood of its passing from the " religion of humanity " in the positivist sense, to a religion "identified with human life in its widest ranges." Whether it may then be properly called humanism is, perhaps, open to question, for it will be humanistic only in the sense that it emphasizes the human quest in the cosmic order. But all religions, other than the religious cults that have made human life secondary to the adoration of deity, have been humanistic in this sense. That is, they have made fulfillment of life the primary objective of the religious quest. Any form of Christianity that sought to naturalize its fundamentals would obviously make this its objective. Perhaps a more reasonable statement of the matter would be to say that religious humanism is an inevitable, even necessary, transition from the kind of God-centered theology that so minimized man as to render his human venture thoroughly unimportant, even to himself, to a reality-centered philosophy that emphasizes the fulfillment of human life through devotion to the cosmic realities or creative order in the universe that sustain and promote organic life.

It is to be hoped that in passing from the strictly humanistic stand of its earlier prophets religious humanism in its new form will not lose the vision of the "New Humanity," but that in finding reinforcement of spirit through a growing sense of at-homeness in the natural order, humanists may strive even more zealously to impel modern man to come into fuller realization of his powers as an earth-creature.

Religious humanism has had vigorous advocates also outside of strictly religious and philosophical circles. Writers like Harry Elmer Barnes, Joseph Wood Krutch, Walter Lippmann, Robert Morss Lovett, John Cowper Powys, and Llewellyn Jones have all made contributions to its literature and influence. Lippmann in particular has given a searching and significant presentation of its view.

WALTER LIPPMANN

Only one book among the many Walter Lippmann has written on social issues has been devoted to the subject of religion. But this one, *A Preface to Morals,* was probably read more widely than any other dealing with this interest. He has a magic pen that writes alluringly. He stands somewhat apart from other thinkers in this field. The other religious humanists hardly claim him as one of themselves, yet he certainly belongs with them more than with any other group. His religion is undoubtedly naturalistic: the object of religious devotion, he makes plain, should be no deity or other power but it should be a certain ideal of how one ought to live.

All the religious humanists set up a humanly formulated ideal as the highest loyalty for the religious life. But Lippmann is unique in the kind of ideal he places in this lofty place. This supreme ideal which should command our highest loyalty should be the ideal of a disinterested self. This concept of disinterestedness is central to his philosophy of religion and must be understood if his thought is to be grasped at all.

To be disinterested means not to be uninterested, but it means to have all interests dominated and shaped by a superinterest. In this sense almost all acceptable philosophies of religion would say that the great gift of a worthy religion is disinterestedness. Lippmann has made a great contribution in lifting this concept out and setting it in the clear light. But religions and philosophies of religion differ in respect to the nature of this superinterest. Lippmann's own philosophy is distinguished from others by his formulation of this master concern of the nobly religious soul.

This superinterest, he declares, is to discover the nature of the universe and conform to its requirements in such a way as to attain whatever maximum satisfaction is possible. This does not mean, however, that all other interests shall be subordinated to the interest in bare knowledge for its own sake. On the contrary it requires the organization of all interests in such a way as to adapt them to circumstances and to ally oneself with whatever one can find that sustains and promotes the good of life when right adjustment is made to it.

The man who lives under the dominance of this ideal is described by Lippmann thus:

And so the mature man would take the world as it comes, and within himself remain quite unperturbed. When he acted, he would know that he was only testing an hypothesis, and if he failed, he would know that he had made a mistake. He would be quite prepared for the discovery that he might make mistakes, for his intelligence would be disentangled from his hopes. The failure of his experiment could not, therefore, involve the failure of his life. For the aspect of life which implicated his soul would be his understanding of life, and, to the understanding, defeat is no less interesting than victory. It would be no effort, therefore, for him to be tolerant, and no annoyance to be skeptical. He would face pain with fortitude, for he would put it away from the inner chambers of his soul. Fear would not haunt him, for he would be without compulsion to seize anything and without anxiety as to its fate. He would be strong, not with the strength of hard resolves, but because he was free of that tension which vain expectations beget. Would his life be uninteresting because he was disinterested? He would have the whole universe, rather than the prison of his own hopes and fears, for his habitation, and in imagination all possible forms of being. How could that be dull unless he brought the dullness with him? He might dwell with all beauty and all knowledge, and they are inexhaustible. Would he, then, dream idle dreams? Only if he chose to. For he might go out simply about the business of the world, a good deal more effectively perhaps than the worldling, in that he did not place an absolute value upon it, and deceive himself. Would he be hopeful? Not if to be hopeful was to expect the world to submit rather soon to his vanity. Would he be hopeless? Hope is an expectation of favors to come, and he would take his delights here and now. Since nothing gnawed at his vitals, neither doubt nor ambition, nor frustration, nor fear, he would move easily through life. And so whether he saw the thing as comedy, or high tragedy, or plain farce, he would affirm that it is what it is, and that the wise man can enjoy it.[12]

In support of his thesis that this is the way to live in the modern world, Lippmann traces the recent development of business, government and sex-love, to show that these all are forcing men out of their self-centered and egoistic interests. In following the logic of the analysis set forth in these chapters one might think that Lippmann was pointing to a process which is forcing men on pain of disaster and futility to live as functional members one of another — to live for the community of men and not for any lesser interest. But Lippmann does not put it just that way. Rather, he says, the lesson to be learned from these developments in our social life is that each must live pre-eminently for achieving the ideal of a regenerate and mature personality. This kind of personality and this kind of life is made clear in the quotation we have made from his writing.

[1] *The Mystery of Religion.* Harper, 1924.

[2] *The Psychological Study of Mysticism* and *God or Man?*

[3] *The Scientific World View.* Macmillan, 1928.

[4] See Burnham's *Wholesome Personality.*

[5] See B. E. Meland's *Modern Man's Worship,* Chapter X, for a discussion of this point. The same article is found in *The Christian Century,* Oct. 10, 1934, under the title, " Religion: Devotion or Solace? " See also Wieman's *Wrestle of Religion with Truth,* Chapter I.

[6] *Humanism States Its Case:* J. A. C. F. Auer. Beacon Press, 1933.

[7] " Religious Humanism," *The New Humanist* (May–June 1933), p. 12. For a full statement of Sellars' philosophical position, see his recent book, *The Philosophy of Physical Realism.* Macmillan, 1932.

[8] In *Mysticism and Logic.* Longmans, Green, 1917.

[9] A. E. Haydon. From unpublished lectures.

[10] See also sermons by John H. Dietrich, E. Burdette Backus, *et. al.* in *Humanist Sermons.* The Open Court Publishing Company, 1927.

[11] I am basing this observation upon the statements of both Edwin H. Wilson and Raymond B. Bragg, editors of *The New Humanist.* See also the articles: E. H. Wilson, " Mysticism, Reason, and Social Progress," *New Humanist* (March–April 1934); James H. Hart, " A Religious Mood," *Ibid.* (January 1933); Rupert Halloway, " The Mystical Mood," *Ibid.* (May 1933); and E. Burdette Backus, " Mystic Naturalism " (Feb.–Mar. 1935).

[12] *A Preface to Morals.* Pp. 329–330.

CHAPTER XV

EMPIRICAL THEISTS

THE convergence of insights coming from the social, psychological, and biological sciences has given rise to a new form of theistic thought, less metaphysical than philosophical theism, yet more inclusive of cosmic interests than religious humanism. The key insight into this mode of thought lies in the idea that man has been produced by the natural universe, and that through healthful relations with its environing processes, he may fulfill his life. Commenting upon the interpretation of the universe set forth by M. C. Otto in *Things and Ideals,* Gerald Birney Smith wrote:

It may be seriously questioned, whether there is any real need of accepting quite so depressing a view of the cosmic order. Granted that supernaturalistic theism is too vulnerable, it is at least legitimate to inquire whether some modification of that theory may not suit the facts, when *all* the facts are taken into consideration. Humanity has been produced by the cosmos. The aspirations and activities of mankind are expressions of cosmic force, expressed through the functioning of an organism which nature has produced. Mankind can accomplish nothing save as he uses the forces of nature in accordance with limitations which nature herself imposes. Protest as we may against what we call the heartlessness of nature, we cannot escape from nature. Is it not a true instinct which leads us to believe that we may in some fashion share the meaning of the cosmic process in our conscious experience as truly as we are compelled to live physically in terms of nature's established process? Is it quite satisfactory to affirm on the one hand the inescapable physical dependence of man on natural forces, but on the other hand to bid man in the evolution of his ethical and social life defy the very nature on which he is dependent?

It is my conviction that such a dualism between the cosmos and the life of man can scarcely be successfully maintained. The majority of persons will continue to feel that man belongs to the cosmic order in his spiritual as well as in his physical existence. They will then either attempt to interpret the cosmic order in such a way as to feel that their moral enterprises are in some sense supported by that order, or else they will conclude that since the cosmos is indifferent to spiritual values, they, as products of the cosmos, may also be indifferent. I seriously question whether a merely naturalistic idealism, declared to be something qualitatively different from the cosmic process, will actually engender the enthusiasm which these humanists expect. In the long run mankind will decide to have the universe on his side rather than to defy it. If it is clear that the cosmic process cares nothing for human ideals, man will adjust himself to the inevitable. And the inevitable, on this hypothesis, is a nonhuman heartless evolution. I should be much more afraid that such an antitheistic position would lead to moral indifference than I should be that theism would weaken moral idealism.[1]

The development of a theistic interpretation of the universe along the empirical and naturalistic lines suggested by this statement, has taken several forms. Philosophers like Ames and Dewey, working wholly within the tradition of pragmatism, have centered attention chiefly upon man's relations with his social environment, and accordingly have undertaken to define God and religion in terms of the empirical social process. Their views might best be described as *humanistic theism*. Shailer Mathews, approaching the study of God and religion with the socio-historical method, makes a similar discovery regarding the social nature of religious concepts, yet is led to think of the concept of God in relation to actual cosmic activities which produce and promote personality. He has preferred to speak of his position as *conceptual theism*. A similar approach was made by the late Gerald Birney Smith, although he refrained from formulating a definite concept or doctrine of God. The outlines of his thought seem to point in the direction of a *mystical naturalism*. The most aggressive effort to discover the grounds for and to formulate a naturalistic theism has been put forth by Henry Nelson Wieman. Although his thought, to some extent, reveals the metaphysical bent of the philosophical theists, his essential emphasis and interest clearly disclose the empirical approach to the problems of religion.

Despite the differences that divide these thinkers, their points of view proceed from a common basis. They are environmentalists first and foremost, steeped in the lore and language of the empirical method. If at times they seem openly critical of one another's views, it is probably because they are near enough in basic aspects to be sensitive to the slightest difference. Their divergences occur most frequently at the point of sharpening up the concept of God in relation to the cosmic environment. Where Wieman chooses to designate a particular process in environment as God, Ames and Dewey, and to a modified extent, Mathews, prefer to use the term symbolically and qualitatively as descriptive of the world's life in relation to human life. Where the former seeks to ascribe unity to deity, the latter are content to acknowledge the pluralistic elements which, taken collectively, describe God.

Perhaps the most important issue dividing their positions is whether the reality called God is essentially human or superhuman in scope and character. Wieman and Dewey differ most sharply on this point, the former declaring for the superhuman character of God, the latter insisting that the activity called God is the work of human imagination and will. Between these two extremes are the positions of Ames and Mathews, the former inclining toward the humanistic view of Dewey, the latter siding more with Wieman in recognizing the more-than-human aspect of God. An adequate evaluation of these similarities and differences is possible, however, only through careful inquiry into their respective philosophies.

HUMANISTIC THEISTS

EDWARD SCRIBNER AMES
JOHN DEWEY

The concern to go *beyond humanism* has found support in both Ames and Dewey. Ames' book, *Religion,* and his essay, " Beyond Humanism," mark the first significant evidence of this trend within humanism. Dewey's widely read lectures on *A Common Faith* provide the most recent pointing in this direction. To say that their philosophies of religion move beyond humanism to theism, however, overstates the extent of their transition. The shift that has taken place in their thought represents more a change of emphasis than a fundamental reconstruction in their philosophy of religion. They are still ardent proponents of the philosophy of pragmatism, and therefore could not embrace theism in the sense that philosophical theists or theologians have held it. Their position is best described by the phrase, *humanistic theism,* for they use the word " God " to denote certain portions of the world's life taken in its *ideal aspects,* or related to activities within that world that bring those ideal aspects into actuality. This is theism of a new sort, if it be acknowledged as theism at all. A. E. Haydon, who prefers to be known as a *religious humanist,* holds to a position very similar to that of Ames and Dewey. His objection to using the word " God " to designate these ideal aspects is that they have not as yet become sufficiently realized within the social environment to warrant their being formulated into a concept that implies a basis for loyalty and devotion. The term " God " according to Haydon is a word of the future.

When the practical values belonging to the traditional idea [of God] are actually achieved in the organization of human life, there could be no objection to the use of the term " God " to signify the real guardian of our ideals, guide of our destiny, and center of our loyalties. But the continuation of the evolution of the planet by a social organization, eventuating in a unified world intelligence, heart and purpose, is a " must be " rather than an " is."   God in this sense of unified cosmic support and leadership belongs to the far future.[2]

The positions of Ames and Dewey go beyond the position of religious humanism, then, in the sense that they bring into focus this ideal aspect of human striving as a present, active *divine* objective, worthy of men's devotion.

Humanistic theism, however, is not theism as theologians and philosophical theists use that term, for it applies the term " God " to conditions and activities within the social process that are distinctly human conditions and activities, from the standpoint of theologian or philosophical theist.

This characterization of their views may become open to misinterpretation, however, in minds unsympathetic to the humanistic mode of thought.   Neither Ames nor Dewey thinks of the social process in the restricted social sense.   For them, the social reality is co-terminous with the vast cosmic reality which we know as nature.   Both Ames and Dewey make plain that they are dealing with ideal aspects that are *rooted in nature,* not mere ideal imaginings of the social idealist.   But one needs to follow the humanistic exposition of the social environment as *the-planet-come-to-consciousness,* nature at the personal level, before he can be clear as to what Ames implies by social value idealized, or reality idealized, and what Dewey means by activities that connect the ideal with the actual.   A more definitive statement of their respective positions may help to bring this point of view into clearer focus.

EDWARD SCRIBNER AMES

To understand Ames' philosophy of religion, one must first understand his approach to the realities of religion.   He is an empiricist of the John Stuart Mill tradition.   He holds that the only reality we may know is the reality that comes to us in the experience of living.   We come to know God, then, not through speculative flights into realms of the abstract, but through discerning awareness of the quality and order of cosmic life as it reaches us through the social process.

Ames has abandoned the search for God as an entity in space-time, just as he has ceased to look for a specific entity known as the " soul " or " mind." For just as *soul* has come to be viewed as the qualitative character of personality, and *mind* as descriptive of the peculiar organization of human behavior, so all concepts are to be understood in terms of their function in the experience of man's life. " An analogous procedure is taking place with reference to the conception of God," he points out. " Instead of trying to locate God as an object in space the search is made in the nature of the life of the world including man and the human cultures which the world sustains. Here again the conventional habit is to envisage the world as a physical substance and to seek God as an object outside or inside of this material universe, just as men have taken the bodily organism as a physical or material thing and the mind as an object alongside or inside of it. But it is possible that a more fruitful course is to inquire whether God may not be more truly and more fully understood as the reality of the world in certain aspects and functions — in what is here characterized as reality idealized." Orderliness, love, intelligence, these are the characteristic aspects of cosmic life which, idealized, constitute for Ames the reality that is God.

Ames has tried to make this view of God explicit by analogies such as Alma Mater, Uncle Sam, the Spirit of the Group, or the Commonwealth. In the minds of many, these figurative expressions have generally served to discredit his position. Much of the objection, however, reveals a lack of appreciation of the full import of these social symbols and of the wealth of operative reality implied by them. For Ames, the term Alma Mater is no mere mythical term, but stands for the total significance of the college life: its physical form, evidenced in the campus and buildings; its administrative personnel and traditions and policies; its faculty and the corporate devotion and insight issuing from its members; its student body, not only of the present, but of former years, manifested in part in its alumni throughout the land, yet not fully focused in them; as well as the many friends and benefactors who promote its enterprises, together with all the values and ideals signified by them. Here we have a great wealth of sentiment, fact, and organized devotion woven into a social process that sustains, constitutes and shapes the college life. Much of it is too elusive to be observed, but on commemorative occasions it may be envisaged as a vital reality. Other aspects are so real that they may be observed, counted, and appraised. To the spectator this may be just another social structure or enterprise; to the student or the graduate who feels his dependence upon it, who cherishes its sentiments and ideals and feels a loyalty and devotion to it, it is his *Alma Mater*.

There are many forms of group enterprises similar to the college life in which personalities, traditions, sentiments, ideals, and material facts are woven together as a social whole: the clan, the city, the state, the nation, perhaps the world, viewed as a political state. In all of these one beholds a corporate life that is sustaining, carrying with it possibilities of greater social value. Now "religion," says Ames, "carries this process to its highest form."

In religion the self stands in relation to the largest whole, to the universe, to God. This relation appears in those situations where the self meets the supreme crises of life, as when facing death, or the ultimate demands of honor. The whole meaning and urge of life then enters into the Other. This Other is of the same nature as all the lesser "others," constituted of social groups of varying scope and function. It is not a figment or an illusion any more than the state or the family is an illusion. It has the substance of the actual world of things and people, of history and projected action. Philosophy calls it the Universal or the Absolute; science designates it as Nature or Life; religion names it God. Psychologically it belongs to the inescapable experience of the relation of the self and the other. The "other" may be another human being, or a set of human beings held together as a family or a city or a nation, or it may be Humanity or the Universe. In every case this other is reality functioning vitally and impressively in the behavior and emotions of the self. We love God as surely and as intelligently as we love our country or our Alma Mater, but with deeper and more consummate affection.

It is to be noted that Ames does not identify God with *all that is* in this "largest whole." Just as "the intentions, plans, hopes, and purposes of founders and of great statesmen furnish the true measure of their nation," so the idealized realities of the cosmic existence — intelligence, love, and order — furnish the true measure of the reality which is God. Thus "God is the Power which makes for righteousness."

JOHN DEWEY

Dewey interprets religious value wholly in terms of the actualizing of ideal possibilities. "Any activity," he writes, "pursued in behalf of an ideal end against obstacles and in spite of threats of personal loss because of conviction of its general enduring value is religious in quality." Now these statements must be viewed against the full background of Dewey's own philosophy of life. Life, says Dewey, is in a state of continuous change. We are moving, not toward one goal, but many goals. In his Credo in *Living Philosophies* he has said:

> It is impossible, I think, even to begin to imagine the changes that would come into life — personal and collective — if the idea of a plurality of interconnected meanings and purposes replaced that of *the* meaning and purpose. Search for a single, inclusive good is doomed to failure. Such happiness as life is capable of comes from the full participation of all our powers in the endeavor to wrest from each changing situation of experience its own full and unique meaning. Faith in the varied possibilities of diversified experience is attended with the joy of constant discovery and of constant growing. Such a joy is possible even in the midst of trouble and defeat, whenever life-experiences are treated as potential disclosures of meanings and values that are to be used as means to a fuller and more significant future experience.

Now this notion of *life in flux* is fundamental, I believe, to an understanding of Dewey's conception of religion and of its structural concepts. It throws the direction of emphasis forward, never backward. It identifies higher value always with the potential, never the existent. That is not to say that religious value has no relevance to existential value, for the significance of the ideal lies in the fact that it is potentially realizable. But for Dewey, the distinctively religious attitude is this preoccupation with, even absorption in, the act of bringing into actuality the embryonic possibilities of every moment of existence.

Dewey is no dreamer about future possibilities. He is fundamentally an activist. He keeps his interest focused upon the process and method whereby ideal possibilities are to be brought into existence. Accordingly he insists that " the future of religion is connected with the possibility of developing a faith in the possibilities of human experience and human relationships that will create a vital sense of the solidarity of human interest and inspire action to make that sense a reality." And he defines God as the *active* relation between ideal and actual. God, in other words, is the actualizing of the ideal, meaning that this bringing to birth in concrete form of these goods that are " relatively embryonic " is that operation in life to which men need to give supreme devotion. God, the object of faith, is the transmutation of the ideal into action. Once the ideal becomes action, it then becomes the new frontier of experience in flux, surging toward new possibilities. Dewey is not saying that the term " God " is to be applied to all actualization of projected ideals. His God has selective meaning. " It selects those factors in existence that generate and support our idea of good as an end to be striven for. It excludes a multitude of forces that at any given time are irrelevant to this function." The " divine," then, from Dewey's standpoint, is the operation of human intelligence, choice, and directive will, acting upon the course of events in such a way as to bring to fruition the tendencies toward the ideal goods, thereby actualizing the ideal.

How does this differ from religious humanism? It does not differ in any vital way from that kind of humanism that relates man and his striving to the natural world in a co-operative way. But it does differ in theory from the anti-theistic type of human-

ism that posits man living in an indifferent and hostile world.
" A religious attitude," Dewey writes, " needs the sense of a
connection of man, in the way of both dependence and support,
with the enveloping world that imagination feels is a universe.
Use of the words ' God ' or ' divine ' to convey the union of
actual with ideal may protect man from a sense of isolation and
from consequent despair or defiance. . . . A humanistic religion, if it excludes our relation to nature, is pale and thin, as
it is presumptuous when it takes humanity as an object of
worship."

   Not until one views human intelligence, choice, and directive
will from Dewey's standpoint, however, does the full meaning
of his concept of God become apparent. Human intelligence
and the volitional activity accompanying it, is the operation of
the vast stream of experience at the conscious and responsible
level. Now Dewey uses the term *experience* in a definitive
manner. It is experience in the nominative, historical, cultural
sense. Throughout the millenniums of human striving there
has been accumulating a heritage of insight and habituated
practice. All that is involved in the emergence of this human
heritage is experience in the inclusive sense. For " the denota-
tions that constitute experience point to history, to temporal
process. . . . Experience denotes both the field, the sun and
clouds and rain, seeds, and harvest, and the man who labors,
who plans, invents, uses, suffers and enjoys. Experience denotes what is experienced, the world of events and persons, and
it denotes the world caught up into experiencing, the career
and destiny of mankind. Nature's place in man is no less significant than man's place in nature. Man in nature is man
subjected; nature in man recognized and used, is intelligence
and art. . . . The fact of integration in life is a basic fact, and
until its recognition becomes habitual, unconscious and pervasive, we need a word like experience to remind us of it, and
to keep before thought the distortions that occur when the integration is ignored or denied." [3]

But experience has been growing increasingly reflective, discriminative, and capable of experimental advancement. Thus, in *Living Philosophies,* Dewey writes: "Experience now owns as a part of itself scientific methods of discovery and test; it is marked by ability to create techniques and technologies — that is, arts which arrange and utilize all sorts of conditions and energies, physical and human. These new possessions give experience and its potentialities a radically new meaning. . . . This possession of a new method, to the use of which no limits can be put, signifies a new idea of the nature and possibilities of experience. It imports a new morale of confidence, control, and security."

Given this enlarged and enriched experience, made intelligent and reliable through the possession of new methods, the singular and important objective is to press on toward the further fulfillment of experience in terms of actualized ideal goods, made attainable by new reliable methods. The function of religion, then, is clear. It is to promote faith in the greater possibilities of human experience and human relationships. It is to turn experience, with its new methods, toward ends that yield greater human value. And the *active relation* — or operation that brings those ends to actual fulfillment — is God.

The question might be raised concerning Dewey's concept of God, is it too narrowly defined? There are, we might say, two poles of religious devotion: one is devotion to the existing, sustaining conditions and activities that promote life; the other is devotion to the possibilities of further values which become imaginatively apparent when existent activity is projected and idealized. Since these existing, sustaining activities, which Dewey designates experience, are the carriers of new possibilities, and, in fact, "the forces in nature (including society) that promote the growth of the ideal and that further its realization," they demand man's adjustment and devotion. Dewey recognizes this fact. (See *A Common Faith,* pp. 47–51.) This aspect would be more genuinely dealt with were the concept of God made more inclusive than Dewey makes it, defining God, not only as the *active* relation between the ideal and the actual, but also as the active relation between the non-ideal and the ideal toward which it moves. We should say, then, God is the collective representation of the total process or community of activities that sustain, promote, and bring life to high fulfill-ment. Even if it *is* admitted, as Dewey claims, that "the ob-jects of religion are ideal in contrast with our present state," it must be further acknowledged that the "present state" carries the conditions and forces that both create the ideal and make for its actualization. The divine activity, then, must not only be related to the non-ideal; it must, to some extent, include it. This correction would turn religious devotion in two direc-tions, rather than one as in Dewey's philosophy: first, toward such existent reality as sustains and promotes value; and second, toward ideal possibilities, as Dewey has said.

Dewey's distinction between *religion* and the *religious* is a further aspect of interest in his philosophy of religion. Reli-gion he identifies with organized forces and institutions which have undertaken to maintain and propagate a certain form of faith and doctrine. The *religious* is every and any act of man, or of groups, however related or unrelated to conventional forms of religion, which contributes to the actualization of the ideal. The scientist laboring in the laboratory to further the frontier of human knowledge and *experience;* the artist fash-ioning an unformed mass into an object of beauty; the parent or teacher delicately encouraging the process of growth in the child through intelligent and sacrificial guidance; men of state, or of any noble enterprise, unselfishly giving their genius to the promotion of the common good — these and many similar acts of devotion destined to further the frontier of human ex-perience and the vista of human ideals through progressive actualization of men's highest and noblest dreams, constitute, in Dewey's thought, *religious effort*. This is a clear formulation of the humanistic conception of religion. And it is in complete accord with his doctrine of God.

Dewey has called attention to an important distinction, we feel, in contrasting these two terms. Yet it would seem that the term *religion,* when used in the humanistic sense, would carry the meaning which Dewey gives to the word *religious.* As long as there are basic differences in the world-views of philosophers, there is little likelihood of concepts carrying the same content of meaning. Abstractly defined, their usage may be consistent. It is when one becomes concerned for the practical or concrete implications of concepts, that he becomes sensitive to the confusion in terms, imposed by the underlying differences in world-view. Abstractly defined, the term God stands for that reality which is worthy of all men's devotion. Now it will readily be seen that one's world-view and basic interests will largely determine what one designates as *that reality.* In supernaturalism it becomes a being of the sort defined in traditional theologies. In idealism and in romanticism it becomes some form of Cosmic Mind active in the universe. In naturalistic views attentive to metaphysical as well as human aspects, it becomes a process or order that is basic in the shaping of *cosmic* value. But in naturalistic views that are thoroughly humanistic, the term God, meaning that reality which is worthy of all men's devotion, becomes a process or order that is basic in the shaping of *human* existence. Both Ames and Dewey have been true to this conception of *that reality.* Their theism is clearly a humanistic theism. Given this form of theism, religion logically follows as meaning devotion to that activity which actualizes the ideal. For again, regardless of world-view, religion has a consistent abstract meaning: It means living in devotion to that reality which one designates as worthy of all men's devotion. Accordingly, in supernaturalism religion is pursuing such activity as glorifies transcendent deity and renders man acceptable to a holy Being. In idealism, religion must mean commitment to the sway of Absolute Mind or to the lure of Divine Personality. In naturalistic views, inclusive of metaphysical interests, religion becomes adjustment and devotion to the process or processes that shape and fulfill highest cosmic values. But in humanism, religion must mean devotion to those ends which serve and promote the actualization of human ideals.

All humanistic theories of religion proceed from this basic conviction that religious realities are wholly within human experience, and therefore distinctly social phenomena. This is a normal deduction from the pragmatic view, and religious humanism may very properly be regarded as the philosophy of religion of pragmatism. For just as the philosophy of pragmatism turned a deaf ear to metaphysical matters, so religious humanism reveals indifference to problems of religious inquiry that go beyond the realm of human affairs.

In one striking sense, the theories of religion set forth by religious humanists and those held by the ethical intuitionists are on common ground. Indeed, it would not be beyond the facts to say that religious humanism is liberal theology carried to a scientific conclusion. Both the humanists and the ethical intuitionists narrow the scope of essential religion to social or empirical dimensions. Each makes practical social consequences the ultimate test of truth. Ethical intuitionism, which is the philosophical expression of liberal theology, arrived at this position through a gradual recedence from supernaturalism in which the concepts of supernaturalism were rationally reconstructed in terms of a social theology and an empirical philosophy. Religious humanism, following much the same procedure, carried the rationalizing tendency to its logical conclusion and thus came to a thoroughgoing humanistic and social conception of religion without cosmic overtones. Ethical intuitionism, on the other hand, committed essentially to Christian tradition rather than to a world-view of modern science, relinquished the rationalizing procedure at the point where it began to dissipate the essential structure of Christian faith. As a means of preserving this structure, it has reared a formidable apologetics, as we have seen, bulwarked by argument and persuasive appeals drawn from many sources. As compared with this procedure, the logic of religious humanism is more defensible, however else one may choose to judge its religious and philosophical consequences. The present plight of liberal theology is the inevitable judgment upon its precarious procedure. It could not long continue to affirm with acclamation what it was denying by implication. And the present tendency of one-time ardent liberals to turn back with a vengeance to modified forms of supernaturalism is a sobering commentary upon the inherent weakness in the logic of the liberals' position.

Now if one is inclined to accept or to remain within the philosophical bounds of pragmatism, he doubtless will select religious humanism as the more logical alternative to liberal theology. If, however, one is concerned to integrate religion with the wider area of metaphysical inquiries, which pragmatism and religious humanism abjure, he will choose one of two alternatives: either he will revert to supernaturalism in modified form (as many disheartened liberals are now doing), or he will take up some mode of naturalistic theism that undertakes to construct a modern metaphysics on scientific and philosophical bases consonant with the modern world-view. In either case there will be a radical departure from the restricted view of religion as pre-eminently a social phenomenon, implicit in liberal theology, and explicit in religious humanism. Religion will again be orienting itself in the wider context of metaphysical relations.

SHAILER MATHEWS: CONCEPTUAL THEIST

Shailer Mathews has developed a distinctive approach to the concept of God through the study of history and social experience. The study of man from early times onward, says Mathews, discloses men seeking help from the environment upon which they felt themselves dependent. Their efforts have been of two sorts: (1) impersonal, as in agriculture, invention, and organized control of natural forces; (2) personal, as in ritualistic worship and moral codes, intended to express devotion to the sustaining forces. Out of the first approach have come the sciences; out of the second, religion. Thus religion, understood historically, says Mathews, " stands for the attempt on the part of man to treat the mysterious forces, at whose mercy he finds himself, in the same way he would treat social superiors; or, more formally, religion can be described as actions, more or less rationalized, seeking to gain help through the establishment of personal relations with those forces of the universe which are judged capable of such relationship. Every religion is a technique by which this end is sought." [4]

This effort to get help from the mysterious environing forces of the universe has led to the development of the idea of God. The idea of God has had a natural history, following closely the emergence of human civilization. For out of the developing forms of social organization have come the patterns with which men have formulated their concepts of God. Thus men's thoughts about God have run the gamut from personified nature powers of primitive society to God as a political monarch of medieval and modern times. But the passing of these patterns for envisaging the reality defined as deity has not left men without God. For each generation, finding itself dependent upon forces outside of man, is impelled anew to set up personal relations with this mysterious environment.

Modern man's thought concerning the universe is dominated, not by political or legal patterns, but by concepts drawn from the sciences. Accordingly, the God of modern life " must be conceived of as activity that is both creative and environing." The pattern in which this concept is cast " must involve the conception of process which now dominates our scientific thought." [5] But to define God merely as process, Mathews continues, gives us a metaphysical, but not a religious view of God. The religious characterization of God demands a focusing of the personal relations of man with the environing universe. The question then presents itself: Can modern man, following the insights of science, conceive these mysterious forces in the universe in personal terms? The vital issue here is " whether the universe in which we live as persons, has any power to produce us as persons." On this issue, Mathews has clear convictions:

No matter how self-centered or subjective a man may be, he cannot escape the forces in the midst of which he has to live. Those that are physical are easily discovered. Man lives under the pressure of the atmosphere; he is a peripatetic laboratory in which chemical elements are continually combining; he is subject to the laws of gravitation and to radioactive forces. The change of a few degrees in the heat of his environment means death. He lives on a planet from which he cannot stray ten miles and live.

But these are by no means all the cosmic relations which condition human life. Otherwise there would be no man to write about. At the best there would be only animals. But here man is. He is unlike any other chemical compound or organism, for he is capable of at least limited self-direction, of ordering life to distant ends, of generalized thought, and of the organization of social institutions, art, and morals. How can such an order of life be accounted for?

The answer is the universe. The mysterious process which we roughly call evolution brought man into being. But if that be the case, then there must be activities within the cosmos sufficient to account for the evolution of the human species with its personal qualities. There must be personality-evolving activities in the cosmos.[6]

Accordingly, modern man, following in the path of his ancestors, proceeds to establish personal relations with these forces that have produced him. His procedure is not different from that employed in ordinary social experience. Just as he employs the word " friend " to aid his social adjustments in society, so he uses the term " God " as an instrumental concept to aid his adjustment to these personality-producing and sustaining forces in the cosmic environment.

It is important to note that Mathews grounds all thought of God in the behavior of humanity. The word " God " is an instrumental concept that stands for the reality relating man and these activities. God is not a Being, nor a principle, nor simply these activities; for the word " God " is our conception and experience of such activities in human relations. " To that extent," he continues, " it must vary in content, being instrumental rather than exclusively ontological." Both the metaphysician and the strict pragmatist, according to Mathews, " fail to give the correct definition of God, for the reason that each omits the relationship between the elements which the other describes." [7]

Mathews is insistent that the concept of God is not primarily a metaphysical matter. Metaphysics will always remain a field of vital human interest, for the human mind will persist in its search for " some ultimate unity from which the various elements of experience may flow," but " metaphysical discussion," he continues, " may easily pass beyond the area of experience represented by the word " God." It is not the thing-in-itself with which religion deals, but that experience of organism and environment which makes a relationship with objective activities possible. A conceptual theism is more vital than a metaphysical theism for its vanishing point is not an Absolute or a Principle or a Being, but personal relations with personality-creating, personally responsive, personally conceived activities of the cosmos." [8]

It thus becomes apparent that Mathews is not concerned to press his inquiry beyond the experienced relationship.

Like a vast parabola, the personality-evolving activities of the cosmos touch our little circle of experience. We know not whence they come or whither they go, but we cannot evade them. We set up relations with them similar to those which we set up with persons. And thus we derive new strength and courage and moral motive for facing the tasks of life and building up a world-order in which personal relations will be more perfectly adjusted and human life happier.[9]

This view seems strikingly pragmatic upon first reading, but careful scrutiny will disclose that its basic ideas have little, if anything, in common with pragmatism. Its functional emphasis is its one, essential pragmatic trait. But its theistic assumptions issue from a rationale of the cosmos which the pragmatist does not share. Ames and Dewey, for example, seem to identify the word "God" with relations growing out of man's experience with environment; yet the locus of their theism is the social process, rooted in nature, to be sure, but qualitatively determined by the social consciousness. But in Mathews' view, while the idea of God is a product of the social consciousness, the reality which is God, relating the cosmic activities and man is a more-than-social phenomenon.

The difficulty of expressing Mathews' concept of God so as to bring out the full import of his meaning grows out of the fact, partly, that we are accustomed to thinking of God either as a Being, a Principle, or perhaps a defined Process. For Mathews, none of these defines God. What we have is an organism personally related to an environment in which personality-producing activities are operative. The relationship evokes a response in the organism, impels him to search out this relationship which is his very life, to declare his gratitude, to commit himself to its sustaining power, and to avail himself of its creative energies. This projection of man toward the personal, sustaining environment, when it gives rise to language, expressive of this vital relationship, calls forth the word *God*. The phrase *conceptual theism,* therefore, aptly characterizes this view.

Now religion, from this standpoint, consists in coming into personal adjustment with these personality-producing activities, thus causing our lives, their interests and activities, to become increasingly personal.

By making our social relations more personal and by controlling our physical urges in the interests of those ends which are super-animal and timeless, we come into harmony with the eternal personality-producing activities of the cosmos and so share in their creative vigor.[10]

MYSTICAL NATURALISM

GERALD BIRNEY SMITH
BERNARD E. MELAND

The clearest formulation of Gerald Birney Smith's views has been set forth in his essay, " The Modern Quest for God," yet Smith did little more than point the way to this mystical venture of the naturalistic sort. Problems of religious thinking, he said, should be stated in terms of human adjustment to environment. The character of God, he felt, is to be found in the experienced reciprocity between man and his environment. He thought of life as adjustment between organism and environment, and religion as an aspect of this life-process. The central problem then becomes, what kind of adjustment is possible? Shall it be conceived as making the best terms obtainable from an indifferent or hostile cosmos? Or is it possible to make an adjustment of such a kind that in it there is an experience of spiritual oneness with the cosmic mystery? If the latter kind of adjustment is possible, Smith reasoned, there has been a religious discovery of God. For he held that belief in God means that there may be found, not merely within the circle of human society but also in the non-human environment on which we are dependent, a quality of the cosmic process akin to the quality of our own spiritual life. For those who think in terms of our modern science, according to Smith, religion would consist in a great mystic experiment in the effort to become helpfully related to that sustaining quality of cosmic process.[11]

The suggestion that religion might become *a great mystic experiment* may seem to imply a reversion to mysticism. But the naturalistic mysticism that Smith was urging has little in common with the creed of the traditional or even of the modern mystics. Bertrand Russell has pointed out in *Mysticism and Logic* that mysticism may be either a creed or simply an attitude toward life. The mysticism of naturalism is of this latter sort, which simply means an emphasis upon the approach to reality which reverses the discursive and analytic approach. G. B. Smith was fond of pointing out that the sciences were given to extracting portions of reality for purposes of controlled observation; while religious worship, in contrast to this laboratory procedure, impels one to respond appreciatively to reality envisaged as a whole. The objective pursued in the laboratory is to secure knowledge for a purpose; while the objective sought in religious worship is emotional adjustment to the cosmic environment, taken in the large. Accordingly the method employed in the laboratory places emphasis upon analysis. Worship, on the other hand, enables one to respond to reality in synthesis.

Now the objective of mystical worship may go beyond enjoyment and appreciation to a kind of discernment, peculiar to its method. This sounds like a reversion to the mystic's claim of special knowledge, but it is not of that esoteric sort. The naturalistic mystic, like other aesthetic naturalists, approaches life with the sensitivity of the poet. His mystical experience is akin to the experience of the poet, the artist, or the lover of nature: charged with a profound fullness, evocative of great emotion and feeling. It is profound and full and stirring because of the dimension of its grasp, not because of any occult feeling that accompanies the envisagement. Like the poet, he includes immense ranges in his grasp. He envisages reality in synthesis. This marks the essential difference between the kind of insight that comes to the mystic and the knowledge discerned by the analytic thinker. The naturalistic mystic is sensitive to the full impact of the event rather than the detailed meanings involved. Does he get a special kind of knowledge then? Yes, in the sense that the artist and the poet get distinctive glimpses of objects and events. Unless one reduces the aesthetic view of things to sheer subjective imagination, one will recognize that the poet and the artist see things in certain relations. Their eyes are sensitive to lines and hues that are hidden to prosaic vision. Their characterizations of objects and events therefore present us with these realities in certain aspects peculiar to vision that has been disciplined for such seeing — aspects that yield the rich fullness of the objects and events in what approximates their total meaning. So with the mystic, when he views life naturalistically. He sees the realities of the world in certain relations. He envisages the world with a scope and a fullness that far exceed the circumscribed perspective of the activist or the discursive thinker who, of necessity, thinks within narrowly defined environings. The insight of the mystic, therefore, is the insight that comes with the approach of openness and wide receptivity. By itself, its meanings remain ambiguous and perhaps even futile (so far as application and usage are concerned). In alternation with the active and analytical judgment, however, it may yield meaning and insight precious beyond all expectation.

Gerald Birney Smith did not live to develop his philosophy of religion. Just what conception of God would emerge from *the great mystic experiment,* we cannot yet tell, he said. But whatever conception is formulated, he concluded, it would " express the experience of kinship between man and that quality in environment which supports and enriches humanity in its spiritual quest." We may be venturing with undue boldness in undertaking to project the outlines of another man's religious philosophy, but the hypotheses to which Gerald Birney Smith's mystical naturalism would seem to lead, might be stated in this manner.[12]

1. The basic one would seem to be: man may feel at home in the universe. There is more than mystical kinship with nature that leads to this affirmation. The whole story of man and his climb to civilization tends to document it.[13]

2. A second hypothesis which mystical naturalism would seem to affirm arises from the first proposition. The realization that man through the ages has been sustained and brought to higher and higher degrees of fulfillment seems to point to a *Creative Order* in the universe, a community of activities, a sus-

taining process (whatever best describes the reality) that sustains and promotes human life. Wholly apart from its wider implications, it is clear that it fulfills human ends. This Creative Order, the mystical naturalist calls *God*.

3. A third hypothesis to which mystical naturalism would seem to be committed is that this Creative Order, which is God, may be progressively better known. We may achieve this to the degree that we are able to discover the conditions of adjustment and control which contribute to the fulfillment of life and its possibilities. This seems to suggest the possibility of developing a " science of God " — that is, a co-operative inquiry into the operations of this sustaining reality with a view to making our adjustments to its demands more intelligent and fruitful. Since the fulfillment of man's life proceeds along several levels — physical, psychical, mental, social, appreciative and mystical — the Creative Order may be conceived as operating at these many levels. Accordingly, the physical sciences, the social sciences, the arts, philosophy, and mystical worship, as well as the humble experiments of everyday living, become the areas of inquiry and the sources of insight into the working of this Creative Order.

4. A fourth hypothesis of mystical naturalism would follow from this conception of God, namely, that religion is to be conceived as adjustment and devotion to this Creative Order that sustains human life and brings it to high fulfillment. Man becomes saved, that is, finds the route toward fulfillment of his being with all its possibilities, through progressive adjustment to this Creative Order which is God.

At the physical level, right adjustment and devotion to the Creative Order bring health to the organism. At the psychical level it makes for a unified life, fortified to endure the pressure of living. At the functional level it integrates the individual's powers and faculties in such a way through creative labor as to give maximum release to his energies and full expression to his unique capacities. At the social level right adjustment and devotion to the Creative Order promotes the social growth and maturity of the individual, enabling him to integrate his life in the wider connections of meanings and values. Beyond these utility levels gifted individuals may continue toward richer participation in the world of meanings through cultivation of reflective and appreciative ends. And the rare individuals, through strenuous adjustment and devotion, may attain the purity of heart known only to those who ascend the mystical heights. Mystical naturalism, then, seeks the maximum fulfillment of human life through intelligent devotion to the Creative Order at every level of its operations.

HENRY NELSON WIEMAN: [14] NATURALISTIC THEIST

Wieman's thought is akin to that of Dewey, Ames, Mathews and Smith in that he starts with the experience of value in the environing world of events as the means of deriving criteria for his definition of God and religion. He differs from them, however, in that he pursues the empirical path to the end of its trail, holding literally to its method by insisting that God is actually an object of experience, apprehended and discerned as any other object in environment. In the philosophy of Dewey, Ames and Mathews, God is not an *object* of experience, but a symbol designating a certain ideal or sustaining aspect of the world's life; for Dewey, the activity relating the ideal and the actual; for Ames, the universe idealized; and for Mathews, the concept expressive of the reality which relates man and the personality-producing activities. From these points of view, God is seen to be more a symbolical representation of activities that transpire, a conceptual, though not a *perceptual* reality. In Wieman's thought, God is clearly an object of immediate experience, *perceived* as well as *conceived*. Thus he speaks of God as *a* process, *a* movement, *a* growth, that operates in our midst, shaping and fulfilling the good. One might say his view differs from the theism of Dewey, Ames and Mathews in ascribing to God dynamic participation in the spatial world.

God *is* and *moves* in our midst in discernible ways. To this view neither Dewey, Ames nor Mathews would agree. In the philosophy of Ames and Dewey, the term God is applied to a functioning that is essentially human in scope and character. This is particularly true of Dewey who frankly states that the *unification* of the ideal and actual, to which he gives the name "God," is "the work of human imagination and will." [15] While Mathews is inclined to relate God more vitally with the cosmic process, he definitely recoils from identifying God *with* that process. For in his view, *all thoughts of God are grounded in the behavior of humanity.* "God is *our conception,* born of social experience, of the personality-evolving and personally responsive elements in our cosmic environment with which we are organically related." [16]

Another basic distinction, growing out of this divergence between the thought of Wieman and that of Ames, Dewey and Mathews, is the difference in their concern with respect to the amplification of the concept of God. For these latter, God is an abstract pattern, characterizing certain present functionings of the world's life. The term God is employed specifically for the purpose of bringing into focus that peculiar aspect or significant form of human activity which merits men's devotion and which, when contemplated and pursued, lures men into co-operative action that creatively fulfills ideal ends. Consequently, in their philosophy, there is no need to amplify the concept of God. To be sure, there is need for extending the ideal aspects, and for pursuing more effective means of unifying the ideal and the actual; but that is not identical with pursuing the discovery of God. The concept God is an instrumental symbol, useful for denoting the ideal aspects to which men should devote themselves. In Wieman's philosophy, however, the progressive discovery of God is fundamental. God being a creative activity in our midst, shaping our lives for good or ill, according as we come to terms with its functioning, the most imperative undertaking becomes the pursuit of a fuller knowledge of that *working,* a clearer discernment of its full implications for all of life to the end that human life may serve it more wisely and completely. This fact will help to explain the tentative element in Wieman's philosophy. He is committed to no final definition of God, except the minimum statement that God is the supremely worthful for all mankind. Thus his quest for the Supremely Worthful becomes a patient and faithful concern to clarify and enrich its meaning for human devotion.

Wieman began his search with the simple assertion that "Whatever else the word God may mean, it is a term used to designate that Something upon which human life is most dependent for its security, welfare, and increasing abundance." [17] As such, he pointed out, God is an object of immediate experience. Being an object of experience, his character and scope are discoverable, providing men can devise methods for inquiring into his nature, and develop the kind of sensitivity requisite for such awareness.

> In moving toward a more adequate, i.e. a more scientific knowledge of God, even though we approach from afar off, three things are required: 1) a clarification of that type of experience which can be called distinctively religious; 2) an analysis or elucidation of that datum in this experience which signifies the object being experienced (God); and 3) inference concerning the nature of this object. (P. 33.)

This prescription was laid down in his first book, *Religious Experience and Scientific Method.* His efforts in succeeding years have been directed largely toward fulfilling these requirements. In pursuing this search, Wieman has committed himself to a rigorous method. He will have nothing to do with emotive appeals, grounded upon intuitive persuasion or moral imperatives; nor with speculative flights that soar toward logical mansions in the sky.[18] His method is strict adherence to observation and reason. That only is knowledge, in religion as in every other area of intellectual search, which has been attained through the tested methods of observation and reason.

He does not decry mystical awareness nor ignore its importance for religion. On the contrary, he stresses its great importance as complementary to scientific method. But mystical awareness is not knowledge, nor does it yield knowledge of God or reality, unless its synthetic grasp be subjected to such tested methods as observation and critical reflection.

On this rigorous basis, Wieman has projected his search for God. Starting with the one criterion that God is that which is supremely worthful for all mankind, he has sought to designate, with all the accuracy and clarity possible, what, in man's environing world, answers to that characterization. This has led him to formulate his theory of value. Value, says Wieman, is *that connection between enjoyable activities by which they support one another, enhance one another and, at a higher level, mean one another.* This condition of mutual support, mutual enhancement, and mutual meaning brings into a situation an organic functioning that makes for the continual increase of good and the progressive retirement of evil. For the friction and frustration that ordinarily accompany unrelated striving would thereby be transmuted into co-operative and impelling energy, mutually shared and enjoyed. Aimless endeavor would become purposive and take on the sense of function. Thus living, in the midst of this organic functioning, would acquire a dimension of devotion not present in the self-sufficient existence. This would lift it from the level of mere expenditure of energy to the level of investment of effort in purposive and worthful endeavor. The man with a cause to serve presents an instance of value greater than one who shifts along as a lone individual, serving only his own demands. Wieman has many figures to illustrate his thesis: A tree is a thing of greater value than a brush pile. A house presents more value than a pile of bricks. A symphony is an event of greater value than a mass of musicians playing individual tunes. A community, pursuing the shared life, offers greater degree of value than a crowd of self-sufficient individuals.

What, then, is Supreme Value to which all men may devote themselves? Conceivably it might be the universe taken as a whole, were it true that all its activities were so related as to mutually support, enhance, and mean each other. But the life of the universe obviously presents no such picture of itself. There is a vast portion of its life that is avowedly indifferent to the ends of other activities; hence the magnitude of conflict, frustration, suffering and evil. Supreme value, then, is not to be identified with the universe as a whole. Neither is it to be thought of as this ideal aspect, taken as a concept alone. For God is not simply an idealization of the universe. The Supremely Worthful is that activity in our midst which shapes life toward that progressive attainment of mutual support and meaning. Supreme value, then, is growth of meaning in the world. Why is this growth Supreme Value? It is Supreme Value for the following reasons:

1. In it the greatest value that can ever be experienced at any time is always to be found.
2. It carries the highest possibilities of value, possibilities reaching far beyond the specific meanings we now know.
3. All increase of value is found in it.
4. The best conceivable world can be approximated in existence to some degree through this growth, and in no other way.[19]

Wieman justifies his claim that this Supreme Value is God on five grounds:

1. Growth of meaning commands our supreme devotion and highest loyalty by right of its worthfulness.
2. It creates and sustains human personality.
3. It carries human personality to whatsoever highest fulfillments are possible to it.
4. It has more worth than personality, hence human personality finds its highest destiny in giving itself to this growth to be mastered, used and transformed by it into the fabric of emerging values.
5. The greatest values can be poured into human life only as we yield ourselves to the domination and control of this growth. When we try to dominate and use it, we lose these values.[20]

This growth of meaning which is God shows itself in the social process and in the shaping of history quite as much as it does in the intimate groups and in the development of personality.

Watch the spirit of a community grow. No mere aggregation of people can ever have this spirit, no matter how rigidly each individual strives to conform to an elaborate system of regulations. This spirit is made up of an intricate multiplicity of habits, sentiments, interests all connected in such a way that the whole system supports, enhances and gives meaning to each separate activity and feeling of each individual. Such a system of organically related habits, sentiments, loyalties, memories, hopes, must grow. It requires years. For the fullest development, it requires thousands of years through which successive generations accumulate the sentiments and bring to each new-born babe a massive body of meanings with which to refine and develop his personality until he becomes like a tuning fork that throbs with every pulse of a great culture.[21]

Criticism of Wieman's thought has come chiefly from two sources: (1) humanists who contend that this process or movement to which Wieman gives the name " God " is nothing more than a human functioning, related, to be sure, to the wider-than-human realm; but significant and spiritual only by reason of its functioning through the human environment; (2) orthodox theists who object to representing God as an activity which, at best, as they say, appears to be an impersonal process, emptied of all the qualitative character and meaning essential to the God of worship.

These objections need to be considered carefully. How does Wieman meet the humanist's criticism that this Supreme Value, which he designates God, is but an expression of *human* activity? We quote his statement:

This growth of meaning in the world is superhuman. Superhuman does not mean supernatural. Neither does it mean something outside of human life, for humans obviously can never experience or know anything that is wholly outside their living. Growth of meaning can occur only in and with human experience. Growth of meaning must always appropriate the materials of human life. In like manner a flower can grow only by using the materials of air, light and soil. But the growth is not the work of the air, light and soil. It grows by reordering these elements. So growth of meaning occurs by reordering human life. It is not the work of human life. It is superhuman because it operates in ways over and above the plans and purposes of men, bringing forth values men cannot foresee, and often developing connections of mutual support and mutual meaning in spite of, or contrary to, the efforts of men.

One of the most common cases of this superhuman growth is found in the friendship and love that grows up between two or more persons. When two complex personalities meet in such a way that the meanings of the one begin to modify and be modified by the meanings of the other, new activities are elicited in the individuals concerned, quite beyond any plan or intent in their minds. Also new activities, unforeseen by them, are elicited from their operative environment, in response to these new activities in their respective ways of living. Some of these new activities in the several persons and their environment enter into connections of mutual support and mutual control. They do this not because of any planned effort on the part of the persons, but because human organisms so function in relation to one another and with other features of environment, and the environment with them, that such connections develop. Thus the world takes on a richer body of meanings and values than it had before. Such is the creative process by which a friendship or love or a beloved community grows.

Such enrichment of the world is a genuine creation in the sense that these meanings did not pertain to the existing world at all, prior to this kind of interaction between the persons and their operative environment. They were, of course, possibilities. But they could not be foreseen or known in their specific nature until this particular interaction occurred. This augmented enrichment of the world was not produced by men except that human personalities entered into the total process by which this greater system of value was brought forth. But the human personalities involved did not plan to bring forth these values, these meanings and this enrichment, because they could not have foreseen them or known them prior to their emergence. Therefore human purpose and human intelligence could not possibly have worked in bringing them forth.[22]

To the humanist, however, these accompanying activities, shaping human ends, appear as *sub-human* rather than superhuman activities. They aid the human organism and human society in its climb toward higher ends, just as the physical and chemical elements of the natural world combine and interact to make and sustain the human body and its functioning organs. But the humanist's thesis being that man, the-planet-come-to-consciousness, is the highest expression of cosmic life, the frontier of spiritual achievement, he cannot be led to acknowledge activities beyond human control as superhuman in any spiritual or religious sense. That they are superhuman in the sense of overpowering, he will admit; but only in that sense. Considered from the standpoint of value, humanism would characterize them as sub-human.

This seems to be the *impasse* into which discussion between these two opposing views invariably leads. Until this dilemma is resolved, there seems little possibility of a constructive interaction of ideas between them.[23]

The objections raised to Wieman's concept of God by conventional theists proceed from the same basis, except, of course, the implications of their criticisms are on the opposite side of the issue. It is important to note, however, that humanism and conventional theism stand together in what they consider to be the God of worship. In their philosophies they differ, to be sure: the one denying the existence of such a Being, the other affirming it. But their definition of terms is at this point in agreement. This raises the pertinent question as to whether the *impasse* to which we have referred, rendering the differences between these two forms of naturalistic thought impossible of resolution, is not a direct effect of the truncation, brought about by the humanistic reaction against theocentric religion, which, in turn, is bolstered up by appeals to the philosophy of pragmatism. If that be the case, the problem would seem to resolve itself into an issue between the pragmatic and the metaphysical approach to religion.

But consider now the conventional theist's objection to Wieman's " impersonal God." Two facts should be kept in mind here. One is that what lies behind this objection is, in some cases, perhaps, more significant for a solution of the problem than the direct assertions themselves. Theism has expressed itself in two forms: one, revealing a marked concern for the sentimental attachment between man and God; the other, a sober recognition of the active implications of the fact of God. The one has carried with it a strong moral optimism; the other, a persistent concern to know reality for what it is. Thus, invariably, the sentimentally inclined theist has shown greater concern to maintain the particular formulation of the idea of God that seemed to warrant such optimism than to inquire resolutely into the problem, *what, in fact, is God like?* Doubtless it is this exaggerated sentimentalism that impels some to recoil from the naturalistic doctrine of God. Facts and arguments to the contrary, sentiment demands for them a warmer view. It would be grossly inaccurate to say that all who insist upon a personal conception of God are motivated in this way, for we have noted eminent theorizers in this study who approach the matter purely upon logical grounds. Furthermore, there are personal theists who are at the same time *dynamic* theists. Yet, much of the popular objection to naturalistic theism is of this emotive sort.

The dominant concern of the dynamic theists is to discover what in actual fact does constitute God? Their thought is motivated by the deeper desire to commit themselves in full devotion to that reality, not through sentiment alone, but through submission to it, allowing themselves to be shaped by it and fulfilled through it, and giving themselves devotedly to promoting its wider fulfillment in the world.

Now just how this operation of God, conceived as the naturalistic theist views it, is to be represented adequately in personal terms, is a problem that needs to be considered carefully — a problem, however, that may be dealt with more properly, perhaps, by the theologian than by the philosopher. Mathews has proposed the analogy of man's use of the term friend. " The anthropomorphism which is involved in setting up personal relations with human beings," he writes, " I see extended to the setting up of relations with the cosmos. Just as the word 'friend' indicates a relationship with that which we deem personal, so the word 'God' appears as our conception of those powers in the universe with which we can be personally adjusted because they originated us. As a concept it aids this adjustment as does the concept 'friend' in social adjustments."

Wieman would not object to this analogy, applied to the *growth of meaning,* which he designates the Supremely Worthful, providing it is taken to imply an active functioning as well as a symbolical relationship. Men *will* set up personal relations with that movement in their midst, not only through the language of worship, but through adjustments in personality, yielding to its sovereign power, to be transformed, shaped, and fulfilled by it. Thus the personal relation between man and God, in Wieman's thought, rests upon more than the symbolical behavior of mankind; it is genuine interaction between the system of forces known as persons and the unifying process called God.

This suggests one other fact to be kept in mind in considering the problem of the personal aspect of God. Personality, as the term is commonly employed, carries a rather restricted meaning. Obviously the pattern of thought nearest at hand is *human* personality; consequently the assumption that seems to follow most readily is that God is like man in this personal sense. What is sought in this analogy, doubtless, is the assurance that the relations between man and God proceed upon the basis of conscious awareness. Whether this marks a limitation in our capacity to envisage value apart from conscious awareness, or reveals inadequacies in our view of consciousness, I am not prepared to say. Both may be true. For the concept of personality as well as our understanding of consciousness has been greatly modified in contemporary thought. This ambiguity in its meaning, together with the limiting, even distorting, meaning implied by popular conceptions, has caused naturalists like Wieman, whose minds seek accuracy of meaning, to recoil from the assertion that God is personal or that he has personality. Theologically it expresses an important religious fact: the responsiveness of reality to man's approach. This Wieman would readily ascribe to God. Philosophically, however, the assertion that God is personality creates confusion rather than clarity.

Naturalism offers more possibility of religious motivation than has yet become recognized or, for that matter, apparent. Its thought is still in the formative period, if, in fact, it may be said to have gone beyond the initial or embryonic stage. Just what may emerge out of the present interchange of conflicting theories, no one, perhaps, is competent to foresee. But it is clear that religious thought today is in transition. And the vigor with which the various currents of thought are pursued, together with the soundness of their respective appeals, will doubtless determine whether the future of religious thinking lies with religious humanism, or with a rehabilitated supernaturalism, or with a theocentric naturalism. And there is the possibility that the philosophy of religion of the future may go beyond all of these present forms of thought. Meanwhile each, according to his persuasion, may give himself devotedly to the developing of what may eventuate in *a common faith*. If, however, these divergent views in contemporary thought reflect differences in men's make-up, more basic than mental outlook, as well as interests more vital than logic, the outlook for a common faith must give way to more co-operative venturing in the face of inevitable differences. The outlook in contemporary philosophy of religion is alluring with promising tendencies; but the lines of development are by no means clearly drawn.

1 *Current Christian Thinking.* University of Chicago Press, 1928. Pp. 159–161.
2 *The Quest of the Ages,* pp. 120–21.
8 *Experience and Nature,* p. 28.
4 *Religious Life,* edited by Baker Brownell. Van Nostrand. Pp. 38–39.
5 *Growth of the Idea of God,* p. 207.
6 *Ibid.,* pp. 213–214.   7 *Ibid.,* pp. 219.   8 *Ibid.,* p. 229.   9 *Ibid.,* p. 230.
10 *Immortality and the Cosmic Process.* Harvard University Press, 1933. P. 47.

[11] This approach to a philosophy of religion has been developed in the writer's, *Modern Man's Worship*. Harper, 1934.

[12] The statements that follow express the outlines of the writer's (Meland) own philosophy of religion, the basis of which I undertook to work out in *Modern Man's Worship*. I present them as a possible projection of Gerald Birney Smith's point of view for the reason that I am deeply conscious of his influence upon my own thoughts. If I have erred in identifying his thoughts with mine, I have done so out of a sense of devotion and indebtedness to the spirit of mind I discerned in him.

[13] See Haydon's *Quest of the Ages*, pp. 110–19, for a suggestive statement on this point. See also Meland's *Modern Man's Worship*, Chapter X.

[14] The manuscript for this book was completed without any discussion of the philosophy of religion held by the authors and it was their intention to publish it without reference to themselves. But several philosophers of religion who read the manuscript asserted that Wieman's work should be discussed along with the others. In response to this comment B. E. Meland has given the following account of Wieman's thought.

[15] *The Christian Century*, Dec. 5, 1934. P. 1551.

[16] *The Growth of the Idea of God*, p. 226.

[17] *Religious Experience and Scientific Method*, p. 3.

[18] Hence he follows Whitehead sympathetically in his theory of the primordial nature of God, but forthrightly rejects his views on the consequent nature of God.

[19] *Normative Psychology of Religion*: H. N. Wieman and Regina Wescott Wieman. Crowell, 1935. P. 51.

[20] *Ibid.*, pp. 51–52.   [21] *Ibid.*, p. 551.   [22] *Ibid.*, pp. 52–59.

[23] For further consideration of this problem, see the article, "Is John Dewey a Theist?" *Christian Century*, Dec. 5, 1934; also *Normative Psychology of Religion*, pp. 52–62.

A SYMPOSIUM

THE PRESENT OUTLOOK IN PHILOSOPHY OF RELIGION

THE PRESENT OUTLOOK IN PHILOSOPHY OF RELIGION

EDITORIAL INTRODUCTION [1]

THE future of religious thought in America is as unpredictable as our economic and political trends. In fact, the course of one is to a marked degree bound up with developments in the other two fields. Already we have sensed the effect of the social crisis upon religious thinking. Theologians and philosophers alike have been impelled to bring reflective thought nearer to the scene of social action, and the reactive spirit so manifest in our public life has become a motivating force also in the realm of religious thought. But more basic than this, the creative patterns that are reshaping political and economic reflection are becoming increasingly articulate in philosophical and religious thinking. Tillich, in his penetrating work, *The Religious Situation,* has called attention to one important expression of this trend. The most significant religious symptom of our times, he suggests, is the reaction against the capitalistic spirit — the protest against self-sufficient individualism. This he finds manifest, not only in political and economic movements, but in the arts, the sciences, and the theories of metaphysics and religion. Now the positive aspect of this reaction seems even more significant. Not only is contemporary

thought protesting against the spirit of individualism; it is
heartily embracing the corporate emphasis. Clearly this is the
distinctive emphasis both in modern metaphysics and in contemporary theology. To be sure, it is not everywhere expressive of the same concrete meaning: In metaphysical doctrines
it implies a cosmic *Gestalt*. In humanistic thought it relates
to social objectives. While in modern theology it implies a
correlation of the metaphysical pattern with social imperatives. Yet, the fact that in all three areas thinking inclines
toward a corporate rather than toward an individualistic emphasis signifies that a radical change in basic concepts is taking
place. Just what this may mean for the thought of the future,
one hesitates to suggest. That it is a fundamental turn of
thought, potent with significant meaning, no thoughtful
observer can fail to discern. And the fact that corporate concepts are assuming such major importance in all of our public
affairs argues that we are witnessing, not only a basic turn of
thought, but a crucial change in the course of our cultural
life.

If this be the case (and there are many discerning thinkers
of our day who are confident that it is) the future of religious
reflection is with the philosophies and theologies that build
upon the corporate premise. It does not follow that religious
thinking will become any less diversified; for, as we have suggested, the corporate emphasis lends itself to a variety of ap-
plications. But it does suggest that any system of thought that
fails to come to terms with the social imperatives now looming
upon the horizon, cannot be expected to cope favorably with
the temper of times that are now dawning.

One further fact must be recognized, however: The swing
toward corporate concepts carries its own perils. We are only
too familiar with the pendulum action in movements of the
past. The collective spirit of the early tribal and civic life of
Greece and Rome gave rise to a divisive individualism; only to
be followed later in the west by a return to the communal

philosophy of Roman Catholicism. And the reaction against Catholic collectivism has precipitated, through the course of four centuries, the present plight of our individualistic culture. If we are simply to repeat the habits of history, present tendencies point to a drift toward collectivism that will eventually call forth its own antithesis. If one is an Hegelian or a Marxian, this will be the expected, even the inevitable, course. But whether inevitable or simply *likely,* the possibility of such a wide swerve of the pendulum suggests that there will be room for philosophies and theologies that will temper the collective emphasis — not middle-of-the-road theories that hesitatingly incline both ways, but vigorous synthesizing philosophies that seek to correlate the claims of both extremes.

Philosophy of religion, therefore, must be interpreted as a phase of the current cultural revolution. If it is to remain vital, it must continue as an integrated intellectual expression of the times. Its systems of thought must be earnest efforts to give rational ground and direction to the impelling human ventures that project man's mind and spirit toward his higher destiny. Whether he will attain these high ends, depends upon much besides philosophy of religion. But that he may be *possessed with the dream,* that he may envisage the objectives, and feel the urgency of the causes that beckon him, philosophy and religion share together in a responsibility.

This states the general character of the approaching situation in philosophy of religion. To make it more specific in terms of the several systems of thought now current, requires a capacity of appraisal which no single interpreter can hope to acquire. In the effort to interpret the trends toward tomorrow with greater discernment and breadth of perspective, it has seemed wise to the authors to invite four present-day philosophers to join them in a concluding symposium on the present outlook in philosophy of religion. The four men whose comments follow represent the four major streams of religious thought which appear to be current in America today.

I

FROM THE STANDPOINT OF A SUPER-NATURALIST

By GEORGE W. RICHARDS [2]

Now, as always, there are some men seeking God and others waiting for God to find them. These are two different attitudes which men have taken toward the Eternal from the dawn of time. There have been philosophers, as well as prophets, since the world began. Each went his own way to God or to the ultimate reality. Megasthenes (ca. 300 B.C.) recognized this fact when he wrote: " All that was said concerning nature by the ancients is said also by the philosophers beyond Greece; some of it among the Indians by the Brahmans, some of it in Syria by those called Jews."

Each of these ways to God is clearly defined and.persistently followed at the present time. One of the permanent contributions of the Reformation to our age, according to Professor Dilthey, is " the foundation of religious conviction upon one's inner experience." In the words of Troeltsch, the new Protestantism is " the religion of seeking God in one's own feelings, thinking, experience, volition " — this in distinction from the old Protestantism, which found God revealed in Jesus Christ, to whom man responds with faith working love in the power and with the patience of hope. Rosenberg, in his book, *Der Mythus des Zwanzigsten Jahrhunderts,* is in full accord with Troeltsch in regard to the way of finding God, though the two men differ widely in their findings.

The different schools of American philosophy of religion, as they are defined in this volume, with the exception of the Supernaturalists, seek after God in the cosmos about man and in the soul within man. They are in this respect true to the philosophers of Greece and to what Troeltsch calls " Schleiermacher's program of all scientific theology " — that is, the approach to God through man — "which only needs working out, not the substitution of new methods."

There also are men and schools of philosophy, both in America and in Europe, who are lineal descendants of the Hebrew prophets rather than of the Greek philosophers. They boldly announce that there is no way from man to God, but only from God to man. They build upon the thesis of Kierkegaard, who proclaimed "the unlimited qualitative difference between time and eternity," thus reviving a presumably antiquated dualism and contradicting the prevalent idealistic or materialistic monism. Philosophers and theologians on three continents, many of whom do not consider themselves followers of Karl Barth, are coming more and more under the influence of neo-dualism. They accept the accredited results of science, the critical and historical study of the Scriptures, the necessity of striving for the social betterment of mankind; but they are convinced that they must be known by God before they can know him; that they must be laid hold on by God before they can lay hold on him; that changed views of the universe — due, for example, to the adoption of the heliocentric system of astronomy in place of the geocentric, or to the discoveries of the chemist and the biologist, the psychologist and the psychoanalyst — require a restatement of what God reveals of himself in his Word, but do not affect the essential content of the Word itself. The spiritual and ethical purpose of God is never altered by new views of the universe, whether they be ancient or modern, theistic, humanistic, or materialistic. Servetus' or Harvey's discovery of the circulation of the blood in man did not change the relation of the child to his parents; neither does a change of *Welt-bild* change the relation between God and man.

Furthermore, they have revived emphasis not only on evil in the world but on sin in man — sin, which is described in mythical terms as a fall and which separates man from God in such a way that he can neither know him nor obey him. Fellowship with God is not merely something that the natural man has not yet attained but something that he has lost and can recover only through an act of God.

Each of these contemporary ways of approach is determined by the tradition to which those who follow it are the heirs: it may be that of supernaturalism, of idealism, romanticism, or naturalism. Yet each of these traditions is profoundly influenced by the distinctive type of culture of this generation, which more than any other is under the spell of the scientific method, the humanistic spirit, and the secular view of life.

At the same time all religions are facing a world whose disposition toward religion generally is wholly different from that of any preceding age. We are in a period of transition that is also a time of crisis. One world is in the throes of death; another in the travail of birth. This means a change of attitude and disposition toward the ultimate realities of life — God, man, and the universe. De Burgh says of the Greeks and their quest for knowledge: "For the first time in the history of human civilization, the scientific spirit swung free from entanglements with popular religious beliefs." If that was true in the Periclean age it is still more true in our day. The modern man makes the most of his new freedom, however far it may lead him away from Anaximander and Democritus, from Plato and Aristotle, from Jesus and Paul.

Professor Dewey boldly professes faith in a method of inquiry, not in a creed or a book or a fund of truth that comes from the past. He speaks of "a steadily increasing number of persons who find security in methods of inquiry, of observation, of experiment, of forming and following working hypotheses." Such persons can say . . . : "Though this method slay my most cherished beliefs, yet will I trust it."

Professor Machen represents the Supernaturalists in America and opposes all efforts to bring the moral and religious idealism of the world into harmony with scientific thought, so that it may more effectively meet the needs of modern life. He claims that the Westminster Confession " is not a purely denominational affair to those who believe it to be true. Those who believe it to be true will never be satisfied until it has been accepted by the whole world."

Albert Schweitzer denies the ability of philosophy to reconcile secular knowledge and faith, whatever the period of history or the stage of culture may be. He says: " All problems of religion, ultimately, go back to this one — the experience I have of God within myself differs from the knowledge concerning Him which I derive from the world. In the world He appears to me as the mysterious, marvelous creative Force; within me He reveals Himself as ethical Will. In the world He is impersonal Force; within me He reveals Himself as Personality. The God who is known through philosophy and the God whom I experience as ethical Will do not coincide. They are one; but how they are one, I do not understand." [3]

What has been will be — but always in another form. Man cannot rest satisfied without searching for God; though by searching he cannot find a God who enables him either to reconcile the discoveries of science and the objects of faith or to face life joyously and triumphantly in the midst of a sinful and a dying world. A man's philosophy of religion may confirm him in his faith or in his unbelief — but neither faith nor unbelief are begotten in him or in others through his philosophy of religion. Furthermore, religion is for the common man, who is not a philosopher and for whom in the struggle for life the arguments of philosophy so far as God is concerned have little weight. Neither does the philosophy of religion furnish religion, and above all Christianity, with weapons of attack or defense. For the philosopher, the scientist, and the blatant atheist can vanquish the Christian, whether he be philosopher, theologian or common man, when the latter uses the weapons of the former. " Where argument convinces, a contrary argument may destroy." [4] A frontal attack with the enemy's weapons will invariably fail; but the wielding of arms that are not carnal but spiritual — a sincere Christian life — will not subdue but will probably win the enemy. In Christian living, after the opponent is vanquished and won, there is endless room for the most penetrating philosophic thought, the most accurate scientific research, and indefatigable use of the results of science in practical Christianity.

When man has observed the "behavior of the universe" from atom to solar system, or the progress of the race from savagery to enlightenment, he still needs the revelation of God as one finds it in the prophets and the Christ. It matters not whether he listens to the raging storm, the sighing breeze, the rushing torrent, the rippling brook, or whether he beholds the sun at noon, the evening twilight, the midnight stars, while wandering as a nomad on steppes, in forests, on deserts; whether, as a scientist, he penetrates with the microscope to the centre of the atom and beholds an infinitesimal world beyond the reach of the naked eye, or with the telescope steals the secrets of billions of wandering stars in a universe the limits of which cannot be reached by the wildest dreams of human fancy. Both nomad and scientist are in touch with, and will find, only nature's forces; but neither the one nor the other can discover the gospel of God.

It is the essence of paganism or of humanism, in its primitive and in its classic forms, in naive myths and legends or in refined philosophy and art, to seek God *in* the world — in the world *about* man and *within* man. Thus men "seek God, if haply they might feel after him and find him." (Acts 17:27).

In principle the savage and the scientific theologian agree: they differ only in the methods and the instruments with which they seek to understand the "behavior of the universe." One may have reason to ask: "Who is in closer contact with nature, the naked savage who wakes and sleeps under heaven's canopy, or the well-groomed scientist who is a voluntary prisoner in the laboratory or the observatory?" The myth may come a little closer to the mystery than the chemical formula or the astro-nomical law.

Moreover, there always remains in the universe the contra-diction of law and order; of chance and caprice; of the justice which controls the mechanism of the world for righteousness and the fate whose decrees are irreversible and fixed; of the God who provides and forgives and the God who withholds and demands the utmost farthing. This contradiction is the un-solvable problem of philosophers; it passeth all understanding. It has perplexed unto despair gnostics, Marcionites, Manicheans, Cartesians, Darwinians, all sorts of humanists. It can be re-solved not by process of reasoning, but only through revelation by incarnation; in other words, through faith in the gospel of God. For gospel we turn to the men who have heard the call of God and in whom God has revealed his purpose — to the prophets rather than to the philosophers.

What of the present outlook in philosophy of religion? One stands in awe of the erudition, the mental acumen, the mastery of vast areas of matter and mind, the indefatigable quest for God and the complete life, of men individually and socially. Yet one cannot refrain from asking, after one has read scores of books and conversations on God and the pathways to cer-tainty, whether we are nearer the ultimate reality than was Plato, Paul, St. Thomas or Kant.

Each of the three great periods of philosophy in the West — the classic age of Greece, the Thirteenth Century of the Middle Ages, and German idealism — has ended in doubt rather than faith, in despair of human effort to reach the absolute, in re-course to revelation of one sort or another. The most that can be said is that philosophy has made it clear that faith is more reasonable than unbelief, and that there are open spaces in the universe that allow room for God and religion. The philos-opher of religion has done and is now doing what Leverrier did for astronomers. He suspected the existence of an undis-covered planet in the heavens. Guided by mathematical measurements of volume, orbit and location at a specified time, he determined the point where the planet ought to be; and lo, the telescope revealed it in all its splendor. By the study of the nature of the universe, the character of the mind of man, the experience of the race, the philosopher discovers the need of God. He may turn men to the Nazarene; and lo, the Christ! And when men come after him and are on the way with him, they will find certainty of the absolute being, which is wholly different from the certainty of scientific observation and philosophical speculation.

The following words of Albert Schweitzer have haunted me ever since I read them ten years ago: they describe, as I see it, the present outlook in philosophy of religion:

> There are two kinds of *naivete:* one which is not yet aware of all the problems and has not yet knocked at all the doors of knowledge; and another, a higher kind, which is the result of philosophy having looked into all problems, having sought counsel in all the spheres of knowledge, and then having come to see that we cannot explain anything but have to follow convictions whose inherent value appeals to us in an irresistible way.[5]

One may call this defeatism; but I prefer to call it fideism — the final outcome of man's struggle for life in the universe into which he is born and which finally he will transcend.

II

FROM THE STANDPOINT OF AN IDEALIST

By EDGAR S. BRIGHTMAN [6]

It would be well to make clear at the start that what follows is written from the standpoint of a personal idealist, as defined in an earlier chapter. A thinker cannot divest himself of real convictions, and it is futile to pose as having none. It is equally futile to treat convictions as dogmas, incapable of modification by further experience and criticism. No philosopher can be without convictions; no philosopher can treat them as unchangeable. Offering the hypothesis of personal idealism in this tentative spirit, let us inquire into the present outlook in philosophy of religion.

I

The first response of any philosophic mind to a survey of contemporary life tends to be pessimistic. If ever there was an age of reason, it is not here now. The illiterate masses, tormented in body and mind by a collapsing economic system, follow leaders they can understand, and they cannot understand philosophers, hardly a Will Durant. Causes — psychologically, biologically, socially, economically determined — rather than reasons appear to govern human conduct and belief.

But, black as are appearances, the light of reason still shines. If rationalists have sometimes betrayed reason by treating it as though it were a system of abstractions, Hegel, the greatest rationalist of human history, saw reason as a unification of the whole content of experience in a coherent whole. The method of reason was for him the method of striving toward that whole by clear analysis and synthesis. It speaks well for the power of reason today that Hegel is still an influence in the world of affairs. No Hegel, no Marx-Engels-Lenin; no communism and no socialist critique of communist dogma. No Hegel, no Nazi theory of the state and no Liebert to indict it. No Hegel, no Gentile to organize the Fascist system of education and no Croce to defy Mussolini. It is from Hegel that Royce received much of his inspiration; from Hegel that Dewey took his start and to Hegel he still looks as the greatest of systematic philosophers.

Hegel to one side, is it not true that social and religious life today is germinating precisely at the centers where ideas are fermenting? Where you find a Whitehead, a Hocking, a Dewey, a Wieman, a Knudson, a Niebuhr, or a Calhoun there you find vital influences being generated which are bound to affect the religion of multitudes for better or for worse. In a world of force and unreason, there is ground for faith in reason.

2

As the personal idealist surveys contemporary American thought, he is able to point to a considerable number of victories.

(a) Idealists have always contended for the objectivity of value. Today, while some (like Sellars) deny it, many who are not idealists grant this principle: for example, Whitehead, Wieman, Spaulding, and even, in a sense, Dewey. Indeed the objectivity of value is being claimed as a peculiar tenet of realism (so Spaulding and the religious realists). Truth laughs at labels. The main point is that what was an almost uniquely idealistic (and theistic) insight is now much more widely recognized.

(b) For centuries idealists have contended for the proposition that the universe is organic, a whole made up of wholes. Although this principle was denied (or regarded as irrational) during the neo-realistic interlude, it is now accepted by most pragmatists and realists, especially by those who have investigated religion, for example, above all, Whitehead and Wieman, by men as far from each other as Sellars and Calhoun, and also by all purposive, Gestalt, and self psychologists.

(c) Ever since the dawning idealism of Plato and Aristotle, the soul has been considered a principle of motion, and being has come, in Berkeley, Leibniz, Fichte, Hegel, Lotze and Bowne, to be interpreted as activity, and as embodying dialectic movement or — to use other language — purposive entelechy or evolution. Idealists saw evolutionary activity at work in the world long before Darwin. Today, pragmatists, socialists and physicists agree on this idealistic principle.

(d) Historically the idealists have insisted that the social problem is an integral part of philosophy. It was Plato, not Democritus, who wrote the *Republic;* it was Berkeley, and not Hume, who was concerned about the economic sufferings of the proletariat; it was Fichte and not Bolzano who unified his nation; it was Hegel and not Herbart who wrote a *Philosophie das Rechts;* it was the idealistic method that led Marx to write *Das Kapital.* Other philosophers than idealists have also been concerned with the social problem, as Hobbes, the eighteenth century French materialists, and the utilitarians. But idealists, more than others, have uniformly insisted that the whole range of social values is part of the subject matter of philosophical interpretation and criticism. Today, almost all philosophers of religion would concede this truth, although pragmatists often forget that they are reviving an idealistic tradition.

(e) The continuity of the idealistic tradition in American thought, despite hostile polemic and periods of unpopularity, may be regarded as a fifth victory for idealism. It is superfluous to say that Plato abides. Fichte has had his spokesman in Hugo Münsterberg and Jared Sparks Moore. The influence of Hegel is evident in Royce, Calkins, Dewey and Hocking, that of Lotze and Hegel in Ladd, Bowne, and the Bowne school. In Pierce and those influenced by him we have traces of both Leibniz and Hegel. Whitehead is constructing a new tradition which idealists find hard to differentiate from the Hegelian.

(f) A sixth victory for idealism is to be found in the reluctant yet gradual recognition that idealism is empirical. It is true that Plato and Kant created so sharp a contrast between phenomena and noumena that they seemed to regard the empirical as a shadow or an illusion. But it is also true that they were discoverers of aspects of experience neglected in their day. Berkeley and Hegel build their idealisms on the analysis of conscious experience; Theodor Haering calls Hegel " the empiricist of consciousness." Kant's realm of *mögliche Erfahrung* was the basis of Royce's idealism. Experience is the very stuff of reality for almost every idealist. The pragmatic emphasis on experience is another rediscovery of idealism.

Each one of these victories of idealism is so obviously a victory for religion that elaboration at this point is unnecessary. What has been said might be taken to mean that idealism (smelling as sweet under other names) has conquered American religious thought and that the prospect is rosy for the maintenance of this conquest. Such an inference would, of course, be quite unwarranted.

3

Idealism in general faces foes in unexpected quarters, like the Italian invasion by Pareto and the Austrian invasion by the logical positivists. If either of these invasions is successful, anything that may properly be called idealistic philosophy of religion is, at least for the time being, done for. The two invaders, by the way, were pretty well repulsed by Charner Perry and E. Jordan in the October 1935 issue of *The International Journal of Ethics*. Just now, however, our concern is not with the major strategy of idealism, but rather with the prospects for personalism.

There are at present three main challenges to personalistic idealism in particular. The first comes from those who accept its personalism, but reject its idealism. This includes the religious realists — such men as D. C. Macintosh, John Bennett, R. L. Calhoun, J. B. Pratt and others, as well as the neo-supernaturalists, more or less under Barthian influence. The religious realists and the Barthians are both dualists of a sort, and there is bound to be further debate on the question whether there is a fundamental dualism between mind and matter, and also between God and the world. Personalists decline to regard either dualism as ultimate and on this issue stand nearer to the naturalists and pragmatists than to the supernaturalists.

The second challenge to personalistic idealism comes from those who accept its idealism but reject its personalism. Here we have realists like E. G. Spaulding, whose God is a realm of impersonal, eternal values, and idealists like W. M. Urban and Clifford Barrett who either evade or deny the personality of God. Here the essential problem is whether a Platonic or idealistic theory of objective values is really intelligible apart from conscious mind.

The third challenge comes from those who reject both the personalism and the idealism of the view, yet affirm religious values on a naturalistic basis. Dewey and Wieman are great antagonists of personalism. Their differences in no way affect their united front against personalism, although both have much in common with impersonal idealism. What will happen to religion in the concrete if their hypotheses are adopted remains to be seen.

4

There are a few problems about which discussion is bound to center in the years immediately ahead. Let us state them briefly.

(a) The conflict between naturalism and idealism will continue. At present in some quarters naturalism has a specious advantage because of the popular impression that naturalism is dealing with verified facts, whereas idealism is purely speculative. When it is seen, as in the dialectical movement of thought it must be, that naturalism and idealism are both attempts to interpret the facts and that both are speculative, as all thought about anything other than the present moment must be, the artificial advantage of naturalism will disappear and the problem will assume new aspects. We shall then begin to ask which of the two systems takes fairer account of all kinds of facts, and which interprets the facts more coherently.

(b) Back of current discussions of religious experience lies a confusion about the meaning of verification. Until we have a lively and ample discussion of the definition of verification, naturalism will continue to have an artificial advantage over idealism. When verification has been reflected on, it may be that it will be seen always to imply an appeal to reason.

(c) Present debate about certainty and possibility must continue. Should religion be based exclusively on what is undeniably certain (Wieman) or should it renounce certainty and be an exploration of the possibilities of experience (Dewey)? Dewey's view is nearer to the idealistic conception of the dialectic of reason, and may be taken more seriously by personal idealists than hitherto.

(d) The fact of creation is now pretty well established by "emergent evolution," but theories of creation are in confusion. There is need for further definition. There has recently been discussion of the sense in which mind is or is not creative. It is obvious that if God is a mind, as personalists believe, his mind possesses many properties that differ radically from those of human minds, as well as many that resemble them. If a mind were truly creative, would it cease to be a mind? Is it conceivable that a divine mind could create?

(e) The problem of evil can be disregarded only if and when religion proposes to give up its task entirely. Religion must choose between optimism and meliorism. Complete pessimism is incompatible with any religion. The phenomenal pessimism and noumenal optimism of many supernaturalists is not merely dualistic; it is from a rational standpoint incoherent and cannot find wide or permanent acceptance. In the long run, religious thought must choose between the optimism of traditional theism, with its blind faith in the absolute omnipotence and benevolence of God, and a meliorism which recognizes that the power for good in the universe works under limits. This view, held in various forms by John Stuart Mill, F. C. S. Schiller, William James, Hastings Rashdall, H. N. Wieman, H. B. Alexander, R. A. Tsanoff, W. P. Montague, W. K. Wright, John Bennett, R. L. Calhoun, and others, must be taken into account by any future philosophy of religion.[7]

(f) Last, and most important, the social implications of religion need more precise investigation. If it can be shown that religion is a rationalization of capitalism and that all churches are hopelessly committed to the *status quo* in economics and politics, the prospect for philosophy of religion is black. But perhaps in religious, as in other, institutions there is a perpetual conflict between free truth and economic determinism. The relations of religion to legislation, to revolution, to labor, to capital, to war, and to the state in general are just beginning to be considered in American philosophy of religion. The social aspects of idealism equip idealists for a large share in this task.

5

Differences of opinion will continue. But creative differences are more valuable than reduction to any " common faith " that sacrifices individual creative energy. Nevertheless we are destined more and more to witness a decline in the importance and authority of individual thinkers and even of " schools " — be they naturalistic or idealistic. What is to be hoped for above all is an increase in co-operative labor on the task of interpreting religion, such as is exemplified in the present volume. Without any arbitrary compromises or sacrifices of individual conviction a new truth may gradually be discerned, larger and more inclusive than any present insight.

III

ROMANTICISM OR REALISM, WHICH?

By DOUGLAS C. MACINTOSH [8]

There is a disturbing plausibility about Comte's law of the three stages of thought which many theologians and religious philosophers must have felt. In fact there is a great deal of truth in it. Desiring to understand his world, man has employed successively a more or less mythical theology, abstract metaphysical concepts and arguments, and finally scientific laws based on facts of experience. This last, the " positive " method, has in practical relations an acknowledged and growing prestige, which is considerably more than can be said, at the present time, of the other two.

It is to be noted, however, that human thought moves in cycles. Satiated with mere scientific knowledge of fact the mind seeks a comprehensive philosophical interpretation of the meaning of things, and even tends to return to a religious world-view. But what is equally important, though not so often recognized, is that the last of the three stages, the positive or scientific, has application in the religious realm itself. Popular religious thought contains a larger ingredient of myth; speculative philosophy assumes the task of proving all things by reasoning and holding fast only that in religious dogma which can be taken as literally true; but what has been left almost unnoted is that there is no good reason why some of our religious thinking and experience should not pass into the positive or scientific stage. What I mean, essentially, is that there is now within our reach a body of verified and verifiable information as to the dependable working, within human experience, of a factor or factors with powers which coincide with those, or some of those, which discriminating religion is most concerned to discover in the object of its faith.

The view I would defend is religious realism. The term covers two meanings, the one a theory of religious knowledge, the other that realistic attitude in religion which insists on due recognition of all the facts of evil as well as those of good. The realistic theory of religious knowledge, as I hold it, posits a Divine Reality which exists whether it is recognized or not, which may be directly experienced and known, and which may not only have qualities which do not appear to us but may also have, as presented in our experience, apparent qualities which cannot be taken as valid revelation of what the independently existing Divine Reality is.

More specifically, what is claimed is based, in the first instance, on the possibility and actuality of a dependable experience of salvation, of deliverance from evil and achievement of good, on condition of a describable and practicable religious adjustment on man's part. That there is such a religious experience, repeatedly experienced and dependably experienceable, on conditions which can be and have often been specified, is a verified and verifiable fact. The deliverance from evil is obviously not immediate complete deliverance from all evil; but it is real deliverance from real evil, and that primarily in the realm of individual will and action. There is a reality which dependably conditions an experience of salvation in response to a certain discoverable religious adjustment. This reality is what practical religion is interested in, so that the statement just made is at once scientific and theological.

Unfortunately this verifiable fact seems to have been overlooked or inadequately recognized by many of those who have passed from the more or less mythical traditional theology through a transitional stage of abstract metaphysical speculation to the modest but relatively dependable ways of positive science. John Dewey is one of these. In the course of the early changes in his thinking he passed from traditional supernaturalistic theism to speculative absolute idealism, and later from this to naturalistic, non-theistic humanism. This latter transition does not involve so great a change as is sometimes supposed. Absolute idealism is naturalism still wearing the halo of theism; but a few rather easy changes suffice to transform its "single, all-inclusive conscious Experience" into the experience, human but social, which is the ultimate philosophical term for Dewey and his humanistic disciples. The rational ideal element in the Absolute is dropped, ideas being taken as mere transitory instruments of biological adjustment. The subjectivism of the experience-philosophy is cured — or obscured — by being applied to the subject itself: reality comes to be just experience without any necessity of a conscious experiencer, which is explained as being nothing but a functional distinction reappearing from time to time when the reaction of the organism to its environment is temporarily impeded and the situation becomes problematic. From the point of view of this humanistic empiricism the God-idea is a mere optional symbol for social values, or (as an after-thought) for undisputed natural and human factors supporting such values, apart from any adjustment to a specifically religious object.

But if we do not despair of experimental religion so easily as these humanistic neo-positivists do, we may discover that at its best it is not merely accidentally good for something, but, as we have intimated, dependably good for something imperatively important. The gaining of empirical religious knowledge will then be possible. Laws can be formulated stating in generalized form the experiences which tend to be conditioned by some functioning reality when certain discoverable adjustments to superhuman reality are made and maintained. That functioning reality is the object of religious interest; the laws of its functioning are theological laws.

In its general features we can say what the right, dependably effective religious adjustment is. It is no mere superficial, self-confident, self-dependent "decision" or "commitment" in favor of a certain ethical or "Christian" way of life. Remember what happened to Vain-Confidence in By-path Meadow! Neither can we recommend the opposite course of those Barthian prophets who would inhibit any voluntary approach to God with the warning, "There is no way from man to God!" There is a way from man to God. It is not the way of mere self-confident volition, but the way of absolute surrender of one's will and life to the will and working of the religiously all-sufficient God. We do not need to wait, stalled and panicky in the face of approaching destruction, hoping against hope for some unpredictable miracle of the "Divine Initiative." The divine initiative has already been taken and is a constant factor of our situation. We have but to respond and rightly adjust our spiritual receptors to the divine stimulus, ever accessible to the faith which is ready to surrender absolutely to the God of the absolute Ideal. " Ye shall seek Me and ye shall find Me, when ye search for Me *with all your heart.*" This constant availability of divinely functioning power, when approached in the faith that is not afraid of absolute self-surrender, constitutes the *permanent possibility of divine revelation.*

"Religion without revelation," according to Barth, " is what Feuerbach said it was." With this statement it is possible to agree more fully than with the Barthian dictum previously quoted. For Feuerbach religion was essentially wishful thinking; all the gods of all the religions he regarded as mere projections of human wishes. And it is true enough that if there be no dependable response of reality to any discoverable religious adjustment, experimental religion is but the futile gesture of a being driven by vain wishes and deceptive fantasies. But, in opposition to the Barthian view, genuine revelation in the religious realm, as in that of sense-perception, is not a different process from discovery; it is simply another aspect of the same thing. Religious revelation is discovery of Divine Reality and Power. It is conditioned on the one hand by the constant stimulus of divine educational processes (including the testimony of those who have already found the way to God). On the other hand it is conditioned by the human response, by that self-abandon to the divine will and working which is comparable to the opening of the eyes to the ever-potential stimulus of the sunlight. There always is a divine initiative, and there always is also a human responsibility for response. Without the divine initiative and the beginnings of revelation doubtless man would never have faith enough to surrender his will and life to God; and without that faith and voluntary self-surrender revelation will never be adequately realized by man.

As for the historic Jesus, his meaning for us is the permanent possibility of divine revelation. In him we see what divine power can do in and for and through one whose will was fully surrendered to the divine will. He lost his life in consequence, but only to become the world's greatest deliverer, God's best revealer. But in relation to us, the revelation in Christ is at second hand. High enough to be ever normative for measuring the divine in the human, the revelation in Christ is, for the world, of the first importance. But what is religiously essential for each of us is a revelation of the saving power of God in his own personal experience.

This empirical knowledge of divine process, presence, reality and power, operating for the salvation of man from sin and therewith from its consequences, may be supplemented (still within the domain of knowledge in the scientific sense) by considering the evidence for power transcending humanity, and working, *as if* with intelligent and moral purpose, first for the evolutionary but creative emergence of persons, and then for their education in the school of experience. Man is being taught, as fast as he will learn the lessons of experience, the need of and the way to scientific knowledge, good moral character, and social co-operation. The way current events are teaching the imperative necessity of international peace may serve as an illustration of this last. Finally, man is being taught in the school of experience the need of a dynamic, regenerating religion. Thus even beyond and prior to the special revelation of divine process and causality in specifically religious experience there is this general revelation of the presence in the universe of a functionally divine reality, working in many ways toward a unitary and ideal end, namely, the being and spiritual well-being of man; working against opposition, but steadily for man; working not only beyond man but, as permitted by man, with man and indeed in and through man; working, therefore, *as if* intelligently and with moral purpose.

Up to this point our concern has been with revelation in the sense in which it coincides with discovery of God, that is, with religious perception, or adequately critical empirical intuition of reality or power which is of supreme value, or divine, *func-*

tionally (delivering man from the supreme evil, sin) and thus divine *qualitatively* also and therefore worthy of supreme adoration. It would make for clearness and distinctness if the term revelation were to be restricted to this experience of divine reality which makes possible strictly verified theological knowledge. But it is customary in modern theology to apply the term revelation to that spiritual illumination which brings subjective certitude, not amounting to full objective demonstration, of religious reality and truth. Furthermore, religious liberals of the Ritschlian persuasion have commonly spoken of such subjective awareness as " religious knowledge." I think it better, because more accurate and less confusing, to use the term " faith " for that subjective certitude and merely imaginal (as opposed to perceptual) intuition. A subjectively assured faith or intuition may be taken as a religious working hypothesis, but I suggest that we limit the application of the terms religious revelation and religious knowledge to the verifying experiences and the verified judgments respectively.

Consider, for example, the intuitive certitude, which many religious persons have, that the functionally divine reality of which we can have experimental knowledge is, beyond what we *know* it to be, really unitary and of the nature of self-conscious spirit, supremely intelligent and supremely good. Such religious thinking may be highly assured and is, as it seems to me, a highly reasonable faith; but it is not knowledge in the sense of demonstrated certainty. The subjective certitude of intuition is not to be taken as infallible. It ought to be tested, as far as possible, by its value and by the facts. A demonstration of its value for the development of ideal personality and ideal society will show not so much its truth as its interest for us. But at least a partial test of its truth is undertaken when the general affirmation of faith is made a principle from which inferences are drawn in order to be compared directly with the facts of experience, as for instance when from the power and love of God something is inferred as to the answer of prayer, in the sense of a dependable response of divinely functioning reality to some discoverable religious adjustment.   The verification of the logically inferred hypothesis about prayer would not fully prove the truth of the major theological principle from which it was inferred, but it would have positive evidential value as making in a thoroughly critical way for the conclusion that that original subjective intuition of faith was perhaps, or even probably, true.   And where subjective intuitions of faith are subjected to philosophical tests of value and scientific tests of truth, due care being exercised not to draw conclusions which are not logically justified, realism, it seems to me, rather than "romanticism," is still the more appropriate descriptive term for the attitude and point of view.

IV

FROM THE STANDPOINT OF A NATURALIST

By EDWARD SCRIBNER AMES [9]

Pragmatism is a relatively recent development in philosophy. With the exception of William James, its great representatives have not undertaken definite application of its point of view to religion with such thoroughness as they have treated logic, ethics, education and social psychology. This has not been due to any feeling that pragmatism is not applicable to religious problems but only to the fact that its spokesmen have been more concerned with other problems. Those problems, however, lie in the path of a significant approach to religion. Pragmatism shares John Locke's interest in "a new way of ideas." That novelty consists largely in dealing with ideas in an empirical, matter-of-fact manner. It seeks to avoid mere verbalisms, vain speculations, and metaphysical dialectic. The whole history of empiricism has emphasized this critical, analytical, practical procedure. Naturally the application of this method to the sanctities of religion has often been interpreted as hostil-

ity to religion itself. It has involved a new vocabulary, a tentativeness, and a recognition of the constant need for criticism
and reconstruction all of which are disturbing to the craving
for certainty and finality. Moreover, this method and these
attitudes are characteristic of modern science and there still
persists on the part of many religionists a suspicion, if not an
antipathy, in regard to " science." It is only the short and
superficial view which falls into this error. As the scientific
method is more widely and adequately employed it yields
its positive and satisfying fruits, and it is already rendering constructive results in various fields. I think it is so in
religion, and as this method is further extended in the treatment of religious problems its fruitfulness will be increasingly
evident.

An illustration may be seen in the conception of a " finite
God " as set forth by James. This was part of his onslaught
against all Absolutes. He could not make out an Absolute,
either as fact or as inference, from any sane and fair estimate
of the world of observed fact and experience. A finite God
fitted the scene better and elicited a deeper religious response,
for such a God could need our human effort and make our
struggles and adventures for his cause real and decisive in the
battles of the Lord. The adoption of this finite God by personalists like Professor Brightman, and realists like Professor
Lyman, shows the growing realization of the positive value
of the idea. Nothing indicates better than this tendency toward new conceptions of God the value of freedom to criticize
and restate the most basic conceptions. It is possible, in the
history of religions, to see how ideas of God have changed under the pressure of new experience, as when the Hebrew exiles
expanded their idea of Jahveh to fit their needs. But such
changes have been only vaguely conscious, whereas with religionists today there is critical search for more vital and satisfying conceptions.

Some of the pragmatists have been occupied with specific

problems which had implications for religion but were left undeveloped. Such is the " generalized other " and the " concrete universal " of Professor George H. Mead. The generalized other arises out of the process in which the self arises. In conversation a person must put himself at the point of view of the other and see himself as the other sees him. He reacts according to the responses he understands the other to be making. In a group, such as that of the playground or the family, the individual finds these responses built up in a way that gives him a sense of an Other toward which his own responses are made. It is through this " other " that the social process influences the behavior of a person, and it is through this other that the community exercises control over the conduct of its individual members. The process of thinking is a conversation with this generalized other. Though Professor Mead did not so employ this significant insight, it easily suggests a fruitful enrichment of the idea of God and of the nature and function of prayer!

Such a functional, social conception can readily answer the charge that the idea of God is involved in individual subjectivism. It likewise points the way to a refutation of social subjectivism, for the social processes are constantly interwoven with the objective world of physical fact and process, of space and time. This is partly the force of the analogy of " Alma Mater " in reference to the idea of God. Here it is evident that the reality is not the picture in the mind but the whole institution, including buildings and grounds, and a complex congeries of " natural " phenomena. They have their place in the objective order, and are subject to the realm of fact and existence. In the same way I assert that God is Reality idealized and personified.

In this connection it is pertinent to indicate the source of the conception of absoluteness which accompanies the function of the idea of God. This I have set forth in terms of the " practical absolute." The original formulation was given in an article in the *International Journal of Ethics,* published in 1922, as follows:

> Why are the values of religion accompanied by such a sense of validity in the active effort to realize them? . . . The definition of religion as a practical endeavor to realize values implies that it is primarily a matter of action, an affair of overt deeds. In this respect it is sharply contrasted with the reflective attitude of philosophy. Now it is characteristic of overt action that it requires the definite selection of an end or plan. Since only one plan can be followed at one time, the one chosen must be carried out as if it were the only possible one and as having, at least at the moment of action, absolute worth and validity. If a person cannot bring himself to choose one line of action with such definiteness and exclusiveness then he either does not act at all or acts without force and effectiveness. He wabbles and hesitates and vacillates. . . . He develops a Hamlet-like hesitation. . . . So long as he refrains from action he may enjoy the contemplation of the alternatives, of the numerous possibilities which play through his thought. The approach of the moment when he must act is repellent because in order to launch himself into the objective deed he must abandon all but one of his cherished potentialities. This line of inquiry has led me to the conception of the *practical absolute,* the absolute of the moment of action and the absolute of predominantly practical modes of life. . . . This suggests a deeper reason for the authority of religious attitudes than those explanations which refer its absoluteness to its natural conservatism or to the fact that it is a product of custom or of revelation. This deeper reason lies in the nature of religion as a life of action.

To this conception of the practical absolute, which alternates with other moments of critical reflection and revision, I now add the equally significant idea of the *honorific absolute.* It is a matter of common experience that we ascribe perfection to objects of appreciation. The objects of our supreme devotion appear as wholly satisfying. Love puts a halo round the idol of affection. The mystical mood of wonder and rapport begets the attitude of complete acceptance. At such moments the intrusion of questioning or limitation is sacrilegious. Such are the great experiences of aesthetic fulfillment. Most of all they appear in religious contemplation. The attributes of omniscience, omnipotence, perfect goodness, love and beauty are the honorific appraisals of loyalty and adoration felt in the contemplation of God as the supreme Reality. They are poetic appreciations which give release and emotional fulfillment. As such they do not demand nor depend upon proof or logical justification. They are generated by the impulsion of desire and the extension of felt goods of existence. They are more than phantasies for they carry into magnified dimensions actual satisfactions and experienced goods. Court salutations, and the lover's unrestrained avowals, are the expressions in human relations which reveal the patterns in which religious devotion honors the divine.

Pragmatism escapes many difficulties of traditional theologies by its view of human nature. It does not accept the mythological story of the fall of man but it holds the scientific theory of what might be called the rise of man. It does not minimize the frailties of human nature nor exaggerate its nobler qualities. Taking the view that man has emerged from an animal ancestry, the important point of emphasis is the manner and the process by which man has achieved his development and high aspirations. It is a long story of growth through trial and error; of remembering, at first in myth and legend and later in records and codes, experiences of success and defeat. It is the story of making tools, organizing groups, discovering means of subsistence, learning the ways of nature, and extending mutual aid. Everywhere man is driven by his hungers, his felt needs, toward experiments and self-discipline. His moral development has been involved in having regard for the established ways of living and in venturing into new activities. Satisfactions and frustrations have been his guides. His goodness and his badness have been relative to the standards and ideals generated in this process of living. Individuals have been better or worse, never absolutely good or absolutely bad. The evolution has not been in a straight line nor by inevitable steps. It has not been guaranteed, nor is it now.

Pragmatism has therefore thrown off the weight of the doctrine of original guilt, as it has surrendered the notion of election to final bliss. Life and its goods continue to be problematic but not capricious. Some stabilities have been discovered, and others have been established at least to a degree. It remains an imperfect world, a hazardous and precarious world, but yet a world in which many goods and satisfactions have eventuated and continued to appear. And in the complex process man takes a real though modest part. He is dependent upon processes of nature and yet is able to avail himself of her resources, and in a scientific age to participate amazingly in her operations and creative forces. More and more he finds the problems and the promise of his existence in the shared life of his fellows. It is by co-operative living that the great achievements in morality, science and art have been secured, and it is toward this social enterprise that his hopes turn in new visions. The religious spirit of love manifest in some degree in the most primitive life becomes embodied in larger and finer forms of endeavor and control.

The most recent extension of pragmatic religious faith has been made by Professor John Dewey in his Yale lectures, *A Common Faith*. Here he has added the great weight of his word to the support of a religious view of life. He sets forth the "natural piety" from which spring the ceremonials, institutions and ideologies of religion, although he also insists that these often obscure and hinder that natural piety. He announces a new and vital conception of God and shows the significance of its function in the fulfillment of significant ideals. He exposes the basic error of atheism and gives clarification and emphasis to the religious character of all sincere devotion to the ideals appearing in the natural values of noble human relationships. Thus pragmatism makes another important advance in the understanding and illumination of the spiritual life of mankind.

V

SUMMARY STATEMENTS

By BERNARD E. MELAND

These presentations by representatives of four distinctive types of philosophy of religion are indeed instructive, not alone for what they contribute toward an analysis of the present outlook, but for what their statements reveal regarding the vigor of these several approaches.

That supernaturalism will continue as an important expression of current religious thought, particularly in the form of the new critical interpretation described by President Richards, seems assured. And there is the likelihood that its decisive stand upon the spiritual versus the secular aspects of culture, as expressed in the recent books, *The Church Against the World* by H. Richard Niebuhr, Pauck and Miller, *Religious Situation* by Paul Tillich, and several provocative volumes by Reinhold Niebuhr will give neo-supernaturalism an important leadership in the religious situation that seems imminent.

Idealism, according to Professor Brightman, bids fair to assume increasing power and influence in the era that is ahead. Doubtless he would be confirmed by many eminent thinkers in the field today. The stirring prophecies of Professor Boodin in the closing chapter of his recent book, *God,* should be heartening to idealists. Whether idealism will hold the prestige that it once enjoyed as a commanding philosophy of the times, may be questioned by some, however. What Professor Brightman says regarding the growing vindication of idealistic postulates is in great measure true. It might be suggested, however, that such recrudescence of these idealistic hypotheses as seems to be occurring is taking form, not under the banner of idealism, but as adaptations of idealistic theses within other types of thought, modified and tempered by their respective emphases. Idealism, that is to say, will doubtless hold sway over a vast area of religious thought in the future, not as a cause new-born, but as a parental influence working through its many offspring within other circles and associations.

The romantic tradition, in the form in which it has existed in this country, that is, as a liberal theology grounded in religious experience, or as an aesthetic expression of the religious response, may not be expected to have a wide appeal in the immediate years that are ahead. For both assume a complacent optimism which our present cultural life decries. That their days are over, however, we cannot feel is true. For both involve elements that transcend the passing mood. The *liberal* temper of the romantic theology which took its rise from Schleiermacher's thought is far too precious to be lost to the human spirit. Its eclipse at present we feel is due in part to the limitations of the particular historic movements that embraced it and in large part to the tensions of modern times. That it may survive in potential form to emerge again in a new renascent period, every truly cultivated mind must hopefully anticipate. The present relinquishment of this ideal on the part of those who choose to be known as religious realists is in some measure inspired by the desire to correct a faulty emphasis; but there is danger that too wholehearted a swing from this emphasis may give rise to a condition in religious thought that will develop more serious limitations. It may be that here the steadying influence of idealism will provide a needed ballast.

Liberalism as well as the aesthetic and contemplative attitude belong essentially to matured periods of thought. They find their fullest expression during times and among groups that have passed beyond the combative, the confused, and the resurgent stage. The close of the nineteenth century and the dawn of the twentieth were periods ripe for such a temper. But the mood of impartial reflection and appreciation has fled the earth today. It may return. It must return! But the tensions of today have dispelled its lure for the present generation and for those who are approaching the tasks of tomorrow.

Dr. Macintosh is right, therefore: it *is* realism rather than romanticism that characterizes the mood of those who once wore the badge of liberalism. Yet that does not erase the fact that this present-day expression of realistic theology and philosophy of religion, arising out of liberal circles, is rooted in the romantic tradition. And a careful scrutiny of the method and spirit of reasoning manifest in Dr. Macintosh's presentation will disclose the essential traits of that way of thinking.

No one could state the outlook for pragmatism more confidently than Dr. Ames, for no one among modern philosophers of religion is more confident than he that pragmatism points the way. A moment ago we stated that if the spirit of liberalism were to prevail in any effective form in our day, idealism would probably give it survival power. Perhaps we should modify that statement to say that pragmatism as an *idealistic* expression of naturalism may be depended upon to exert that influence. No one in our day, for example, stands out more boldly and uncompromisingly for the liberal tradition than Professor John Dewey. And his contemporaries who call themselves pragmatists are equally outspoken in their acclaim of his stand.

Thus pragmatism, as an expression of the naturalistic tradition, may do more than contribute to the growing prestige of the naturalistic outlook. It may turn the naturalistic outlook more and more toward ideal and liberal ends, and thus bring together in its *common faith* the elements of idealism, liberalism and naturalism that give promise of serving the cause of human fulfillment.

We now turn again to consider the prospects of change in current ways of thinking in relation to the developing cultural situation. Refinement of logic and the growth of knowledge bring new insight with which to fashion our systems of thought more perfectly; but philosophy of religion, when it is a vital intellectual expression of an age, is never purely a matter of logic. Like every other creation of the human spirit, it tends to ride the wave of events. For the thoughts of men, however disciplined or refined, are as much the reflex-currents of life surging about them as they are instruments for guiding its course; which is but a way of saying that ideas are called into being by the causes they are to serve. Thus the religious reflection of tomorrow waits upon the rise and fall of tidal waves whose movements no theologian or philosopher can, with certainty, foretell; except as thunder or dawn upon the horizon announce its forebodings. To this matter of perilous prophecy Professor Wieman will address his remarks. His discussion will conclude the symposium.

VI

CONCLUDING PERSPECTIVES

By HENRY NELSON WIEMAN

From the standpoint of practical living the chief purpose in studying the past and present is to forecast the future. If we are to live with any intelligence, religiously or otherwise, we must know something about the direction which the course of life is taking. So we ask, What can be said in the light of our study about the future?

If one follows closely the movements of religious thought in America today he will discover two divergent trends, one toward naturalism and the other toward supernaturalism. The thinkers we have listed under the traditions of idealism and romanticism are dividing in these two directions. The idealists and the intuitionists make up what have generally been called liberals in religion. It is among them that the two separating propensities toward naturalism and supernaturalism are clearly discernible. Some have moved over the border line into the beginnings of naturalism. These we classified under the head of evolutionary theists. Another set have gone in the opposite direction across the border line into supernaturalism. These we presented under the heading of neo-supernaturalists. Most of the evolutionary theists and the neo-supernaturalists were once liberals. Neo-supernaturalism is a revised and improved form of supernaturalism with relinquishment of liberalism. Naturalism is a revised and improved form of liberalism with relinquishment of supernaturalism.

Shall we cast off the old and inadequate forms of liberalism and supernaturalism and become a new kind of supernaturalists called neo-supernaturalists? Or shall we cast off the old and inadequate forms of supernaturalism and liberalism and become a new kind of liberals called religious naturalists? Or shall we do neither, but sink through increasing social and intellectual confusion into a kind of religious dogmatism where scientific inquiry and all free inquiry is throttled wherever it touches on religious questions? These would seem to be the three alternative possible courses before us.

Of course many idealists and intuitionists have not become neo-supernaturalists or religious naturalists, and probably never will. But most have moved in one direction or the other without going all the way. Professor Brightman, for example, has marked leanings toward naturalism. On the other hand, Professors W. A. Brown, H. P. Van Dusen, Walter Horton and others are turning toward a renewed supernaturalism. One way these men like to express it is to say that they are moving " theologically to the right and socially to the left."

All this would seem to indicate that the fourfold division of American philosophies of religion will tend to become twofold. Perhaps it would be more accurate to say that it will become weighted more and more at the extremes and less and less in the middle. The intuitionists and idealists will become more supernaturalistic or naturalistic while the positions of naturalism and supernaturalism will become more powerful. In other words, the mediating positions will become weaker and weaker while the extremes will become stronger and stronger. The actual shifting of positions which is now occurring would seem to make this evident. Perhaps the idealists, so far as they undergo any change, will move toward naturalism because of their emphasis upon intellectual tests. The intuitionists more commonly seem to shift in the direction of supernaturalism because they discount the power of the intellect in religious matters.

We have based our forecast on actual events now transpiring. The same prognosis issues from an examination of the structure of thought found in the philosophies under consideration. Let us look at the matter from this standpoint.

Idealists and intuitionists have both been mediators between the rising claims of naturalistic science and the ancient claims of supernatural religion. The idealists have done it by well-wrought and magnificent systems of philosophy. The intuitionists have done it by supplementing and reinterpreting the findings of the sciences by means of intuition variously called " religious experience," " value judgments," " moral optimism," the claims of conscience, mystic insight, the teaching of great seers. In these ways the accepted body of religious sentiment, belief and practice has been conserved with as little modification as possible in the face of an emerging scientific view of the world. They who rendered this service of conservation and gradual modification we call mediators. They were on the one hand the idealists, on the other hand the intuitionists.

Now as long as the religious attitude could be intelligibly retained only by mediating between the growing naturalistic interpretation on the one hand, and a traditional supernatural religion on the other, the idealists and intuitionists had great work to do. They flourished and became numerous. But the need for this service of the mediator is passing, because of two changes that are occurring within Christianity itself. On the one hand, Christianity has developed a form of neo-supernaturalism which is able to accept the totality of all natural knowledge without a qualm or question and still retain its faith in the realm of the supernatural. The neo-supernaturalist no longer needs the services of the mediator, either as idealist or intuitionist, to help him swallow the whole of modern science. On the other hand, Christianity has found a way of basing itself squarely and fairly on the naturalistic view of the world. The religious naturalist also no longer needs a mediator to negotiate differences between the scientific view and the religious view.

Thus the need for mediating between science and religion diminishes. The religious person who is informed can today go all the way over into naturalism or all the way over into supernaturalism without experiencing any religious difficulties with science. It is true that the mass of religious people are not yet sufficiently informed to be able to do this and will not for a good while yet to come. It is not necessary that the total mass be able to do it. It is only needful that the great majority have access to a guide and mentor who can do it for them. But even this will take time. So there will still be work for the mediator. Also, when this problem of adjusting the religious and naturalistic viewpoints has been settled, there will be other advances in human life requiring the services of contact-men to mediate between the pioneers and the masses. But so far as concerns the mediation between supernaturalism and naturalism as represented by idealists and intuitionists, we believe all the evidence points to a decline in the need for this kind of service, even though the demand for it may continue for an indefinitely long time.

Thus far we have considered supernaturalism and naturalism together as over against the idealists and intuitionists. But which will prevail over the other, supernaturalism or naturalism? Or will the two hold the field together with neither winning? This, we believe, is a more difficult question to answer than the one we have been considering. It will depend in no small part on the course taken by economic and political developments, for these profoundly influence religious thought and life.

If we are moving toward coercive regimentation in public life so that free inquiry, criticism, creative imagination and investigation will be fettered more and more, then the domination of supernaturalism or of naturalism will depend on what attitude the economic and political rulers take toward religion. If they endeavor to foster religion as a means of augmenting their power of control over the people and of bringing comfort and courage to themselves, religion will probably assume that form of supernaturalism which most readily lends itself to these uses. On the other hand, if the rulers are opposed to religion and succeed in greatly weakening professed and conscious religion by impoverishment and neglect (weakening by direct persecution is impossible), we are likely to have a growing religion that is naturalistic but is unconscious and unprofessed. It will be a spontaneous but unconscious growth of religion such as we see in Russia today. It will be naturalistic because it will be a natural growth in a world dominated by the natural sciences. When at last it comes to consciousness and is recognized to be a religion by its adherents, its naturalism will be so well established that it will not be likely to disappear.

On the other hand, if we are moving toward a time when free inquiry and criticism shall be released, and the mind of man stimulated to search out all things by his natural powers, there will ensue the growth of a naturalistic religion which is conscious and professed. That will avoid serious break with the past and loss of its rich cargo of tradition and insight. The spontaneous growth of an unconscious, naturalistic religion could not avoid such a break.

It may be we are going into a transitional period of coercive regimentation after which will come a time of greater freedom for the questioning and inquiring mind. In that case we shall probably have an increase of supernaturalism during the regimentation, followed by a period of increasing naturalism when stability and freedom are gained.

There is still another possibility. Our economic and political life may be entering a period neither of coercive regimentation nor of free inquiry, but of disorganization and increasing chaos. In that case dogmatic supernaturalism is almost sure to grow from more to more.

While no one knows which of these several courses may be followed by our economic and political life, we believe the most probable is something like this. First a time of difficult and dangerous reconstruction with social control more or less dictatorial but finally emerging into a state where there will be more leisure, better distribution of material wealth and more free inquiry. Will the religion of such a society be naturalistic or supernaturalistic?

Whatever the outcome it is highly probable there will be strong surges and resurgences of supernaturalism. This way of religious thinking and feeling has too strong a hold on the human heart to pass lightly away. These powerful revivals will be led by prophets having a wide appeal. But these waves of renewed supernaturalism will not endure because they will come from the power of prophetic leadership and not from the gradual growth of basic presuppositions and methods. A recent book by supernaturalists, *The Church Against the World* by H. Richard Niebuhr, Pauck and Miller, makes plain that they themselves see that the only hope of revived supernaturalism is in a prophet whose coming they await. But a prophet is never so strong as a growth, however spectacular for a time may be his achievements and gains. Through and underneath these powerful revivals of supernaturalism will be growing the presuppositions and methods which must finally determine the kind of religion that prevails.

If the scientific method continues to develop, if the scientific view continues to include more and more, if scientific findings shape life increasingly, if the scientific ideals of knowledge and intellectual integrity spread further among men, we believe that basic presuppositions and methods of human living will lead on most surely to a naturalistic religion. Most important of all, a great change that is coming over the scientific method and scientific interpretation of the world, points in this direction. We must look at this change.

As long as science is immature it must limit itself to mechanical relations and ignore organic connections. This is so because the mechanistic is much simpler and easier to handle. But as it rises to higher levels of maturity it becomes able to deal with the organic connections found throughout natural existence. Physics, the most mature of all the sciences, has quite definitely passed over to this stage of its development. Biology had to begin with mechanisms but it also is fast coming to discern the place of organic relations. Psychology and sociology are the least mature of the sciences and so are laggards here. But that form of psychology which makes *gestalten* the objects of inquiry, shows that psychology is also moving in this direction. R. S. Woodworth is developing an improved form of this approach.[10]

Now when scientific method could only explore mechanisms and the scientific view could only recognize mechanistic connections, it was inhospitable to the interests of religion. It could not give sufficient room for the higher outreaches of the human spirit. But when organic connections come fully into view from the scientific standpoint, that limitation is removed. That is precisely what is now occurring.

Even after the specialized sciences have passed over the great divide from mechanisms to organic connections, it will still take some time for common sense, which is the starting point of all naturalistic inquiry including the religious, to make the great transition. It will also take time for the basic presuppositions of our total view of reality to make the change. Not until this occurs will we have a naturalism which can give ample room for the highest aspirations of love and faith, hope and beauty. The deepest currents are running in this direction, we believe.

Before we can have a satisfactory naturalistic religion naturalism must outgrow the crudity of its beginning with the crassly mechanistic and materialistic viewpoints that then prevailed. Such a beginning was inevitable, for the reasons noted. But those beginnings are being left behind.

All this, we believe, points to the slow but sure growth of basic presuppositions and methods which will bring forth a naturalistic religion to sustain, guide and inspire human life toward the most worthful reality.

[1] By Bernard E. Meland.

[2] Dr. Richards is President of The Theological Seminary of the Reformed Church, U. S., Lancaster, Pennsylvania. He is a recognized leader both as a churchman and as a scholar. His book, *Beyond Fundamentalism and Modernism,* is an arresting presentation of the new emphasis upon supernaturalism in modern thought.

[3] *Christianity and the Religions of the World,* p. 83.

[4] *The New Testament Idea of Revelation:* Ernest F. Scott, p. 104.

[5] *Christianity and the Religions of the World,* pp. 80–81.

[6] No American philosopher of recent times has propounded the cause of idealism with greater vigor than Doctor Brightman, who is Professor of Philosophy in Boston University. While he holds to a distinctive form of personal idealism, he may be regarded as a representative voice of the tradition of idealism.

[7] Professor Brightman has himself presented this thesis in a striking manner in his recent writings. See his book, *The Problem of God.*

[8] Doctor Macintosh, who is Professor of Theology and Philosophy of Religion in Yale University, prefers to be known as a religious realist rather than an ethical intuitionist of the romantic tradition. Whatever the caption, the view he represents proceeds upon the basis of the intuitive appeal tested by reason and practical experience. As an exponent of this view, Dr. Macintosh has gained an important leadership among a representative group of theologians and philosophers of religion, and has exerted a wide influence among clergymen and religious leaders in this country.

[9] Doctor Ames has long been identified with the philosophy of pragmatism, and is recognized as a pioneer in the effort to formulate a philosophy of religion on a naturalistic basis. His statement gives the view of pragmatic naturalism. He is Professor Emeritus of Philosophy, The University of Chicago.

[10] In an unpublished lecture delivered before the Psychology Club of the University of Chicago, November 8, 1935, Professor Woodworth called this new approach to psychological problems by the name of " the Situation-and-Goal Set." He is proposing that this be made the fundamental concept in psychology.

ACKNOWLEDGMENTS

SEVERAL persons have been helpful in the preparation of this volume. The authors are deeply indebted to Edgar S. Brightman, Edward Scribner Ames, George W. Richards, and Douglas Clyde Macintosh for their contributions to the symposium and for their helpful criticisms and suggestions regarding the manuscript as a whole. A memorable night on which the authors discussed their work with Professor Robert Lowry Calhoun of Yale University resulted in some important revisions which measurably improved the book. For Dr. Calhoun's searching, critical suggestions they are therefore grateful. The authors are indebted also to Dr. Regina Wescott Wieman for critically reading some of the chapters and for her helpful suggestions.

In presenting the thoughts of certain contemporary philosophers, it seemed advisable to quote liberally from their works. The authors wish to acknowledge the generous co-operation and courtesy of the following authors and publishers who made this possible:

The Abingdon Press for permission to quote from *The Philosophy of Personalism*, by Albert C. Knudson, copyright 1927.

Dr. Hartley Burr Alexander for permission to quote from his essay "God and Philosophical Thinking," which appeared in

Alfred A. Knopf, Inc., for permission to quote from *Joseph and His Brothers,* by Thomas Mann.

Liveright Publishing Corporation for permission to quote from Sherwood Anderson's *Notebook.*

The Macmillan Company for permission to quote from the following volumes: *Contemporary American Philosophy,* edited by Adams and Montague, copyright 1930; *The Idea of God,* by C. A. Beckwith, copyright 1922; *Cosmic Evolution,* by J. E. Boodin, copyright 1925; *History of Modern Philosophy,* Volumes I and II, by H. Hoffding, copyright 1900; *Religious Foundations* and *New Studies in Mystical Religion,* by Rufus Jones, copyrights 1923 and 1927 respectively; *Preface to Morals,* by Walter Lippmann, copyright 1929; *Growth of the Idea of God,* by Shailer Mathews, copyright 1931; *The Next Step in Religion,* by R. W. Sellars, copyright 1918; *Process and Reality,* by A. N. Whitehead, copyright 1929; and *Religious Experience and Scientific Method,* by H. N. Wieman, copyright 1926.

The editors of *The New Humanist* for permission to quote from an article by R. W. Sellars in the May-June issue of 1933.

W. W. Norton & Company for permission to quote from *The Enduring Quest,* by H. A. Overstreet, copyright 1931; and *Mysticism and Logic,* by Bertrand Russell.

The Open Court Publishing Company for permission to quote from *Experience and Nature,* by John Dewey, copyright 1925; and *Humanistic Sermons,* edited by C. W. Reese, copyright 1927.

Charles Scribner's Sons for permission to quote from the following volumes: *Pathways to Certainty,* and *God At Work,* by W. A. Brown, copyrights 1930 and 1933 respectively; *God and the Common Life,* by R. L. Calhoun, copyright 1935; *The Meaning and Truth of Religion,* by E. W. Lyman, copyright 1933; *Beyond Fundamentalism and Modernism,* by G. W. Richards, copyright 1934; and the following books by George Santayana: *The Sense of Beauty,* copyright 1896; *Poems,* copyright 1901; and *Reason in Religion,* copyright 1905.

Sheed and Ward Company for permission to quote from *Medieval Religion,* by C. H. Dawson.

Simon and Schuster, Inc., for permission to quote from John Dewey's Credo in *Living Philosophies.*

The University of Chicago Press for permission to use material by E. S. Ames from *The International Journal of Ethics,* and to reprint as Chapter II of this volume, an article which appeared in *The Journal of Religion.* Also for permission to quote from *Current Christian Thinking,* by G. B. Smith, copyright 1928.

D. Van Nostrand Company, Inc., for permission to quote from an essay by Shailer Mathews in *Religious Life,* Vol. 11 of series *Man and His World,* edited by Baker Brownell, copyright 1929.

The John C. Winston Company for permission to quote from *Social Law In The Spiritual World,* by Rufus Jones, copyright 1904, and for permission to reproduce an illustration taken from this volume in Chapter VII.

Yale University Press for permission to quote from *The Dilemma of Religious Knowledge,* by C. A. Bennett, copyright 1931; *A Common Faith,* by John Dewey, copyright 1934; and *Belief Unbound,* by W. P. Montague, copyright 1930.

HENRY NELSON WIEMAN
BERNARD EUGENE MELAND

BIBLIOGRAPHY

CHAPTER I

AUBREY, E. E., *Present Theological Tendencies.* New York: Harpers, 1936
BAILLIE, J., *The Interpretation of Religion.* New York: Scribners, 1933
BENNETT, C. A., *The Dilemma of Religious Knowledge.* New Haven: Yale University Press, 1931
HOERNLE, R. F. A., *Studies in Contemporary Metaphysics.* New York: Harcourt, Brace, 1920
HOCKING, W. E., *Types of Philosophy.* New York: Scribners, 1929
KNUDSON, A. C., *Present Tendencies in Religious Thought.* New York: Abingdon, 1924
MONTAGUE, W. P., *The Ways of Knowing.* New York: Macmillan, 1925
PERRY, R. B., *Recent Philosophical Tendencies.* New York: Longmans, 1916
ROBINSON, D. S., *Anthology of Recent Philosophy.* New York: Crowell, 1929
SPRANGER, E., *Types of Men.* (Translated from the German by P. J. W. Pigas) Stechert, 1928
WALLAS, G., *The Art of Thought.* New York: Harcourt, Brace, 1926

CHAPTER II

AUBREY, E. E., *Present Theological Tendencies.* New York: Harpers, 1936
BENNETT, JOHN C., *Social Salvation.* New York: Scribners, 1935
CALHOUN, R. L., *God and the Common Life.* New York: Scribners, 1935
DAWSON, CHRISTOPHER, *Christianity and the New Age.* London: 1931
HORTON, W. M., *Realistic Theology.* New York: Harpers, 1934
JUNG, C. G., *Modern Man in Search of a Soul.* New York: Harcourt, Brace, 1935
KELLER, A., *Religion and Revolution.* New York: Revell, 1935
KRUTCH, J. W., *The Modern Temper.* New York: Harcourt, Brace, 1929
LIPPMANN, W., *A Preface to Morals.* New York: Macmillan, 1929
MELAND, B. E., *Modern Man's Worship.* New York: Harpers, 1934
MORRISON, C. C., *The Social Gospel and the Christian Cultus.* New York: Harpers, 1933
NIEBUHR, R., *Does Civilization Need Religion?* New York: Macmillan, 1927
NIEBUHR, R., *Reflections on the End of an Era.* New York: Scribners, 1934

SPERRY, W. L., *Signs of the Times.* New York: Harpers, 1929

SPERRY, W. L., " *Yes, But —* " *The Bankruptcy of Apologetics.* New York: Harpers, 1931

TILLICH, P., *The Religious Situation.* New York: Holt, 1932

VAN DUSEN, H. P., *God in These Times.* New York: Scribners, 1935

VLASTOS, GREGORY, *The Religious Way.* New York: Woman's Press, 1934

WIEMAN, H. N., " The Present State of Religious Thought," in *The Wrestle of Religion with Truth.* New York: Macmillan, 1927

WIEMAN, H. N., *The Issues of Life.* New York: Abingdon, 1930

WIEMAN, H. N., with WIEMAN, REGINA WESCOTT, *Normative Psychology of Religion.* New York: Crowell, 1935

CHAPTER III

ALIOTTA, A., *The Idealistic Reaction Against Science.* Translated by Agnes McCaskill. New York: Macmillan, 1914

BAILLIE, J., *The Interpretation of Religion.* New York: Scribners, 1933

BURTT, E. A., *Metaphysical Foundations of Modern Physical Science.* New York: Harcourt, 1925

CROSS, GEORGE, *What is Christianity?* Chicago: University of Chicago Press, 1918

DEWEY, JOHN, *Reconstruction in Philosophy.* New York: Holt, 1920

HARNACK, A., *History of Dogma.* 7 vols. (English edition). London: Williams and Norgate, 1894

HOFFDING, H., *History of Modern Philosophy.* 2 vols. New York: Macmillan, 1900

LAKE, K., *The Religion of Yesterday and Tomorrow.* Boston: Houghton Mifflin, 1926

McGIFFERT, A. C., *The Rise of Modern Religious Ideas.* New York: Macmillan, 1915

McGIFFERT, A. C., *Protestant Thought Before Kant.* New York: Scribners, 1911

MATHEWS, SHAILER, " The Development of Christian Doctrine," in *A Guide to the Study of the Christian Religion,* edited by G. B. Smith. Chicago: University of Chicago Press, 1916

MERZ, *History of European Thought in the 19th Century.* Edinburgh: 1903

MOORE, E. C., *Christian Thought Since Kant.* New York: Scribners, 1911

PARRINGTON, V. L., *Main Currents in American Thought.* 3 vols. New York: Harcourt, Brace, 1927–30

PFLEIDERER, *The Development of Theology Since Kant and its Progress in Great Britain Since 1825.* New York: 1893

RANDALL, J. H., JR., *Making of the Modern Mind.* New York: Scribners, 1926

RILEY, W., *American Thought.* New York: Holt, 1915

ROGERS, A. K., *English and American Philosophy Since 1800.* New York: Macmillan, 1922

ROYCE, J., *The Spirit of Modern Philosophy.* Boston: Houghton Mifflin, 1892

ROYCE, J., *Lectures on Modern Idealism.* New Haven: Yale University Press, 1919

SABATIER, A., *Religions of Authority.* New York: McClure, Phillips, & Co., 1904

SMITH, G. B., *Social Idealism and the Changing Theology.* New York: Macmillan, 1913

SMITH, G. B., *A Guide to the Study of the Christian Religion.* Chicago: University of Chicago Press, 1916. Chapter IX

SMITH, G. B., *Current Christian Thinking.* Chicago: University of Chicago Press, 1928

TOWNSEND, H. G., *Philosophical Ideas in the United States.* New York: American Book Co., 1934
WEBB, C. C. J., *A History of Philosophy.* London: Thornton Butterworth, Ltd., 1915
WHITEHEAD, A. N., *Science and the Modern World.* New York: Macmillan, 1925
WORKMAN, H. B., *Christian Thought To The Reformation.* New York: Scribners, 1911

CHAPTER IV

MACHEN, J. G., *Christianity and Liberalism.* New York: Macmillan, 1923
MACHEN, J. G., *What Is Faith?* New York: Macmillan, 1925
MULLINS, E. Y., *Freedom and Authority in Religion.* Philadelphia: American Baptist Publication Society, 1913
MULLINS, E. Y., *Christianity at the Cross Roads.* New York: Doran, 1924
MULLINS, E. Y., *Faith in the Modern World.* Nashville: Baptist Sunday School Board, 1930
PATTON, F. L., *Fundamental Christianity.* New York: Macmillan, 1926

CHAPTER V

CELL, G., *The Rediscovery of John Wesley.* New York: Holt, 1935
LEWIS, E., *A Christian Manifesto.* New York: Abingdon Press, 1934
NIEBUHR, H. R., (with Pauck and Miller), *The Church Against the World.* Chicago: Willett, Clark & Co., 1935
NIEBUHR, H. R., " Religious Realism in the Twentieth Century," in *Religious Realism,* edited by D. C. Macintosh. New York: Macmillan, 1931
NIEBUHR, R., *Does Civilization Need Religion?* New York: Macmillan, 1928
NIEBUHR, R., *Moral Man and Immoral Society.* New York: Scribners, 1932
NIEBUHR, R., *Reflections on the End of an Era.* New York: Scribners, 1934
NIEBUHR, R., *An Interpretation of the Christian Ethic.* New York: Harpers, 1935
PAUCK, W., *Karl Barth: Prophet of a New Christianity.* New York: Harpers, 1931
PAUCK, W., " The Crisis in Religion," in *The Church Against the World.* Chicago: Willett, Clark & Co., 1935
RICHARDS, G. W., *Beyond Fundamentalism and Modernism.* New York: Scribners, 1934
TILLICH, P. Y., *Religionsphilosophie,* in *Lehrbuch der Philosophie,* Vol. II. Berlin, 1925
TILLICH, P. Y., *The Religious Situation* (Translated by H. R. Niebuhr). New York: Holt, 1932
TILLICH, P. Y., *Das Daemonische.* Tuebingen, 1926
TILLICH, P. Y., *Kairos.* Darmstadt, 1926

CHAPTER VI

ADAMS, G. P., *Idealism and the Modern Age.* New Haven: Yale University Press, 1919
HOCKING, W. E., *The Meaning of God in Human Experience.* New Haven: Yale University Press, 1912
HOCKING, W. E., *Human Nature and Its Remaking.* New Haven: Yale University Press, 1918
LADD, G. T., *Philosophy of Religion,* 2 vols. New York: Scribners, 1905

LADD, G. T., *Knowledge, Life, and Reality.* New York: Dodd, Mead & Co. 1909
LEIGHTON, J. A., *Man and the Cosmos.* New York: Appleton, 1922
LEIGHTON, J. A., *Religion and the Mind of Today.* New York: Appleton, 1924
LEIGHTON, J. A., "My Development and Present Creed," in *Contemporary American Philosophy,* Vol. I, New York: Macmillan, 1930
ROYCE, J., *Religious Aspects of Philosophy.* Boston: Houghton Mifflin, 1885
ROYCE, J., *Conception of God.* New York: Macmillan, 1897
ROYCE, J., *The Spirit of Modern Philosophy.* Boston: Houghton Mifflin, 1892
ROYCE, J., *The World and the Individual.* New York: Macmillan, 1901
ROYCE, J., *Sources of Religious Insight.* New York: Scribners, 1912
ROYCE, J., *The Problem of Christianity,* 2 vols. New York: Macmillan, 1913
ROYCE, J., *Studies in Good and Evil.* New York: Appleton, 1915
ROYCE, J., *Lectures on Modern Idealism.* New Haven: Yale University Press, 1919
URBAN, W. M., *Valuation: Its Nature and Laws.* New York: Macmillan, 1909
URBAN, W. M., *The Intelligible World.* New York: Macmillan, 1929

CHAPTER VII

BENNETT, C. A., "An Approach to Mysticism," *Philosophical Review,* 27:392
BENNETT, C. A., "Religion and the Idea of the Holy," *Journal of Philosophy,* 23:460
BENNETT, C. A., *A Philosophical Study of Mysticism.* New Haven: Yale University Press, 1923
BENNETT, C. A., "Poetic Imagination and Philosophy," *Yale Review,* Winter, 1931
BENNETT, C. A., *The Dilemma of Religious Knowledge* (posthumous publication edited by W. E. Hocking). New Haven: Yale University Press, 1931
JONES, R., *Social Law in the Spiritual World.* Philadelphia: J. C. Winston Co., 1904
JONES, R., *Studies in Mystical Religion.* New York: Macmillan, 1909
JONES, R., *New Studies in Mystical Religion.* New York: Macmillan, 1927
JONES, R., *Some Exponents of Mystical Religion.* New York: Abingdon, 1930
JONES, R., *Pathways to the Reality of God.* New York: Macmillan, 1931
JONES, R., *Religious Foundations,* Chapters I–III. New York: Macmillan, 1923
JONES, R., *Preface to Christian Faith in a New Age.* New York: Macmillan, 1932

CHAPTER VIII

BOWNE, B. P., *Metaphysics.* New York: Harper, 1882
BOWNE, B. P., *The Philosophy of Theism.* New York: Harper, 1902
BOWNE, B. P., *The Immanence of God.* Boston: Houghton Mifflin, 1905
BOWNE, B. P., *Personalism.* Boston: Houghton Mifflin, 1908
BOWNE, B. P., *The Essence of Religion.* Boston: Houghton Mifflin, 1910
BRIGHTMAN, E. S., *Religious Values.* New York: Abingdon, 1925
BRIGHTMAN, E. S., *The Problem of God.* New York: Abingdon, 1930
BRIGHTMAN, E. S., *The Finding of God.* New York: Abingdon, 1931
BRIGHTMAN, E. S., *Is God A Person?* New York: Association Press, 1932
BRIGHTMAN, E. S., Personality and Religion. New York: Abingdon, 1934
BUCKHAM, J. W., *Religion as Experience.* New York: Abingdon, 1922
BUCKHAM, J. W., *The Humanity of God.* New York: Harpers, 1928
FLEWELLING, R. T., *Creative Personality.* New York: Macmillan, 1913
FLEWELLING, R. T., *Personalism and the Problems of Philosophy.* New York: Methodist Book Concern, 1915

FLEWELLING, R. T., *Bergson and Personal Realism*. New York: Abingdon, 1920
FLEWELLING, R. T., *Reason in Faith*. New York: Abingdon, 1924
KNUDSON, A. C., *Philosophy of Personalism*. New York: Abingdon, 1927
KNUDSON, A. C., *The Doctrine of God*. New York: Abingdon, 1930
KNUDSON, A. C., *The Doctrine of Redemption*. New York: Abingdon, 1933
McCONNELL, F. J., *The Divine Immanence*. New York: Methodist Book Concern, 1910
McCONNELL, F. J., *Is God Limited?* New York: Abingdon, 1924
McCONNELL, F. J., *The Christlike God*. New York: Abingdon, 1927
McCONNELL, F. J., *Borden Parker Bowne: His Life and Philosophy*. New York: Abingdon, 1929
WILSON, G. A., *The Self and Its World*. New York: Macmillan, 1926

CHAPTER IX

BECKWITH, C. A., *The Idea of God*. New York: Macmillan, 1922
LYMAN, E. W., *Theology and Human Problems*. New York: Scribners, 1910
LYMAN, E. W., *The Experience of God in Human Life*. New York: Scribners, 1918
LYMAN, E. W., *The Meaning and Truth of Religion*. New York: Scribners, 1933
MACINTOSH, D. C., *Theology as an Empirical Science*. New York: Macmillan, 1919
MACINTOSH, D. C., *The Reasonableness of Christianity*. New York: Scribners, 1925
MACINTOSH, D. C. (with others), *Religious Realism*. New York: Macmillan, 1931
MACINTOSH, D. C. (with Wieman and Otto), *Is There A God?* Chicago: Willett, Clark & Co., 1932

CHAPTER X

BENNETT, J., *Social Salvation*. New York: Scribners, 1935
BROWN, W. A., *Christian Theology in Outline*. New York: Scribners, 1906
BROWN, W. A., *Beliefs That Matter*. New York: Scribners, 1928
BROWN, W. A., *Pathways to Certainty*. New York: Scribners, 1930
BROWN, W. A., *God At Work*. New York: Scribners, 1933
HORTON, W. M., *Theism and the Modern Mood*. New York: Harpers
HORTON, W. M., *A Psychological Approach to Theology*. New York: Harpers, 1930
HORTON, W. M., *Theism and the Scientific Spirit*. New York: Harpers, 1932
HORTON, W. M., *Realistic Theology*. New York: Harpers, 1935
VAN DUSEN, H. P., *The Plain Man Seeks For God*. New York: Scribners, 1933
VAN DUSEN, H. P., *God in These Times*. New York: Scribners, 1935

CHAPTER XI

ALEXANDER, H. B., *Poetry and the Individual*. New York: Putnam, 1906
ALEXANDER, H. B., *Nature and Human Nature*. Chicago: Open Court, 1923
ALEXANDER, H. B., *Truth and the Faith*. New York: Holt, 1929
ALEXANDER, H. B., "The Great Art Which is Philosophy," in *Contemporary American Philosophy*, Vol. I. New York: Macmillan, 1930
BROWNELL, B., *The New Universe*. New York: Harpers, 1926
BROWNELL, B., *Earth is Enough*. New York: Harpers, 1933
PARKER, DeW., *Human Values*. New York: Harpers, 1929
RANSOM, J. C., *God Without Thunder*. New York: Harcourt, Brace, 1930
SANTAYANA, G., *Interpretations of Poetry and Religion*. New York: Scribners, 1900

SANTAYANA, G., *Reason in Religion*. New York: Scribners, 1905
SANTAYANA, G., *Winds of Doctrine*. New York: Scribners, 1913
SANTAYANA, G., *Skepticism and Animal Faith*. New York: Scribners, 1923
SANTAYANA, G., *The Realm of Essence*. New York: Scribners, 1928
SANTAYANA, G., *The Realm of Matter*. London: Constable & Co., 1930

CHAPTER XII

BOODIN, J. E., *A Realistic Universe*. New York: Macmillan, 1916
BOODIN, J. E., *Cosmic Evolution*. New York: Macmillan, 1925
BOODIN, J. E., " Nature and Reason," in *Contemporary American Philosophy*, Vol. I.
    New York: Macmillan, 1930
BOODIN, J. E., *Three Interpretations of the Universe*. New York: Macmillan, 1934
BOODIN, J. E., *God*. New York: Macmillan, 1934
CALHOUN, R. L., *God and the Common Life*. New York: Scribners, 1935
WRIGHT, H. W., *Faith Justified By Progress*. New York: Scribners, 1916
WRIGHT, H. W., *The Religious Response*. New York: Harpers, 1929
WRIGHT, W. K., *A Student's Philosophy of Religion*. New York: Macmillan, 1922
    (new edition, 1935)
WRIGHT, W. K., " God and Emergent Evolution," in *Religious Realism*. New York:
    Macmillan, 1931

CHAPTER XIII

CONGER, G. P., *World of Epitomizations*. Princeton: Princeton University Press, 1931
CONGER, G. P., *Horizon of Thought*. Princeton: Princeton University Press, 1933
NOBLE, E., *Purposive Evolution*. New York: Holt, 1926
NORTHROP, F. S. C., *Science and First Principles*. New York: Macmillan, 1931
OVERSTREET, H. A., *The Enduring Quest*. New York: Norton, 1931
WHITEHEAD, A. N., *Science and the Modern World*. New York: Macmillan, 1925
WHITEHEAD, A. N., *Religion in the Making*. New York: Macmillan, 1926
WHITEHEAD, A. N., *Process and Reality*. New York: Macmillan, 1929
WHITEHEAD, A. N., *Adventures of Ideas*. New York: Macmillan, 1933

CHAPTER XIV

AUER, J. A. F. C., *Humanism States Its Case*. Boston: Beacon Press, 1933
HAYDON, A. E., *The Quest of the Ages*. New York: Harpers, 1929
KRUTCH, J. W., *The Modern Temper*. New York: Harcourt, Brace, 1929
LEUBA, J. H., *A Psychological Study of Religion*. New York: Macmillan, 1912
LEUBA, J. H., *The Psychology of Religious Mysticism*. New York: Harcourt, Brace,
    1925
LEUBA, J. H., *God or Man?* New York: Holt, 1933
LIPPMANN, W., *A Preface to Morals*. New York: Macmillan, 1929
MARTIN, E. D., *The Mystery of Religion*. New York: Harpers, 1924
OTTO, M. C., *Things and Ideals*. New York: Holt, 1924
OTTO, M. C., *Natural Laws and Human Hopes*. New York: Holt, 1926
OTTO, M. C. (with Wieman and Macintosh), *Is There A God?* Chicago: Willett,
    Clark & Co., 1932
REESE, C. W., *Humanism*. Chicago: Open Court, 1926
REESE, C. W. (editor), *Humanistic Sermons*. Chicago: Open Court, 1927

REESE, C. W., *Humanist Religion*. New York: Macmillan, 1931
REISER, O. L., *Humanism and New World Ideals*. Antioch: Antioch Press, 1933
REISER, O. L., *Philosophy and the Concepts of Modern Science*. New York: Macmillan, 1935
SELLARS, R. W., *The Next Step in Religion*. New York: Macmillan, 1918
SELLARS, R. W., *Evolutionary Naturalism*. Chicago: Open Court, 1921
SELLARS, R. W., *Religion Coming of Age*. New York: Macmillan, 1928
SELLARS, R. W., *Philosophy of Physical Realism*. New York: Macmillan, 1932
WALLACE, W. K., *The Scientific World View*. New York: Macmillan, 1928

CHAPTER XV

AMES, E. S., *Psychology of Religious Experience*. Boston: Houghton Mifflin, 1910
AMES, E. S., " The Validity of the Idea of God," *Journal of Religion* 1:462–81
AMES, E. S., " Religious Values and the Practical Absolute," *International Journal of Ethics* 32:347–65
AMES, E. S., *Religion*. New York: Holt, 1929
DEWEY, J., *Experience and Nature*. Chicago: Open Court, 1925
DEWEY, J., *The Quest For Certainty*. New York: Minton, Balch, 1929
DEWEY, J., *A Common Faith*. New Haven: Yale University Press, 1934
JAMES, W., *Principles of Psychology*, Vol. II, Chap. XXI. New York: Holt, 1890
JAMES, W., *The Will to Believe*. New York: Longmans, 1896
JAMES, W., *The Varieties of Religious Experience*. New York: Longmans, 1902
JAMES, W., *A Pluralistic Universe*, Chaps. V and VIII. New York: Longmans, 1909
MATHEWS, S., " The Religious Life," in *Man and His World* Series, Vol. XI, edited by B. Brownell. New York: Van Nostrand, 1929
MATHEWS, S., *Growth of the Idea of God*. New York: Macmillan, 1931
MATHEWS, S., *Immortality and the Cosmic Process*. Cambridge: Harvard University Press, 1933
MATHEWS, S., " Is God Emeritus? " *The American Scholar,* Autumn, 1935
MELAND, B. E., " Toward A Valid View of God." *Harvard Theological Review,* July 1931
MELAND, B. E., " Kinsmen of the Wild: A Study of Religious Moods in Modern American Poetry." *Sewanee Review,* Oct. 1933
MELAND, B. E., *Modern Man's Worship*. New York: Harpers, 1934
MELAND, B. E., " Mystical Naturalism and Religious Humanism," *The New Humanist,* April–May, 1935
SMITH, G. B., *Current Christian Thinking*. Chicago: University of Chicago Press, 1928
SMITH, G. B., " Is Theism Essential to Religion? " *Journal of Religion,* 1925
SMITH, G. B., " An Overlooked Factor in the Adjustment between Science and Religion," *Journal of Religion,* 1927
WIEMAN, H. N., *Religious Experience and Scientific Method*. New York: Macmillan, 1926
WIEMAN, H. N., *The Wrestle of Religion with Truth*. New York: Macmillan, 1927
WIEMAN, H. N., " God and Value," in *Religious Realism*. New York: Macmillan, 1931
WIEMAN, H. N. (with others), *Is There A God?* Chicago: Willett, Clark & Co., 1932
WIEMAN, H. N., with WIEMAN, REGINA WESCOTT, *Normative Psychology of Religion*. New York: Crowell, 1935

INDEX OF PROPER NAMES

SUBJECT INDEX

366